Lectura Dantis
Newberryana

VOLUME TWO

Lectura Dantis Newberryana

VOLUME TWO

Editors
Paolo Cherchi
Antonio C. Mastrobuono

Lectures presented at
The Newberry Library
Chicago, Illinois
1985–1987

Northwestern University Press
Evanston, Illinois
1990

Northwestern University Press
Evanston, Illinois 60201

Printed in the United States of America

ISSN 1048-5295

The paper used in this publication meets the minimum requirements of American National Standard for Information Sciences—Permanence of Paper for Printed Library Materials, ANSI Z39.48-1984

Contents

Preface

We take satisfaction in presenting to our readers the second volume of *Lectura Dantis Newberryana*. This undertaking, which was meant to be just a local or regional get-together to present Dante research, has now become an object of national and international attention, as favorable reviews of the first issue prove. This success is due primarily to the high quality of the essays, to the formula of our "lecturae," which are not limited to the traditional canto-by-canto readings, and to the inclusion of scholars who are not "professional" Dante scholars. The success is also due to the fact that colleagues from both coasts as well as from Europe have accepted our invitations to lecture. The local audience has been our greatest delight, for it has faithfully attended our lectures in unusual numbers: when R. Hollander and P. V. Mengaldo spoke—one in the morning, the other in the afternoon—there were at least one hundred people in the lecture room of the Newberry; when Mark Musa and Giuseppe Mazzotta gave their lectures, there were no less than seventy people in the audiences. But undoubtedly much of our success is due to the Northwestern University Press for its handsome presentation of the first volume and for its campaign to find subscriptions.

Not everything has been smooth; organizing four lectures per year can be a complicated business that has to take into account several schedules: the speakers', the Newberry's, and our own. Also, it is difficult to run the series without financial resources, so we have to rely on nearby universities for assistance. The University of Chicago and Loyola University have been most generous in this respect. Help has also come from the Newberry Library and from the Istituto Italiano di Cultura in Chicago, as well as from our own pockets. We have experienced what many editors are surely familiar with: struggles to meet deadlines for submitting final copy to the press, for correcting proofs, for last-minute changes—but it is all worth it!

This volume contains the lectures delivered in the period from the fall of 1985 to the spring of 1987. These are the lectures announced in the previous issue—the only two we have not included are those of G. Mazzotta and P. Valesio: the former was unable to hand in his paper but promised to submit a new one for the third volume, while the latter presented an Italian version of his lecture that we, in line with our policy, could not print. We hope to see both papers in the next issue. In the meantime, we have substituted for them essays by R. Hollander and C. Cioffi that were to have appeared in the third volume. By doing so, we have fulfilled our commitment to publishing eight lectures per year.

This volume is appearing roughly two years after the first; the third volume is planned for next year. In this way it will be possible to catch up with the backlog of lectures and, by the fourth volume, to achieve the programmed rhythm of one volume every other year.

Paolo Cherchi
Antonio C. Mastrobuono

Lectura Dantis Newberryana

VOLUME TWO

Dante's Hardened Heart: The Cocytus Cantos

LAWRENCE BALDASSARO

The three cantos that portray the ninth and last circle of Hell (32–34) comprise a distinct entity within the *Inferno*, one that is perhaps more unified in tone and visual imagery than any other segment of the first canticle. The poet underlines the newness, and the cohesiveness, of this final segment by providing it with its own invocation (*Inf.* 32.10–12). The harshness and brutality of both landscape and behavior that characterize this circle of treachery are signaled by the opening two tercets of canto 32, in which Dante confesses his inability to find language coarse enough to portray this dismal hellhole:

> S'io avessi le rime aspre e chiocce,
>   come si converrebbe al tristo buco
>   sovra 'l qual pontan tutte l'altre rocce,
> io premerei di mio concetto il suco
>   più pienamente; . . .
>
>   (32.1–5)

If I had harsh and grating rhymes, as would befit the dismal hole on which all the other rocks converge and weigh, I would press out more fully the juice of my conception; . . .[1]

The harsh judgment of the poet upon the sinners in the ninth circle of Hell is evident in the brutal form of punishment reserved for them,

3

the frozen lake of Cocytus, the visual image that most obviously unifies this final trio of cantos. Trapped in that ice are the shades of those guilty of complex fraud, whose punishment is to be submerged in ice up to their necks or, in the case of those in the fourth and final region, Judecca, to be totally entombed beneath the surface. The cold and eerie silence of Cocytus is broken only by the sound of chattering teeth and, because of Dante's presence there, by the voices of the several talking heads the Pilgrim encounters as he makes his way toward the center of the lake.

The unrelenting harshness of the Cocytus episode—evident in its landscape and language, in the demeanor of its treacherous shades, and finally in the grotesque figure of Lucifer as he chews on three souls in his three slobbering mouths—is interrupted only by the sad story told by Ugolino. But, as we shall see, Ugolino's tale of betrayal and suffering proves to be only an apparent, if beguiling, interruption of the pattern of cruelty and hardness that characterizes these cantos.

In spite of the evident signs that Dante has here created a discrete and unified entity within the *Inferno*, critical studies of the ninth circle have been devoted to single cantos, usually in the form of the traditional *lectura Dantis*, or to segments of cantos—most notably, of course, the Ugolino episode. One element of the thematic and structural unity of these cantos that has been neglected by scholars is the role played by Dante the Pilgrim. Perhaps because of the dominant presences of Ugolino and Lucifer, relatively little attention has been paid to Dante's own behavior as he moves across the four regions of the frozen lake. No one, so far as I know, has attempted to examine systematically the pattern of that behavior. The lack of interest shown by scholars in this particular element of the Cocytus cantos is puzzling, considering the active and at times perplexing role played by the protagonist here. In fact, one of the real surprises, and an unsolved problem, for readers of the *Inferno* is precisely the curious behavior of Dante in these final cantos. Far from remaining a passive observer of what he witnesses, he assumes an active role, more so than in any other segment of the *Inferno*. And his actions are both startling and unprecedented, as he behaves with an apparent cruelty that he has displayed nowhere else in his journey through Hell: he kicks a sinner in the head, then pulls out his hair, and he matter-of-factly breaks a solemn promise made to one of the shades he meets. This Dante seems far removed from the one who was overcome by pity for Francesca (5) and Pier delle Vigne (13), and who wept at the sight of the distorted human figures of the soothsayers (20).

Most commentators and critics who do note Dante's behavior in Cocytus limit their observations to specific incidents and attribute his relentlessly pitiless attitude to his political passion; he responds harshly as the exiled Florentine citizen who is witnessing examples of the political treachery that was so offensive to him, in both a personal and moral sense.[2] A more general explanation for Dante's actions in Cocytus suggests that his behavior reveals the progress he has made in the course of his journey through Hell; having come to learn the true nature of sin, and to abhor it, he now accepts, and seconds, the judgment of divine justice.[3] Some even see Dante as a minister of that divine justice, inflicting on the shades just punishment for their sins.[4]

In my opinion, these responses do not fully explain the startling behavior of Dante in Cocytus. Are we, in fact, witnessing the response of an enlightened and knowledgeable Dante who willfully scorns the sinners *because* he recognizes, understands, and condemns their sins, in accord with divine justice? I do not believe that a close reading of the text supports this conclusion exclusively, primarily because it ignores the ironic element that characterizes the Pilgrim's behavior throughout the Cocytus episode. What I propose to do is reexamine these cantos and offer a reading that does take into account that element of irony, and consequently suggests a quite different portrait of the Pilgrim.

As the Cocytus episode begins, Dante is far from being a cognizant and disdainful observer of the ninth circle of Hell. When he is first set down on the ice by the giant Antaeus, the Pilgrim, like a newly arrived tourist, continues to gaze at the high wall surrounding the lake, unaware of where he is until one of the sinners startles him with a warning not to kick the heads protruding from the ice:

> . . . "Guarda come passi:
> va sì, che tu non calchi con le piante
> le teste de' fratei miseri lassi."
> (32.19–21)

"Look how you pass; take care not to tread on the heads of the wretched weary brothers."

Only then does he turn and see the frozen lake and the motionless heads of the sinners condemned to Caina, the region of those who betrayed their kin.

The Pilgrim now assumes an uncharacteristically active role; without any prompting from Virgil (who will, in fact, utter only one sentence throughout cantos 32 and 33), he asks the identity of two shades he sees at his feet, shades who are locked in the ice face-to-face. While these two butt their heads in anger, a neighboring (though not neighborly) shade readily identifies them, an act of betrayal appropriate to Cocytus, where, as we shall soon learn, the shades prefer anonymity to notoriety.

After learning the identity of several of the shades being punished in Caina, Dante moves toward Antenora, the second region of the ninth circle. As he moves from one region to the next, he shivers from the effects of the cold: "io tremava ne l'etterno rezzo" ("I was shivering in the eternal chill," 32.75). We might take this reference to Dante's trembling as a mere device to enhance the realism of the scene. Considering what is about to happen, however, that shiver would seem to indicate that the Pilgrim himself is subject to the effects of the chilling landscape in which he finds himself.

In the very next tercet we learn that the Pilgrim—perhaps willfully, perhaps accidentally—kicks one of the sinners in the head:

> se voler fu o destino o fortuna,
>> non so; ma, passeggiando tra le teste,
>> forte percossi 'l piè nel viso ad una.
>>> (32.76–78)

whether it was will or fate or chance I do not know, but, walking among the heads, I struck my foot hard in the face of one.

Is this a willful act of violence, or is it "destino" or "fortuna"? The ambiguity remains, but we should keep in mind that the first words Dante heard in Cocytus were a warning not to do precisely what he has just done. Whether or not this first act of violence is willful, he will soon commit a violent act whose motive is no mystery.

When the as yet unidentified sinner asks if Dante is kicking him in order to take revenge for Montaperti, the Pilgrim is led to believe that this may be the shade of Bocca degli Abati, whose betrayal of the

Florentine Guelfs led to their defeat by the Ghibellines in the battle of 1260. Dante's suspicion is evident in his request to Virgil: "Maestro mio, or qui mi aspetta, / sì ch'io esca d'un dubbio per costui" ("Master, now wait here for me, that I may rid me of a doubt respecting this one," 32.82–83). To verify his suspicion Dante asks the sinner his name, coaxing him by promising to spread his fame: "caro esser ti puote . . . se dimandi fama, / ch'io metta il nome tuo tra l'altre note" ("if you crave fame, it may be worth much to you that I note your name among the rest," 32.91–93).

The Pilgrim's appeal to Bocca is, of course, deceitful. His intent is not to spread Bocca's fame but to shame and discredit him by letting the world know that he is spending eternity among the most wretched sinners in Hell. The irony concealed in Dante's promise of "fama" is not lost on Bocca, who is himself a deceiver. Like all the shades in Cocytus, he prefers anonymity to the kind of "fame" offered by this intruder into his world. Too shrewd to fall into the trap, he mocks Dante for his feeble attempt to trick him: "Lèvati quinci e non mi dar più lagna, / ché mal sai lusingar per questa lama!" ("Take yourself hence and trouble me no more, for ill do you know how to flatter in this depth," 32.95–96).

His attempt at deceit having failed, Dante now resorts to violence; he grabs Bocca by the hair and begins to pull out chunks of it, threatening to tear it all out unless Bocca identifies himself. Bocca, though screaming in pain, defies his tormenter and still refuses to reveal his identity, but finally he too is betrayed by a fellow sinner who calls out his name. Only now does Dante reveal to Bocca, in a stinging rebuke, the true reason he had asked his name: "a la tua onta / io porterò di te vere novelle" ("to your shame will I carry true news of you," 32.110–11). Like the shades themselves, who are so willing to betray their fellow sinners in this circle by identifying them, Dante will identify, and thereby disgrace, this sinner who did all he could to conceal his identity.

Nowhere else in the *Inferno* has Dante behaved in such a curious fashion.[5] How, then, are we to respond to this combination of trickery and violence? Is the Pilgrim's treatment of Bocca, as some would argue, a personal act of vengeance against the man who betrayed the Florentine Guelfs? Even if we were to agree that Dante displays an unusually hostile attitude toward this particular sinner, and that his behavior is motivated by personal animosity toward him, that conclusion does not in itself account for the mechanism whereby Dante expresses his hostility. If the motivation behind this episode were simply Dante's desire to vent his personal hatred, one could imagine other, less complex ways of generating that response within the framework of the fiction. The dramatic device of Dante's trickery, followed by an act of violence, is certainly an elaborate means of expressing personal animosity. Furthermore, are we to take it as mere coincidence that this combination of deceit and violence mirrors the very sin being punished in this circle?

As I noted earlier, some commentators see Dante's behavior toward Bocca as an act of divine justice and Dante himself as a minister of God. C. S. Lonergan justifies Dante's violent behavior toward Bocca thus: "Dante here intensifies the punishment inflicted by God on Bocca degli Abati; he is acting as minister, as upholder of the divine justice that is violated by men, by traitors like Bocca."[6] Such a reading of the episode raises more questions than it answers. Think of Dante's words as he inflicts "divine punishment" on Bocca: "Either you'll name yourself, or not a hair will be left on you here." Strange words for a minister of God, and hardly the tone one would expect from someone sent on such a somber mission. If Dante is acting as a minister of divine justice, why does he carry out that function here and not elsewhere? Indeed, why not everywhere? Furthermore, the suggestion that Dante is "intensifying the punishment inflicted by God" leads to the untenable conclusion that divine justice, at least in this instance, is defective and must be assisted by a mortal hand. Finally, the notion of Dante the Pilgrim serving as minister of divine justice contradicts the very purpose of his descent into Hell, which is to attain humility. Dante is in Hell to witness and understand the nature of sin, not to mete out punishment for it.

Whether one concludes that Dante's behavior toward Bocca is motivated by personal vengeance or by an impersonal longing for justice, both conclusions depend on the assumption that the author of the poem and the protagonist who attacks Bocca speak with one and the same voice. Both readings ignore the fundamental distinction between poet and protagonist, a distinction which, by now, has become a commonplace of Dante criticism.

There can be no question of the poet's severe judgment of the sinners condemned to Cocytus; the tone throughout is one of unrelenting harshness and brutality. Does his judgment, however, require, or justify, the unprecedented behavior of the Pilgrim? Is there an inevitable, or logical, progression from the poet's judgment, as expressed in the punishment meted out to these sinners, to the Pilgrim's act of trickery and violence? In other words, does the poet's attitude toward this particular sin require that the Pilgrim behave in such a way that his actions, in effect, imitate the very acts of betrayal and violence for which these sinners are condemned to this circle? What is most revealing about Dante's behavior in Cocytus is not that he has suddenly grown harsh toward the sinners—he had earlier displayed at least verbal harshness toward Filippo Argenti (8), Farinata (10), Nicholas III (13), and Mosca dei Lamberti (28)—but that the nature of his behavior coincides with, or mirrors, the very sin that is being punished there.

In these final cantos of the *Inferno* we are witnessing the conclusion of the first phase of the Pilgrim's journey to God—that is, his descent into the self, into his own heart. The goal of that descent is, of course, humility, the necessary counterpoint to the self-sufficient pride that motivated the Pilgrim's failed attempt to climb the mountain when he emerged from the dark wood.[7] The humility to be attained by his descent into Hell represents nothing less than his recognition, and admission, of his own human fallibility as a son of Adam. If the journey through Hell is a descent into his own heart, then Cocytus represents the darkest region of that heart.[8]

This is not to suggest that the Pilgrim's harsh behavior toward the sinners is unwarranted, or that it contradicts the judgment of either the poet or of divine justice. Indeed, it *seems* to be the very manifestation of that judgment. Nevertheless, to see in his curious behavior in Cocytus only the manifestation of the poet's passion for justice is to miss the irony of that behavior. His specific actions, while not contrary to the dictates of justice, nevertheless betray his own susceptibility to the very sin whose agents he treats so harshly. His is not the attitude of a knowledgeable, dispassionate observer who understands and scorns the evil he witnesses. Nor is that the purpose of his descent. He himself is passionate and involved, and that involvement is a dramatic portrayal of his recognition of his own human fallibility. The Pilgrim is in Hell not only to witness the manifestation of evil in others but, more importantly, to recognize, and admit, the capacity for such evil in himself. This is the essence of humility. What he sees in the sinners is a potential self, and he acts out that recognition in his mimetic behavior. Throughout the *Inferno*, the Pilgrim has been participant as well as observer. Here, in the depths of Hell, at the very nadir of the universe, his participation assumes its most active and obvious form. Among the deceitful and violent sinners of Cocytus, he is himself deceitful and violent. His pitiless behavior toward Bocca is thus not only an act of vengeance but a dramatic portrayal of the Pilgrim's recognition of his own capacity, as a fallen human being, for deceit and violence. Without that recognition there could be no humility, and without humility there could be no repentant ascent of the mountain of Purgatory.

The Pilgrim's conduct in the remaining episodes of the Cocytus cantos reveals the consistency of his mimetic behavior as he moves closer to the bottom of the universe. At the end of canto 32, Dante witnesses one of the most grotesque scenes in the *Inferno*: he sees Ugolino chewing on the skull of Archbishop Ruggieri. Perhaps recalling Bocca's ridicule of his failed effort to flatter him, the Pilgrim addresses a more elaborate *captatio* to Ugolino, capitalizing on the shade's obvious hunger for revenge on his fellow sinner:

> "O tu che mostri per sì bestial segno
>   odio sovra colui che tu ti mangi,
>   dimmi 'l perché," diss'io, "per tal convegno,
> che se tu a ragion di lui ti piangi,
>   sappiendo chi voi siete e la sua pecca,
>   nel mondo suso ancora io te ne cangi,
> se quella con ch'io parlo non si secca."
>
> (32.133–39)

"O you who by so bestial a sign show hatred against him whom you devour, tell me the wherefore," I said, "on this condition, that if you with reason complain of him, I, knowing who you are and his offense, may yet requite you in the world above, if that with which I speak does not dry up."

Though Dante acknowledges the bestiality of Ugolino's behavior ("O tu che per sì bestial segno"), he expresses no repulsion toward it. Instead, he strikes a deal with the hungry shade, promising to help him gain revenge on his fellow sinner: if Ugolino will explain the reason for his obvious hatred of Ruggieri, Dante will repay him by retelling the story when he returns to the world, simultaneously denigrating the memory of Ruggieri and restoring the reputation of Ugolino. By now the Pilgrim is well aware how anxious the shades in Cocytus are to keep their identities secret and how willing their fellow sinners are to betray them. Unlike Bocca, Ugolino is willing to reveal his identity, but only because Dante has so carefully assured him that it will be to his benefit to do so.[9] He even prefaces his narrative, in canto 32, with a reevocation of the "convegno" established by Dante: he will tell his story, but only because Dante has promised to repeat it, thereby defaming Ruggieri.

> Ma se le mie parole esser dien seme
>   che frutti infamia al traditor ch'i' rodo,
>   parlare e lagrimar vedrai insieme.
> (33.7–9)

But if my words are to be seed that may bear fruit of infamy to the traitor whom I gnaw, you shall see me speak and weep together.

Coming, as it does, at the very end of the canto, Dante's pact with Ugolino takes on an aura of significance it might not have were it to appear elsewhere in the text. And how curious it is that the Pilgrim should make a deal such as this with a sinner in hell, particularly one of the sinners in Cocytus, since he has just shown such pitiless behavior toward Bocca. But here in Cocytus betrayal is the constant modus operandi, and by striking his bargain with Ugolino the Pilgrim is merely playing according to the local ground rules; not only is he betraying Ruggieri's desire for anonymity, he is also assisting one sinner to wreak revenge on an enemy. Such an act of betrayal of a traitor is certainly appropriate to Cocytus, but in this particular instance it is the Pilgrim himself who is the agent of that betrayal.

The story told by Ugolino in response to Dante's request, of how he and his children were locked in a tower and left to starve by his former ally Ruggieri, is too well known to require any summary. It is a tale of such exceptional treachery and cruelty—the terrifying sound of the hammer nailing shut the tower door, followed by six days of horror as Ugolino watches his innocent children starve to death—that the listener must be moved to pity. At one point in his narrative Ugolino even dares Dante not to weep: "se non piangi, di che pianger suoli?" ("if you weep not, at what do you ever weep?" 33.42).

The episode as a whole provides us with both a succinct model of Dante's way of writing in the *Inferno* and a test of how the reader responds to the text. Ugolino's story, a sort of play within a play, is clearly calculated by the teller to evoke a sympathetic response from the listener. And if, like the Romanticists, we focus our attention on the story itself without regard for its context, we shall find in that story a tale of sorrow—the "dolore" of Ugolino as suffering father and the tragic destiny of his innocent children. If, however, we turn our attention to the descriptive elements that provide the framework, we are more likely to place that story in its larger context. The story is framed, at both ends, by the image of Ugolino's bestial rage as he gnaws on the skull of Ruggieri. It is this "perpetual" image of Ugolino, the beast who will always be chewing on that skull, that puts into proper perspective the other image of Ugolino, the pitiful and helpless father portrayed in the sinner's self-serving narrative.

That Ugolino—the suffering father—is, after all, a character in a narrative recounted by the shade who is submerged in the ice of Cocytus for his acts of treachery. Not that he is a "fictive" character—the story itself is undoubtedly meant to be taken as a historically accurate account of the events as they occurred—but the protagonist Ugolino *is* a creation of the shade Ugolino, who concocts a self-serving image of himself as a loving and suffering father, an image that serves to justify the vengeance he is now taking on Ruggieri. The shade is, in effect, doing exactly what Dante the Pilgrim had asked him to do.

The choice for the reader, then, is either to focus on the story (that is, the self-created image of Ugolino as narrator) or to keep in mind the framework which places that story, and its narrator, in its proper context. The choice we make determines our response to Ugolino's narrative. Dante himself seems to respond directly to the story. Interestingly, however, he does not respond to its pitiful elements as he did when, at the beginning of his journey, he heard Francesca's tale of sorrow. In fact, he shows no pity whatsoever, in spite of Ugolino's admonition: "se non piangi, di che pianger suoli?"

Has the Pilgrim, therefore, progressed since his encounter with Francesca? Has he come to recognize, and disdain, the sins he encounters? In itself, the absence of a pitying response in no way indicates a dispassionate judgment of Ugolino or his sin by the Pilgrim. There is no evidence to suggest that he shows no pity because he realizes that sinners so treacherous deserve none, or that displaying such pity would be offensive to divine justice.

The response that does follow Ugolino's narrative is more problematic than the exegetical tradition would seem to indicate. Immediately upon the conclusion of the sinner's story, Dante launches into a harsh invective against Pisa; blaming the city for the unjust deaths of Ugolino's innocent children, he invokes the Arno to flood and drown every last person in the city: "sì ch'elli annieghi in te ogne persona!" ("so that it drown every soul in you!" 33.84). This invective ends with a reference to the "canto" that names Ugolino's children—"Uguiccione e 'l Brigata / e li altri due che 'l canto suso appella" ("Uguiccione and Brigata . . . / and the other two that my song names above," 33.89–90)—suggesting that the voice we now hear is not that of the Pilgrim on the scene but the poet looking back on the actual episode. If we accept that the voice we hear is in fact that of the presumably objective poet, then we might also conclude, as did Croce, that what we are hearing is the cry of Dante's offended soul.[10] Croce made of Ugolino a spokesman for humanity offended by the excesses of political vendetta and factionalism; consequently, Dante's invective, like Ugolino's anger, is an outcry against such injustice. A standard critical response to the invective, and one that seconds Croce's reading, is to compare Dante's lofty tone and apocalyptic invocation to those of a biblical prophet; Dante assumes this posture as a means of expressing his moral indignation at the injustice done to the innocent children.[11] Read in this way, the invective becomes a rhetorical strategy designed to underscore the intensity of Dante's outrage.

But can we so easily divorce the invective from its narrative context? Whatever we may take to be Dante's motive, we must ask why he chose to render such an awesome and apocalyptic judgment on Pisa. One who did ask that question was De Sanctis, who was certainly a sympathetic reader of the Ugolino episode. Nevertheless, he was perplexed by Dante's outcry, which he called "uno sfogo di crudeltà"—"an outburst of cruelty." He was uncertain who was more ferocious, "Ugolino che ha i denti infissi nel cranio del suo traditore, o Dante, che per vendicarsi quattro innocenti condanna a morte tutti gli innocenti di un'intera città, i padri e i figli e i figli dei figli" ("Ugolino, who has his teeth sunk into the skull of his betrayor, or Dante, who in order to vindicate four innocents condemns to death all the innocents of an entire city, fathers and sons, and the sons of sons."[12]

Our response to the invective depends, to a large degree, upon our reading of Ugolino's narrative. If, like Croce, we read the episode in a historical-political way and conclude that Ugolino is rightfully vindicating the innocent who have suffered, we may conclude that Dante was objectively justified in condemning Pisa as a new Thebes. To do so, however, is to treat the invective as an autonomous segment of the text whose content is determined by factors extraneous to the immediate context. If, on the other hand, we set Ugolino's story within the contextual framework of the ninth circle of Hell, and keep in mind that, for all his humanity and suffering, Ugolino himself was treacherous and violent and ultimately responsible for the death of his innocent offspring, then Dante's invective takes on a strikingly mimetic tone. The same spirit of brutal vengeance that impels Ugolino to chew on Ruggieri's skull is evident in Dante's call for the annihilation of an entire city, presumably including the innocent. How curious that in condemning one injustice Dante would invoke another! His is a strange antidote to factionalism and vendetta—a vindictive judgment that perpetuates the very notion of injustice it presumes to condemn.

In a suggestive reading of the Ugolino episode, John Freccero contrasts the vengeful and selfish political game that results in the death of the innocent children with their own selfless suffering, which culminated in their offer to sacrifice their flesh so that Ugolino might live. According to Freccero, their suffering, couched in Christological language, offers "a redemptive possibility."[13] Ugolino's hardened heart, however, makes him deaf to their sacrificial message which, if heeded, "would put an end to the otherwise eternal series of violent acts, making possible a communion that was not possible before." Ugolino sees in their death not a new way of life but "only a spur to his infernal retribution." Freccero's reading clearly puts the episode as a whole into its larger context. However, it must further be noted that Dante's bitter invective indicates a response to Ugolino's story that corresponds not to the forgiving and healing spirit of the children but to the vengeful and violent spirit of Ugolino. If, indeed, it is only the poet's voice we are meant to hear in the invective, then either Freccero has misread the episode, and the children's language does not bear "redemptive possibility," or Dante himself has both created that message and contradicted it.

Whatever extratextual justification there may be for Dante's invective, a contextual reading demands that we take account of the parallel between Ugolino's bestial hatred and the unforgiving ferocity of Dante's condemnation of Pisa. While Ugolino may not have elicited the pity he had hoped for, Dante's response to the sinner's sad story is sympathetic in the literal sense. His response to the narrative account of the events in the tower is essentially the same as was Ugolino's to the experience of those events: both react with anger and a strong appetite for vengeance.

The Ugolino we see trapped in ice, the one who, in his bestial rage, is likened to a dog gnawing on a bone, is a representation of the distortion of human nature that characterizes all the sinners entombed in Cocytus. The frozen lake is an appropriate image for their hardened hearts, souls so cold and remote, so callous, that they have cut themselves off from any semblance of human warmth or charity. The Pilgrim's behavior subsequent to his encounter with Ugolino further indicates that his own heart has become hardened by exposure to the icy atmosphere of the ninth circle. As he moves toward Ptolemea, the third region of Cocytus, he again feels the physical effects of the numbing cold, to the point that he loses all feeling in his face:

> . . . sì come d'un callo,
> per la freddura ciascun sentimento
> cessato avesse del mio viso stallo
> (33.100–102)

as in a callus, all feeling, because of the cold, had departed from my face.

In his final dramatic encounter in Cocytus, with Frate Alberigo, the Pilgrim's callous and numb physical state will prove to be an objective correlative of his hardened heart. Once more he enters into a pact with one of the sinners. In a vocative address that will prove to be ironically prophetic, Alberigo, thinking that Dante and Virgil are condemned sinners come to take their place in Hell, refers to them as wicked souls ("O anime crudeli," 33.110), then asks them to remove the crust of ice that covers his eyes. Why Alberigo would assume that two shades whom he perceives as "anime crudeli" would come to his aid is not at all clear; in fact, his misperception of Dante and Virgil seems to serve primarily as preparation for the deception that is about to take place. The Pilgrim's first deceptive act is to not correct Alberigo's mistaken perception about his and Virgil's condition and destination. In answer to the request, he promises to remove the ice if Alberigo will identify himself. To seal the pact Dante swears an oath, one that is couched in the same ambiguity as was his promise to bring "fame" to Bocca: "s'io non ti disbrigo, / al fondo de la ghiaccia ir mi convegna" ("if I do not relieve you, may I have to go to the bottom of the ice," 33.116–17). Alberigo, unaware that Dante is still alive and that his journey will of necessity take him beneath the ice, believes that the Pilgrim is calling down upon himself the ultimate punishment, entombment beneath the ice in Judecca. He falls into the Pilgrim's deceitful trap and identifies himself. Then, when he calls on Dante to fulfill his promise, the Pilgrim walks away in disdain, proudly concluding, "cortesia fu lui esser villano" ("to be rude to him was courtesy," 33.150).

The traditional gloss on Dante's betrayal of Alberigo, going back to the earliest commentators, defends his behavior on two grounds: it is no sin to betray a traitor; and to help a sinner would be a violation of divine justice. However, two details of the Cocytus episode seem to contradict the logic of that reading: first, Ruggieri is in Hell because he betrayed a traitor in life and, second, moments earlier Dante himself had helped a sinner: by his covenant with Ugolino he had promised to help one sinner gain revenge on another.[14] More importantly, perhaps, the conventional reading of the Pilgrim's behavior avoids the more fundamental question of why the poet chose to create an episode in which the Pilgrim deceives Alberigo. The nature of complex fraud is that it is a betrayal of a specific bond of trust. Here, the Pilgrim first establishes that bond of trust between himself and Alberigo, then calmly betrays it. Once more his behavior reveals a mimetic response to the sin he encounters in Cocytus.

In Judecca, the final region of Cocytus, where all the shades are totally submerged beneath the ice, there can be no dramatic encounter between Pilgrim and sinner. Yet even here his condition is shown to be analogous to that of the sinners. Soon after he enters Judecca and sees the shades of those entombed in ice, Dante stands before the terrifying figure of Lucifer and is frozen with fear: "gelato e fioco" ("frozen and faint," 34.22).

The poet now focuses our attention on the condition of the Pilgrim at that moment by challenging the reader to understand what he became, neither dead nor alive:

Io non morì e non rimasi vivo;
  pensa oggimai per te, s'hai fior d'ingegno,
  qual'io divenni, d'uno e d'altro privo.
                                    (34.25–27)

I did not die and I did not remain alive: now think for yourself, if you
have any wit, what I became, deprived alike of death and life!

Rarely does the poet intercede so directly in the text, and here he
is obviously asking the reader to recognize that the Pilgrim's frozen
condition is no mere metaphor for the fear he felt as he stood before
Lucifer. In addition to conveying his psychological state at that
moment, the metaphor of the Pilgrim's negative duality, neither dead
nor alive, suggests an analogy with those very shades he sees buried
beneath the ice. Like them, he is "gelato e fioco"—frozen and faint.
And, like him, they are neither alive nor dead; having cut themselves
off totally from humanity through their treachery, they are being punished by being entombed beneath the ice, and thus are not alive. Yet
neither are they dead, for they are alive to the torment that they will
endure for eternity. Given the sinners' physical condition in Judecca,
there can be no dramatic involvement with them as there was with
Bocca, Ugolino, and Alberigo. Nevertheless, the frozen, motionless figure of the Pilgrim is an appropriate analogy to the state of the sinners
in the final region of Cocytus, as well as an apt image of the final step
of his descent into the darkness of his own heart.

The Pilgrim is "like" the shades in Judecca for the same reason he
is "like" all the shades in Cocytus; he shares with them the fallible
human condition, and his mimetic behavior is a dramatic portrayal
of his recognition of that fact. His recognition of sin in the *Inferno*
is not passive; it is, and must be, an act of self-recognition. It is, I
think, no casual remark made to the Pilgrim by Camicion de' Pazzi
soon after he enters Cocytus: "Perché cotanto in noi ti specchi?"
("Why do you gaze so much on us?" 32.54). That unusual verb,
specchiarsi (literally, "to mirror oneself"), found nowhere else in the
Inferno, sums up the Pilgrim's behavior during his journey through
Cocytus. He mirrors the sinners, I would suggest, precisely in order
to acknowledge his potential to be like them.

But just as the Pilgrim is neither dead nor alive in Judecca, so he
is both like and unlike the sinners he encounters in Cocytus. In them

he sees a potential self; but, unlike them, he is still free, because alive, to choose not to be like them. The ice of Cocytus is a symbol of the sinners' choice to seal themselves forever in the coldness of their own treachery, as far removed as possible from the warmth of human or divine charity. Their submersion in that frozen water suggests a parody of the baptismal rite; theirs is a baptism unto death.

The Pilgrim's descent into Hell is also, in Pauline terminology, a baptism unto death; but, unlike that of the sinners in Cocytus, his is a temporary death—the necessary death of the old man to be followed by the birth of the new man. His "death," and its ironic analogy to that of the entombed sinners of Judecca, recalls Paul's reminder, in his Letter to the Romans, that "by baptism we were buried with [Christ], and lay dead, in order that, as Christ was raised from the dead in the splendor of the Father, so also we might set our feet upon the new path of life" (Romans 6:3–6).

The Pilgrim begins to set his feet upon "the new path" at the moment when he turns his body upside-down on Lucifer's flank, a literal conversion that signals the end of his descent—which is, after all, only an apparent one—and the beginning of an ascent out of the darkness of Hell and of his own heart.

Soon after Dante's "resurrection" on the shore of Purgatory, Cato will instruct Virgil to wash the Pilgrim's face with the fresh dew from the shore. That life-giving water of renewal, which removes from the Pilgrim's face the stains of Hell, is the antithesis of the fatal water of Cocytus that seals its inhabitants in eternal life-in-death. No such baptism would have been possible, however, had the Pilgrim not first descended to that lake and there recognized his own potential entombment.

University of Wisconsin-Milwaukee

NOTES

1. All quotations from the *Comedy* are from the Giorgio Petrocchi edition, found in *The Divine Comedy*, trans. with a commentary by Charles S. Singleton (Princeton: Princeton Univ. Press, 1970–75).

2. Benedetto Croce, *La poesia di Dante*, 11th ed. (Bari: Laterza, 1966), pp. 100–102; Natalino Sapegno, ed., *La Divina Commedia* (Florence: La Nuova Italia, 1955–

57), note to *Inf.* 32.90; M. Puppo, "Il canto XXXII dell'*Inferno*," in *Nuove letture dantesche* (Florence: Le Monnier, 1969), 3.139.

3. Francis Fergusson, *Dante* (New York: Macmillan, 1966), concludes that Dante's behavior demonstrates that "he is capable, here in Cocytus, of identifying himself almost completely with the will of God" (p. 124).

4. Attilio Momigliano, ed., *La Divina Commedia* (Florence: Sansoni, 1946–51), note to *Inf.* 32.103; C. S. Lonergan, "The Context of *Inferno* XXXIII: Bocca, Ugolino, Fra Alberigo," in *Dante Commentaries: Eight Studies of the Divine Comedy* (Dublin: Irish Academic Press, 1977), p. 66.

5. In *Inferno* 13, Dante had inflicted pain on Pier delle Vigne by breaking off one of the branches of the tree into which the shade of the suicide had been transformed. Bocca's question to Dante ("Perché mi peste?" 32.79) echoes Pier's question ("Perché mi schiante?"—"Why do you break me?" 13.33). The similarity of Bocca's question underscores the difference in Dante's behavior. Dante had injured Pier unwittingly, having broken off the branch at Virgil's direction, and, contrary to his harsh behavior toward Bocca, he responded to Pier's plea for mercy with pity.

6. Lonergan, p. 66. He also offers another (and seemingly contradictory) explanation for Dante's behavior. Noting that Dante's treatment of Bocca offends a sense of fair play, Lonergan concludes that "with Dante minister there is also Dante sinner and pilgrim, the Florentine activist lost in a dark wood of evil" (p. 68). Dante's violence toward Bocca, then, is "a form of exorcizing that evil from himself" (p. 66). In this secondary explanation of Dante's actions, Lonergan seems to sense the participatory behavior of the Pilgrim (see n. 8 below) but ultimately attributes it to biographical motives: "Dante dwells longest on those sins closest to his heart, and these seem to be the sins connected with politics and the political life" (p. 67).

7. See Charles S. Singleton, *Dante Studies 2: Journey to Beatrice* (Cambridge, Mass.: Harvard Univ. Press, 1958), and "In Exitu Israel de Aegypto," *78th Annual Report of the Dante Society* (1960), pp. 1–24, reprinted in *Dante: A Collection of Critical Essays*, ed. John Freccero (Englewood Cliffs, N.J.: Prentice-Hall, 1965), pp. 102–21; John Freccero, "Dante's Firm Foot and the Journey Without a Guide," *Harvard Theological Review* 52 (1959): 245–81; Anthony K. Cassell, "Failure, Pride and Conversion in *Inferno* I," *Dante Studies* 94 (1976): 1–24.

8. For a discussion of the notion of Dante's journey in the *Inferno* as a journey into his own heart, see Rudy S. Spraycar, "Dante's *lago del cor*," *Dante Studies* 96(1978): 1–20. Spraycar links the image of the frozen lake of Cocytus with Dante's spiritual condition at the beginning of his journey; the frozen lake is a physical portrayal of Dante's hardened heart, which has been frozen by sin. I would argue that the frozen lake is also an objective correlative of the Pilgrim's condition at the *end* of his journey through Hell, where his hardened heart, displayed not only in the image of the frozen lake but in his behavior, is a metaphorical participation in the sins he encounters in Cocytus. For a discussion of Dante's participation, see my article "Dante the Pilgrim: Everyman as Sinner," *Dante Studies* 92 (1974): 63–76.

9. Citing the syntax of reciprocity that ironically links Ugolino and Ruggieri, John Freccero notes that the rule of reciprocity is also evident in the attitude of the Pilgrim when he offers to repay Ugolino for what he has suffered. See "Bestial Sign and the Bread of Angels (*Inferno* 32–33)," *Yale Italian Studies* 1 (1977): 56.

10. Croce, p. 101. Also see M. Sansone, "Il canto XXXII dell'*Inferno*." in *Nuove letture dantesche* (Florence: Le Monnier, 1969), 3.170–80.

11. See, for example, the commentary of Emilio Pasquini and Antonio Quaglio in their edition of *Commedia: Inferno* (Milan: Garzanti, 1982), p. 420, and that of

Tommaso DiSalvo, in *La Divina Commedia: Inferno* (Bologna: Zanichelli, 1985), pp. 565–66.

12.   "L'Ugolino di Dante," in *Lezioni e saggi su Dante*, ed. Sergio Romagnoli, 2d ed. (Turin: Einaudi, 1967), p. 700. Earlier, in his Dante lectures at Turin, De Sanctis concluded, in commenting on Dante's invective: "Qui Dante cade nello stesso peccato che rimprovera ai Pisani" ("Here Dante falls into the same sin for which he reproaches the Pisans"). See "Corso torinese sopra Dante, secondo anno, lezione settima," in *Lezioni e saggi*, p. 313.

13.   Freccero, "Bestial Sign," p. 57.

14.   Dante's refusal to assist Alberigo is all the more striking in light of courtesies he had extended to other sinners earlier in the *Inferno*: he asked Farinata to tell Cavalcante (when he recovered from his swoon) that his son Guido was still alive (10:110–14); and he gathered together the scattered branches of the anonymous Florentine suicide who had been torn apart by a pack of dogs (14.1–3). Alfred A. Triolo, in "*Inferno* XXXIII: Fra Alberigo in Context," *Alighieri* 11 (1970): 39–71, notes these two instances but concludes that Dante refuses to assist Alberigo because such an act would modify the dictates of divine justice and therefore be a discourtesy to God.

"Esto Visibile Parlare": A Synaesthetic Approach to *Purgatorio* 10.55–63

GINO CASAGRANDE

> Nam et innuere quid est,
> nisi quodam modo visibiliter dicere?
>
> Et sunt haec omnia
> quasi quaedam verba visibilia.
> —Augustine, De Trinitate
> 15.10.18; De doctrina cristiana 2.3.4

Introduction

Linguists have been aware for some time that the expressive plane of a language is made up not only of units that can be divided, analyzed, and properly studied in distinctive segmental features, but also that certain phenomena are connected with these features which have been only partially classified and which go under the broad category of paralinguistics. These phenomena are superimposed upon what is strictly called linguistics, and at times they have been found to be characterized by such a strong pertinence over and above the linguistic level that they themselves become the primary channel of communication. Linguists can tell us practically everything about a given word (its origin, formation, history, influences upon other words, and so on), but until recently they could not explain how and why that given word

21

could be pronounced in different ways, with diverse intonations, pauses, rhythms, and various inflections that modify to a certain degree its *normal* meaning. This aspect becomes, of course, much more complex and complicated when we analyze a full sentence, that is, when we consider the word in its syntagmatic role in a given act of communication. In fact, the matter of intonation and modulation has been a concern from the first writers on rhetoric down to our times.

Alongside paralinguistics a whole new branch of investigation into the process of communication has developed in recent years. It goes under the name of kinesics. Kinesics, as a science, is the study of all nonlinguistic and nonvocal forms of human behavior such as gesture, bodily motion, facial and visual expression, and so on, which are intended to designate semantic units. Recent investigations have already provided us with a basic and perhaps preliminary semiotic classification of various gestural expressions.[1] Linguists, educators, anthropologists, psychologists, and psychiatrists have begun to study the laws which regulate this type of communication.[2] These studies, in general, emphasize that the linguistic message is qualitatively modified or changed, strengthened or weakened, by auditory or vocal expressions that are not codified linguistically, as well as by various somatic expressions or bodily gestures. In other words, studies show that such phenomena transmit information either singly or in conjunction with the spoken language; and, from this point of view, they must indeed be considered as a king of "language." The efforts of these scholars and the abundant contributions of their studies lie beyond the scope of this article. From the scientific point of view, the problem of kinesics is that of systematizing the substance of such human expression and constructing a repertoire structurally determined by the complex units of a given culture.

In the following pages I shall consider this kind of communication mainly from the point of view of intersensorial perception and as a tool used by one poet to express and manifest a certain content at the expressive level. I have chosen Dante as an exemplary figure since we find in him (more than in other poets of his time) a high incidence of certain recurring tendencies regarding the metaphoric-metonymic relationship that result from pluridimensional channels of perception. Dante's language has received and continues to receive attention from scholars throughout the world. In the field of paralinguistics, some recent investigations have proven to be a good beginning to what could be an important contribution to Dante criticism.[3]

Here I shall attempt: (1) to shed some light on Dante's precise intention to avail himself of various channels of communication, including the kinetic in its largest sense; (2) to consider the communication conveyed by the various channels as a synaesthetic phenomenon and to construct a framework for synaesthesia in Dante on the basis of some observations provided by the Schoolmen, in particular Thomas Aquinas; (3) to analyze a synaesthetic "episode" from the *Purgatorio* (the "visible speech" of the three sets of sculptures in canto 10, with particular emphasis on the central panel), according to some elementary tenets of structural semantics; and (4) to substantiate the finding through a brief inquiry into the exegetical tradition of some biblical passages related to the point in question.

The Poet's Intention

Let us consider briefly canto 21 of the *Purgatorio*, where an unusual phenomenon occurs. The mountain of Purgatory trembles and all the souls up and down the slope cry out together. In this canto we learn the reason. It is a rejoicing that occurs whenever a spirit has completed its repentance and is ready to rise to Heaven. In this particular case, the spirit whose liberation has produced such a commotion is Statius. Dante of course knows the works of Statius, and Statius himself has a profound admiration for Virgil. Statius, then, not knowing that the addressee of his explanation for the trembling of the purgatorial mountain is Virgil, tells him that on earth he was a poet and that the *Aeneid* was to him both "mother and nurse." He confesses to his unknown interlocutor that in fact he would have consented to stay in Purgatory even longer had he been fortunate enough to live during Virgil's time. It is at this point that a *dialogue* of mimetic gestures takes place between Dante and Virgil. Here the kinesic element, and particularly the facial expressions, are so detailed and mimetically so well studied and described by the text as to deserve our close attention:

> Volser Virgilio a me queste parole
> con viso che, tacendo, disse 'Taci';
> ma non può tutto la virtù che vole;

ché riso e pianto son tanto seguaci
alla passion di che ciascun si spicca,
che men seguon voler ne' più veraci.

Io pur sorrisi come l'uom ch'ammicca;
per che l'ombra si tacque e riguardommi
nelli occhi ove 'l sembiante più si ficca;

e "Se tanto labore in bene assommi"
disse, "perché la tua faccia testeso
un lampeggiar di riso dimostrommi?"

(Purg. 21.103–14)

These words turned Virgil to me with a look that said in silence: "Be silent." But the power of the will cannot do all, for smiles and tears are such close followers to the feelings from which they spring that they least follow the will in the most truthful. I only smiled, like one that gives a hint; at which the shade was silent and looked into my eyes, where the expression is clearest, and said: "So may your great labor end in good, do tell me why did your face just now show me a flashing of smile?"

Some commentators have justly defined this episode as a "luminous study in physiognomy,"[4] although they are inclined to believe that this so-called psychological parenthesis concerning smiles and tears, as expressed by lines 105–8, is not justified poetically. And it may be so. However, this "parenthesis" must be considered as Dante's quasi definition of a type of nonverbal communication—namely, that belonging to facial expressions, and more precisely to tears and laughter. This type of communication, Dante tells us, is so natural and occurs so suddenly in us that one could say it is almost directly proportional to the sincerity and veracity of the emotion which generates it. In addition, our willpower, which is perfectly capable of restraining the words within us, is not able to suppress such a form of communication. Dante elsewhere in the *Divina Commedia* speaks of the face and the eyes as being "i sembianti / che soglion esser testimon del cuore" ("The looks which are wont to be testimony of the heart," *Purg.* 28.43–44). Moreover, the face, and in particular the eyes and the mouth, are also the objects of Dante's consideration in the prose that serves as a commentary to the second canzone of his *Convivio*:

E però che ne la faccia massimamente in due luoghi opera l'anima—però che in quelli due luoghi quasi tutte e tre le nature de l'anima hanno giurisdizione—cioè ne li occhi e ne la bocca. . . . Ahi mirabile riso de la mia donna, di cui io parlo, che non si sentia se non de l'occhio. (3.8.8, 12)

And in fact inner feelings show up on the face, and especially in two places: in the eyes and in the mouth, because in these two places almost all three powers of the soul have jurisdiction. . . . O marvelous smile of my lady which could only be heard by the eye!

Here Dante considers the eyes and the mouth as the most direct channels of communication, because through them we can readily understand the internal "passions" of the soul. By means of an elegant comparison, Dante imagines the eyes and the mouth as the windows and balconies of the edifice of the body, because through them its lady-dweller, the soul, albeit to a degree veiled, often reveals herself. This passage will help us to comprehend more fully a line in the *Paradiso* where the poet affirms that he is overcome by the "light of a smile" from Beatrice ("Vincendo me col lume d'un sorriso" (*Par.* 18.19). Moreover, serious consideration of this passage from the *Convivio* will prevent us from accepting that opinion which considers the encounter between Statius and Dante, quoted above, as a comic episode; indeed, more recent Dante critics have refuted and rejected this view.[5] There also occurs in the prose passage from the *Convivio* an extraordinary concept which I would like to underscore—namely, that the smile of his lady *is heard with the eyes.*[6] I shall return to this point later.

Virgil and Beatrice both transmit their intentions to Dante either by words or by means of nonverbal signs. Having completed his mission as guide, Virgil fixes his eyes on Dante and tells him, "Non aspettar mio dir più né mio cenno" ("Await no further my word or my sign," *Purg.* 27.139). *My word* and *my sign* are expressions that synthesize verbal and nonverbal aspects of communication. They recall other similar expressions. Thus, in canto 18 of the *Paradiso*[7] we find that Dante, in his profound desire to be fully instructed by his guide, turns to Beatrice *to see* and *to hear* from her what he must do:

Io mi rivolsi dal mio destro lato
per vedere in Beatrice il mio dovere
o per parlare o per atto segnato;
(52–54)

I turned to my right to see in Beatrice my duty shown by language or by gesture.

The command of Beatrice is "by *language* or by *gesture* shown." Her gestural signs are most often made through her eyes and smile, which are, of course, the chief characteristics of her beauty. Beatrice's eyes sparkle as she smiles and her smile, as we have seen, is a light that overcomes the wayfarer Dante (see *Par.* 3.24, 42; 5.125–26; 21.4–12; 28.11; 30.14–27). In the Heaven of the fixed stars, Dante, witnessing the hymn sung to God by the blessed, will again use the word *smile*, but this time it is the smile of the whole universe:

> Ciò ch'io vedeva mi sembiava un riso
> dell'universo; perché mia ebrezza
> intrava *per l'udire* e *per lo viso*.
> (*Par.* 27.4–6)

What I saw seemed to me a smile of the universe, because my rapture entered by both hearing and sight.

In this tercet we have what seems an extraordinary statement that once again reveals Dante's intention to combine various channels of sensorial experience. "Extra-ordinary" because here he considers the assimilation of different sense perceptions as a normal semantic process. In this particular example we are confronted with the convergence of the auditory and visual perceptions at the level of a mutual association. In the prose of the *Convivio* that I have quoted above, we have seen that the admirable smile of the lady could only be *heard* by the *eyes*. Here again, a particular sensation is perceived by two senses, the auditory (verbal) and the visual (kinesic), and is integrated and associated at the semantic level.

The Synaesthetic Phenomenon

When we speak of various types of communication that are perceived through the combination of two or more senses and are integrated and focused at the level of meaning, we are of course speaking about the phenomenon which goes under the name of synaesthesia. *Grosso modo*, synaesthesia is a kind of intertransposition based on the interaction of the sensory experience during the act of perception. As such, it belongs to the realm of metaphor. Yet it can be considered as somewhat more than a simple metaphor. In fact, linguistically, in synaesthesia there is no actual displacement of the "real" sign, as in metaphor. Here, neither of the two real signs displaces the other. However, they do enter into a form of simultaneous and synergetic association, and by so doing *create* a virtual image that constitutes a global semantic transposition of each and all "real" signs involved. A synaesthetic perception is one derived from the specific semantic area designated by the lexicon pertaining to sensory images. As such, synaesthesia is a kind of *semantic metaphoric fusion* of two or more sensory perceptions.

It is a commonplace that literary synaesthesia[8] is one of the canonic forms of expression in modern poetry. However, the concept of synaesthetic perception is a very ancient one. In the Western world the idea can be attributed to Aristotle. In fact, it was one of the underlying assumptions that prompted him to develop a theory of the common or central sense as a comprehensive perception and thus constitutes one of the basic structures in Aristotle's conception of man's cognitive powers. The idea was discussed and elaborated first by the Hellenist and Byzantine commentators on Aristotle, who also used the term συναίσθησις ("synaesthesis") for the first time.[9] It was then revived by the philosophical and psychological analyses of the Schoolmen— both in Paris and Bologna as well as at Oxford. Later it captured the attention of poets and writers on poetics in the post–Italian Renaissance. And finally it developed as one of the basic ingredients in Symbolist and post-Symbolist poetics down to our day.

In the theoretical writings of Dante there is no overt evidence for synaesthesia.[10] However, references implying that he was well and directly aware of the concept can be found, at least, in a couple of related passages from the *Convivio* (3.9.6). Making precise references to the two works of Aristotle in which the doctrine of common sense is developed, Dante affirms that only color and light can properly be said to pertain to the visual sense: "Dove è da sapere che, propriamente, è visibile lo colore e la luce, sì come Aristotile vuole nel secondo *de l'Anima*, e nel libro *del Senso e Sensato*" ("One must know that, properly, only color and light are visible, as Aristotle states in the second book of *De anima*, and in the treatise *De sensu et sensato*").

Dante adds that, to be sure, other things come into the field of sight and therefore are visible, but not *properly* visible as in the case of color and light: "Ben è altra cosa visibile, ma non propriamente, però che[11] altro senso sente quello, sì che non si può dire che sia propriamente visibile, né propriamente tangibile; sì come è la figura, la grandezza, lo numero, lo movimento e lo stare fermo, che sensibili [comuni] si chiamano: le quali cose con più sensi comprendiamo" ("Other things are also visible, but not properly since another sense perceives them. Therefore we cannot say that they are properly visible or properly tangible. These are figure, size, number, movement, and stasis. They are the so-called (common) sensible objects as we perceive them with more than one sense").

Here Dante applies the Aristotelian doctrine pertaining to the distinction between the so-called *sensibilia propria* ("Dico autem [sensibile] proprium quidem, quod non contigit altero senso sentiri. . . . ut visus coloris, et auditus soni, et gustus saporis"—"I am saying that proper sensible objects are those which are not perceived by another sense. . . . Sight perceives only color, hearing only sound, and taste only flavor") and the *sensibilia communia* ("Communia autem sunt motus, quies, numerus, figura, magnitudo: huiusmodi enim nullius sensus sunt propria, sed communia omnibus"—"Common sensible objects on the other hand are movement, stasis, number, figure, size. They are not proper to any individual sense, but common to all").[12] This doctrine became one of the basic points of discussion for all the thirteenth-century commentators of the two works of Aristotle mentioned by Dante, from Alexander of Hales and earlier to Thomas Aquinas and later. The discussion centers on the common sense.

According to Aristotle, common sense is the one function of the ψυχή that gains perception of all objects, a common central organ of perception in which the separate communications received by the proper senses are combined into a unity. Common sense also can display synthetic power by grasping the common properties in the qualities of common sensibles; in fact, the common sensibles (movement, figure, and so on) are the *proper* objects of the common sense. In addition, common sense has the power to separate and distinguish among the various sensations, and yet it must preserve the unity of sense perception. In short, it is the common ground, "the fontal principle of all external senses," as Thomas Aquinas puts it in his commentary on Aristotle's *De anima*, and as Dante himself calls it in the same chapter of *Convivio* (3.9.9) quoted above: "Di questa pupilla lo spirito visivo, che si continua da essa, a la parte del cerebro dinanzi, dov'è la sensibile virtute sì come in principio fontale, subitamente senza tempo la ripresenta, e così vedemo" ("The spirit of vision from the pupil is transmitted to the frontal lobe of the brain, where the sensitive power is located, as in a fontal principle. Thus the image is represented immediately, without lapse of time, and we see").

According to the medical tradition of his time, Dante assigns the seat of common sense "a la parte del cerebro dinanzi," namely, to the first of the three ventricles in which, besides common sense, also fantasy, or imagination, is located. This placement is reiterated by Dante in a passage from the *Vita nuova*, which states, "lo spirito animale . . . dimora ne l'alta camera ne la quale tutti li spiriti sensitivi portano le loro percezioni" (2.5): "The vital spirit . . . dwells in the most secret chamber of the heart to which all other sensitive spirits bring their perceptions." While not all Aristotle's commentators were in agreement as to the location of the *sensus communis*,[13] they all agreed that it had the power, through the medium of the proper senses, to bring together and unite two or more sensations. Thus, for Alexander of Hales:

Sensus communis habet primum actum et singularem, scilicet discernere album a dulci vel conferre. . . . Si enim discernit album a dulci et confert, necesse est recipi formam utriusque in uno organo: illud non erit organum gustus nec organum visus . . . [sed] sensus communis. Non differt sensus communis sensibilis in suo sensibili a particularibus: quinque enim sensibilia, quae sunt magnitudo, motus, numerus, figura, quies, quae sunt communia sensuum particularium, etiam sunt propria sensus communis. Apprehendatur etiam sensibilia sensum particularium a sensu communi: nam aliter non posset inter illa distinguere; ergo necesse est differre sensum communem in obiecto a sensibus particularibus.

Common sense is responsible for a fundamental and specific activity: namely, that of discerning white from sweet and of conflating them. . . . In fact, if white and sweet are perceived separately and combined together, it is necessary that the forms of each be perceived by a single organ. This cannot be the sense of taste or the sense of sight, but a common sense. Insofar its own and proper field, the perception by common sense does not differ from that of the particular senses. In fact, the five common sensibles—namely, size, movement, number, figure, and stasis—are common to the particular senses, and proper to the common sense. Particular objects perceived individually by the particular senses are also perceived by the common sense. Otherwise it could not distinguish among them. It is necessary therefore to make a distinction between common sense and particular senses.[14]

Alexander of Hales's point of view was closely followed by other major Schoolmen. Thus, for Thomas common sense, which—again—was "the fontal root of all senses," could be considered in two ways. First, it could be taken as the *terminus* of a sensation perceived by an external sense—for instance, the perception of white by the organ of sight. Second, it could be taken as the *principum* and *terminus* of a sensation perceived by any and all external senses—for instance, the perception of sweet by the organ of taste in relation to the perception of white. In this manner, common sense is able not only to perceive the difference between white and sweet, but also to conceive and realize that in certain cases white is indeed joined with sweet, as in the case of sugar:

> Vis sentiendi diffunditur in organa quinque sensum ab alia una radice communi, a quo procedit vis sentiendi in omnia organa, ad quam etiam terminatur omnes immutationes singulorum organorum: quae potest considerari dupliciter. *Uno modo,* prout est principium unum et terminus omnium sensibilium immutationum. *Alio modo,* prout est principium et terminus huius et illius sensus. . . . Habet igitur hoc principium sensitivum commune, quod simul cognosca plura, inquantum accipitur bis ut terminus duarum immutationum sensibilium; inquantum vero est unum, iudicare potest differentiam unius ad alterum. . . . Ultimum iudicium et ultima discretio pertinet sensum communem.

> The power of perception comes to the organ of the five senses from one common root. The power of perception derives from it, and all perceptions gathered by the individual senses terminate in it. This can be considered from two points of view. One, as beginning and end of all sense perceptions. Two, as beginning and end of this or that individual sense. . . . This common sensitive foundation—which knows many things at once—holds power in two ways: first, insofar as it is taken twice as end of two sensitive perceptions; second, insofar as it is taken as one, it can judge the difference of one and the other perception. The final judgment rests with the common sense.[15]

The same concepts are reiterated by Thomas in several passages of his *Summa*. Thus, for instance, in the question on the "powers of the soul taken specifically," Aquinas dedicates two full articles to the matter we have been considering. He describes what we now call synaesthesia not as the result of a psychic disorder[16] but as the normal process of decodification and integration of various sensory perceptions. Nor does he consider it a simple perception of one sense modality in terms of another, but sees it as a totality that envelops the whole field of perception itself in relation to knowledge, in which fantasy-imagination ("Phantasia sive imaginatio idem sunt"—"Fantasy and imagination are the same thing") and memory—considered respectively as the treasure-stores ("thesaurus") of *sense-forms* and of *intentions*—play a fundamental and indispensable role. A basic schematic diagram illustrating the direction of this totality of perception, as expressed by Thomas in *Summa Theologica* 1ª, Q. 78, a. 4, might loook something like this:

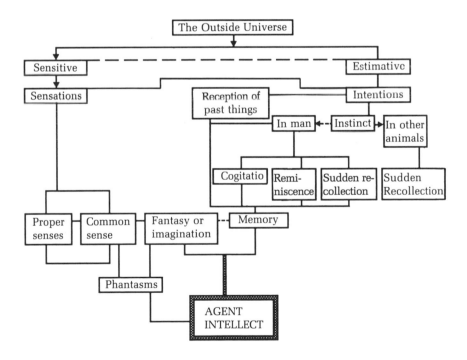

While memory in a way can be considered to contain the total gestalt, in the reflection of Thomas the basic working mechanism to which synaesthesia could be ascribed would be under the control of *common sense* and *imagination*. These two powers, however, work in strict correlation with the *phantasms*. *Phantasmata*, in fact, are not only the images presented to the imagination by the activity of exterior things affecting the different and individual sensory powers (i.e., visual, auditory, olfactory, tactile, and gustatory images), but they also present a "certain natural order linking different images to each other, e.g., a unity accruing to them from a definite area and time that serve as focal points for different sensations."[17] Hence, a synaesthetic operation would topographically occupy the entire lower half of the diagram. When memory seems to have lost the context of an image, what has really happened is that fantasy has taken over. The function of the common sense is to perform a kind of synapse of the sense forms apprehended by the individual senses. So that while sight, for instance, can discern white from black or green, and taste can understand sweet, "neither sight nor taste can discern the difference between white and sweet; because in order to discern the difference between two things it is necessary to know them both. Therefore it is necessary that such a judgement belong to a common sense to which all sense perceptions are referred, as to a common *terminus*" (*S.Th.* 1ª. 78.4.2). In fact, "sometimes we know *separately* things which are *con-joined* in reality; for instance, something is white and sweet, and yet sight knows only the whiteness and taste only the sweetness."[18] Leaving aside momentarily the treasure-store of fantasy, it seems clear that common sense is responsible for the process of decodification and integration of diverse and divergent sensations in order to move toward the level of association.

The idea of common sense as a common terminus is predicated on the analogy Aristotle drew between it and the mathematical point. Thomas says that any point between the two ends of a line can be considered either as one or as two. He underscores this analogy in a comment to *De senso et sensato* where the underlying concept of synaesthesia once again becomes apparent:

> Punctum autem, quod est terminus diversarum linearum, secundum quod in se consideratur, est unum et indivisibile. Et isto modo sensus communis secundum quod in se est unum, est indivisibilis et est unum sensitivum actu dulcis et albi: dulcis per gustum et albi per visum. Si vero consideretur punctum seorsum ut est terminus huius lineae, sic est quodammodo divisibile, quia utimur uno puncto ut duobus. Et similiter

sensus communis, quando accipitur ut divisibile quoddam, puta cum seorsum iudicat de albo et iudicat de dulci est alterum secundum actum: secundum vero quod est unum, iudicat differentias sensibilium.

The point, which is the end of various lines, when considered in itself is one and indivisible. In the same manner, common sense, considered in itself, is also one and indivisible, because it has the power to combine in a single sensitive activity sweet and white: sweet as perceived by taste, and white as perceived by sight. If, on the other hand, we consider the point as the end of a line, the point is divisible because we use one point as the end of two lines. In the same manner, common sense, when taken as divisible (as when it gives judgment on white and sweet) is one or the other according to the activity performed.[19]

It must be noted that the early commentators on Aristotle, such as Alexander of Aphrodisias and Themistius, came to regard the Aristotelian point as the center of a circle from which, *as many*, a number of radii start and in which, *as one*, they all unite. This observation is common to almost all medieval commentators as well, so that by the second half of the thirteenth century the common sense had become firmly and widely established as analogical to the center point of the circle and the relation which the center has with its radii proceeding from the circumference and terminating on it, and vice versa.

The doctrine of the common sense and the underlying concept of synaesthesia—in fact, the concept itself of its tradition, namely, the analogy of the point and its development into the center of a circle— can be well illustrated by the so-called *Wheel of the Five Senses*, a medieval wall painting in Longthorpe Tower (near Peterborough, England), discovered some thirty years ago and said to have been made before 1340. The painting[20] portrays the figure of a king standing behind a five-spoked wheel which he apparently holds in place with his left hand. The king's head is turned toward his right as he seems to look over a spider web outside the wheel. Surrounding the wheel, from the king's right to his left, at the points where the spokes connect to the rim, are five animals: a spider in its web, an eagle or vulture, a monkey, a cock, and a boar. According to a passage from *De rerum natura* by Thomas of Cantimpré, each of the five animals represents a sense.[21] Now for our purpose this painting may be considered as the first known visual representation[22] of the connections among the five senses, both in relation to the sense of touch (scholastically understood as the most important, in that it is the foundation of all the senses and hence the closest "to the fontal root," namely, common sense)[23] and in relation to the king, who may be considered to represent man's *ratio*. Insofar as the process of perception is concerned, we may therefore say that each animal, taken by itself, represents the "aesthetic" or sense level. The fact that in the painting the senses are in a way correlated to the rim of the wheel is quite significant. The spokes may represent the sensorial channels of perception leading to a center, the hub of the wheel—an interaesthetic point where decodification and integration of various sensory perceptions take place. This area is under the control of the common sense, which sets up for the ratio, and hence for the intellect, the associational meaning of two or more sensory perceptions. For our discussion, then, we may call this painting in Longthorpe Tower not simply *The Wheel of the Five Senses*, but *The Synaesthetic Wheel*.[24]

According to Thomas, two activities take place at the sensory level (*in parte sensitiva*). The first, just described and illustrated by the *Synaesthetic Wheel*, is of course effected from the outside by sensible objects. So, at the "aesthetic" level for instance, the sense of sight will only be able to see the color of an apple and not perceive its characteristic fragrance. But the fact that the apple is being perceived without its scent can only be attributed to sight, because in the sense of sight there is only the image of color and not that of fragrance (*S.Th.* 1ª, Q. 85, a. 2, ad 2). It is, as we have seen, the function of the common sense to integrate the two perceptions.

The other activity at the sensory level is a kind of *pro-duction* on the part of the imagination, in that it forms for itself the image of an absent object, or even of an object never seen before. Both of these activities are controlled by the intellect. However, it is by virtue of the second operation that definitions and acts of meaning are formed by the combining and separation of ideas. These, in turn, are expressed through *words*. Single words express the definition, while words in the syntagmatic union of enunciation express the intellectual process of composition and separation—that is to say, *meaning*.[25] The operation of the intellect, as an operation, is closely related to that of the common sense. In fact, the intellect is to imagination as common sense is to common sensations. This is an analogy in the strictest sense and holds true in relation to nonhomogeneous sensations such as white and sweet, as well as opposite sensations such as white and black. As common sense "judges" the sensations of white and black or of white and sweet, so intellect "judges" the phantasms of white and black or of white and sweet (cf. *In de anima* 3, lect. 12, 770). The intellectual process of conjunction is, of course, purely synthetic. The intellect has the power to abstract and synthesize two or more distinct concepts and merge them into one.[26] It seems obvious, then, that between sensation and imagination (and indeed also memory, which when it loses the context of an image is in fact relinquishing it to fantasy) there is a normal condition of anastomosis. It may be said that we have reached the fontal principle from which fine art springs. But with this we are far beyond the concept of synaesthesia, and thus the limited scope of this investigation.

Suffice it to say that while these ideas comprise quite an important stage in the considerations and reflections of Thomas, they were also the object of an intensive and in-depth analysis by other Schoolmen. Naturally, they also formed part of the inheritance of other thinkers and philosophers of the late Middle Ages, including, of course, Dante. What is astonishing is Dante's unique feat of turning these theoretical principles into a vast poetic enterprise. It has been said that the poetic message, in all of its manifestations up to the fifteenth century, is strongly characterized by an almost total absence of sensory notations.[27] From this perspective, the importance of synaesthesia used as a poetic tool by Dante acquires even greater significance. In fact, his use of various sense modalities in the poetic message of the *Divina Commedia* should be considered one of the major elements of the work. These modalities still await a full semiotic analysis.

A Synaesthetic Modality

Dante makes clear the synaesthetic modality of sensory perception at the very beginning of the *Divina Commedia* when he describes the atmosphere of the *Inferno*. He characterizes the *selva oscura* as the realm where "il sole tace" ("the sun is silent," *Inf.* 1.60). As we know, the *Commedia* is literally filled with synaesthesias of varying complexity. To my knowledge, a thorough and comprehensive study of them has yet to be undertaken.[28] It is not the purpose of this article to provide an inventory and a proper classification of the many synaesthesias and synaesthetic concepts found in Dante's masterpiece, much less to suggest a possible semiotic approach to this very complex prob-

lem. Instead I shall try to consider—in a single example of synaesthesia—the interplay between the level of sensation (the aesthetic
level) and the level of association (the synaesthetic level), in order to
arrive at the axis of the elementary semantic structure that unites two
or more heterogeneous sensory perceptions.

Before we proceed, it may be useful to clarify briefly my terminology, which is essentially drawn from A. J. Greimas. In his terms, an
elementary semantic structure is defined by the formula $A / r (S) / B$,
in which the relation (r) of the two terms A / B is given by the semantic
axis (S), which unites the similarities and the differences of the two
terms.[29] As an example, the formula can be elucidated by the synthetic
maxim "homo lupus," in which A (homo) and B (lupus) are related
(r) through the semantic axis (S) understood in terms of "rapacity,"
which as an element connected with the idea of "lupus" thereby
becomes also a connotation of "homo."[30]

Let us now direct our attention to those sculpted figures of white
marble on the cliff in the first terrace of Purgatory:

> . . . io conobbi quella ripa intorno . . .
> esser di marmo candido e adorno
> d'intagli sì, che non pur Policleto,
> ma la natura lì avrebbe scorno.
>
> (10. 29–33)

. . . I perceived that the encircling bank . . . was of white marble and
adorned with carvings such as not only Polycletus but Nature would
there be put to shame.

We are confronting a "sculptured dialogue," the function of which is
to communicate[31] to the proud souls doing penance there exemplars
of the virtue of humility. Dante describes these and hastens to tell us
that he is in fact admiring a "visible speech" (visible parlare) wrought
by God himself and new to humankind because it is not found on
earth:

> Colui che mai non vide cosa nova
> produsse esto visibile parlare,
> novello a noi perché qui non si trova.
>
> (10. 94–96)

He for Whose sight nothing was ever new, wrought this visible speech, new to us because it is not found here.

The expression "visible speech" could be considered as a semic nucleus, which means that these two words can be taken as the *minimal terms* of a denomination of which logos in its two most obvious aspects—that of sound-speech or verbal communication and that of sight-speech or kinesic communication—is the semantic condensation or the semantic axis of an elementary semantic structure. (It may, incidentally, be interesting here to note that John Chrysostom in one of his homilies uses the verb *kīneîn* in a syntagmatic union with the word *logos*).[32] We could also consider the two words "visible speech" as a *single member* of a binary system, the first term of which corresponds precisely to the Dantean *visible speech* of Purgatory and the second term to be defined as *audible speech*, so that we could formulate an elementary semantic structure as follows: visible speech / audible speech.

For the sake of clarity, and at the same time for the purpose of suggesting a certain analogical relationship between the divine sign (the sculptures) and a sign of that sign (Dante's text), we may combine the two possibilities suggested above into a unified pattern in the following manner:

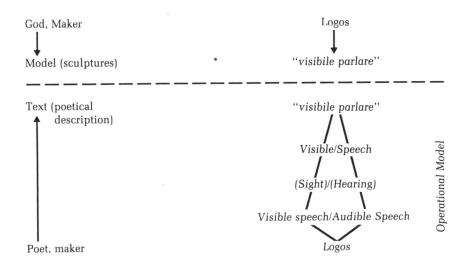

From that part of the diagram portraying the "Operational Model" the two expressions *visible/speech* and *visible speech/audible speech* are for our purposes one and the same, although for the sake of analysis it may be more convenient to adopt the longer form. Now, such a binary opposition can best be analyzed in the form of a semic articulation—that is to say, by establishing the relation among the elements of meaning in each opposite term. In our specific case, we would have to describe each opposite syntagma through the sensory order upon which it depends: in the first expression (visible speech), a visual order (mime, gesture); in the second (audible speech), an auditory order (word-sound). In Dante's lines it seems apparent that the "visible speech" stands out as an *ars nova*,[33] a pure category that has in its reality the value of a divine kinesis. The *new visible-speech* we are concerned with here, of course, is a form of *total art* that can only belong to God as Maker, the divine "fabbro" (Purg. 10.99). In its perfection the model is inaccessible not only for any human artist but even for Nature herself, ". . . not only Polycletus, but Nature herself would there be put to shame" (10.32–33). Here is not simply a creation out of chaos—as was the primal creation—but a special act of love, a *pro-duction* ("produsse"), a leading forth by the divine intellect, an act of *caritas*. The marble itself has become perfectly ductile under the ineffable spirit of the Maker, who is *Logos* and *motus* anterior to any articulated word.[34]

The model of the supreme making (~*poieîn*) is a "language for the eyes and for the soul. Sculpture is a visible art. It is seen, not heard. But Dante, having reached a full understanding of the word as well as of the living dialogue of the high reliefs, associates vision and word, sculpture and poetry, art and life."[35] The model, although inaccessible to man because of its perfection, must nonetheless be described by a second making—that of the poetical operation that makes the first one accessible to us through the synaesthetic word-images of Dante's text. In this text, here and elsewhere, Dante's poetic word—heavy with patristic and Scholastic tradition—becomes ductile as never before under the skillful pen of its master. The assertion of Oderisi da Gubbio that Dante "will hold the glory of the language" by surpassing the most famous poets of his times (Purg. 11.97–99) has already become a reality. From now on, Dante's tremendous task will be an ever-increasing poetic responsibility, to bend his fantasy toward creating a similitude of the word and the Logos insofar as it is possible[36]—in other words, up to the point of the complete and irreversible aphasia at the end of the *Paradiso*: "all' alta fantasia qui mancò possa" ("to the high fantasy here power failed," 33.142). But this, interesting though it may be, lies outside our immediate concern, and I shall pursue it no longer. The important point here is that the above suggestion may be taken as an indication of the infrastructure upon which Dante's poetical expression rests and works.

The tenth canto of the *Purgatorio* is a veritable gallery of divine sculptures. It is composed of three blocks of high reliefs. In the first we find the Annunciation. The Archangel Gabriel is portrayed by Dante as an image that "one would swear was saying 'Ave' " (10.40). Mary herself is described in such a way that the words "Ecce ancilla Dei" (10.44) are as if imprinted in her attitude. The second high relief portrays another fundamental biblical episode (Sam. 6:12–16). Here we find king David dancing "with all his might" (10.65) before the Ark of the Covenant as it is drawn into the city. In the third panel, we have as an example of humility Trajan portrayed by Dante in his imperial majesty and yet in the act of acknowledging the justice of a poor widow's claim. This last high relief is an excellent example of movement and of that "living dialogue" mentioned above. I may add that here Dante translates for us the *kinetic dialogue* between the emperor and the widow into an extremely expressive *verbal dialogue*.

I shall leave aside the long series of gestural signs on which Dante's "visible speech" is based. However, I would like to devote particular attention to an important detail around which the second sculpture seems to revolve. It also can be taken as an example to support the idea of Dante's intention of expressing himself through various means—in this particular case, a tridimensional order of communication based on the visual, auditory, and olfactory perceptions. Following basically the operational model sketched above, our analysis will also clarify the concept of elementary semantic structure proposed at the beginning of this section (p. 36).

In the second set of the high reliefs on humility, the Ark of the Covenant, which is being escorted by David into the city of Jerusalem, is preceded by a group of seven choirs. On the marble walls are also sculpted censers. Now, the smoke that rises from them is so perfect, Dante tells us, that his "eyes and nose bore discordant witness both of *yes* and *no*" (10.62–63). Dante's observation here is based on an olfactory-visual order. This, in turn, is preceded by another observation

based on an audio-visual order: it refers to the hymn of praise chanted
by the seven choirs before the Ark of the Covenant. Again, these choirs
are so perfectly sculpted, Dante says, that they "made two of my senses
say, the one 'No,' the other 'Yes, they are singing' " (10.59–60).

> Era intagliato lì nel marmo stesso
>> lo carro e i buoi, traendo l'arca santa,
>> per che si teme officio non commesso.
> Dinanzi parea gente; e tutta quanta,
>> partita in sette cori, a' due miei sensi
>> faceva dir l'un "No," l'altro "Sì, canta."
> Similmente, al fummo de li 'ncensi
>> che v'era imaginato, li occhi e 'l naso
>> e al sì e al no discordi fensi.
>
> (10.55–63)

There carved in the same marble were the cart and oxen drawing the
sacred ark which makes men fear tasks not committed to them. In front
people appeared, and the whole group, divided into seven choirs, made
two of my senses say, the one, "No," the other, "Yes, they are singing."
In the same way, about the smoke of incense which was shown there,
my eyes and nose bore discordant witness both of *yes* and *no*.

This particular detail is set by Dante precisely and pertinently at the
very center of the divine gallery, both thematically and composition-
ally. I have already mentioned that the Ark of the Covenant is the
central panel of the three sculptures. In terms of composition, we note
that the core of the description of the Ark is preceded by nine tercets
and followed by nine more (10.31–57, 67–93). It seems, therefore, that,
at least as an exemplum, the central sculpture is in a way the carrying
structure of the whole cornice and, perhaps, one of the main emblematic elements of the entire *cantica*. Within the central panel itself, the
smoke of the censers and the song of the choirs come together to form
a double synaesthesia that concerns the pairs ears/eyes and eyes/nose.
From a literal interpretation of the text, it is obvious that the visual
sense is contrasted to the auditory and olfactory senses. Dante does
insist in fact on their "discordance." His textual precision and his
adherence to the doctrine of the proper sensible objects are unmistak-
able. The visual faculty can *properly* see only color. The eyes have no
proper jurisdiction over the fragrance from the censers or over the

chant from the choirs. In the text, the discordance of the secondary senses is an attempt on their part to "correct" the superior sense of sight. Yet a reading of the two tercets conveys the strong impression that the eyes do indeed perceive the voices and the fragrance of the smoke. We know that this is a result of the synaesthetic working of the intellect through the *common sense* and the *phantasmata*, or sense images. The "correction" performed by the ears and the nose is only a synchronic correction of the sense taken in its *proper* function. It has nothing to do, of course, with the function of the intellect. We must, then, draw the conclusion that the poetic image we derive from the reading of the text is a correct one—that is, at the syntagmatic union of the enunciation (at the level of its meaning) there is a synaesthetic blending of sight, hearing, and smell. As we have seen above, this is due to the accumulation, reorganization, reshaping, and storing of previous sensations—a diachronic process in which the eyes absorb more than any other external sense. But in the literature we have been considering so far as the basis for synaesthesia, there is an even more cogent passage suited precisely to our purpose, in that it seems to bear directly on our specific case in point.

In the first chapter of the third book of *De anima*, Aristotle shows that the continued conjunction of two or more qualities perceived by two different senses eventually enables us to perceive both qualities, properly and incidentally, with a single sense. So that if one were to perceive the color and consistency of honey, one would also perceive its sweetness, and, in this case, Aristotle says, the individual would perceive sweetness with the organ of sight. His argument is as follows: "Incidentally we perceive something to be sweet through seeing it, because we have from past experience a perception of two qualities united in one object . . .", so that ". . . the senses perceive incidentally qualities which are proper to other senses, but not in so far as they are separate, but in so far as they constitute one sense, when a simultaneity of perception takes place in regard to the same object" (425a.20– 425b.2).

Perhaps even more important for our specific case is the explanation of this passage given by Thomas Aquinas—more important and more relevant because the example chosen and the expressions used by him are so close to the Dantean text as to make his explanation of Aristotle's passage seem an extremely pertinent commentary on the very lines of *Purgatorio* we have been considering. In his exposition

Thomas asserts that "the senses perceive each other's special objects indirectly, as sight that of hearing, and *vice versa*. Sight does not perceive the audible as such, nor hearing the visible as such (for the eye takes no impression from the audible, nor the ear from the visible) but both objects are perceived by each sense only in so far as 'one sense,' i.e. one actual sensation so to say, bears upon an object which contains both. I mean that both the senses in question are exercised at once upon one and the same sensible thing".[37] It must be noted, however, that both Aristotle's argument on the incidentality of perception and Thomas's explanation of it refer only to the level of sense perception and are predicated on previous knowledge that is furnished by some other cognitive faculty, such as "the cogitative or estimative powers, or intellect." In fact, it is true that "the operation of the intellect originates from the senses, but the intellect knows many things which sense itself cannot perceive."[38] We may then conclude our preliminary observations on Dante's experience when facing this sculpture of *Purgatory* with the following perceptive assertion by Fallani: "No sound reached the ears. The crowd seemed silent, but the eyes felt the movement of the chant and were fascinated by it as if it were a reality. The eyes were deceived in judging that the smoke was rising. The incense wasn't giving out any fragrant aroma, because the nose wasn't perceiving it. But in this relief the senses are mistaken, they clash against matter, except the sense of sight which is the only one to enjoy this real and unreal happening."[39]

At this point, if we are correct in reading the poetic message, we could begin our semantic analysis of this synaesthesia by structuring these three sensory orders in such a way as to constitute an opposition (//) at the olfactory level (the fragrance of the incense) and at the auditory level (the laud chanted by the choirs) through the visual level that partakes of both:

Sensation

(Incidental)   (Proper)   (Incidental)

Olfactory   //   Visual   //   Auditory
Fragrance   //   Laud

A schematic diagram of this specific act of communication could be formulated as follows:

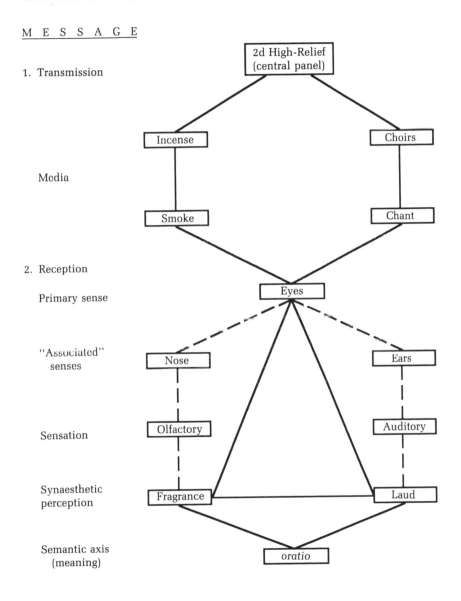

M E S S A G E

1. Transmission

Media

2. Reception

Primary sense

"Associated" senses

Sensation

Synaesthetic perception

Semantic axis (meaning)

2d High-Relief (central panel)

Incense

Choirs

Smoke

Chant

Eyes

Nose

Ears

Olfactory

Auditory

Fragrance

Laud

oratio

A few explanatory remarks are in order. (1) The diagram is basically intended as a visual operational model showing schematically the message in that section of Dante's text. The diagram itself may be considered a meta-message. This, however, is irrelevant to our analysis. (2) In the "Transmission" and "Reception" sides, all the elements (down to the level of "Sensation") are given by the text. (3) In the "Reception" part, the primary receiver (the eyes) has the full burden of "receiving" sensations from nonproper channels (smoke, chant). (4) There is no reception from the sensory data of smoke and chant by the proper senses of smell and hearing. An analysis conducted along Thomistic lines would certainly classify these media as sense-objects *per accidens,* as they (the choirs-*chant* and the censers-*fragrance*) are apprehended by the intellect as soon as this particular *sight* experience of Dante occurs.[40] (5) The secondary senses are "associated" only through a kind of sense reflex. In the diagram this is indicated by dotted lines. (6) In the operational model, the semantic axis is given as such (*oratio*). It will be the task of the following inquiry to prove it correct.

Substantiation of the Semantic Axis

The above diagram shows a synaesthetic connection between the fragrance of the incense and the laud of the choirs. The semantic axis of these two terms is the result of their aesthetic syncretism. As I have said, the axis goes under the denomination of *oratio,* or prayer. It is self-evident that the term *prayer,* in one of its manifestations (namely, the saints' laud that rises to God in the form of a chant), belongs specifically to only one of the two terms in question, that characterized by auditory sensation. However, this connotation of the chant becomes also a denotation of the opposite term in the semantic structure, that given by the smoke of the incense and characterized by olfactory sensation. The net result is that *laud, fragrance,* and *prayer,* under these circumstances, become interchangeable elements of an equation in which *prayer* functions as the central term of correlation. We could say, then, that the fragrance of the incense and the laud of the choirs are in a state of symbiosis. They coexist semantically by virtue of a synergetic exchange that has been taking place between them for a long time. If this is so, the semantic axis (or, if one prefers, its dia-chronic aspect) will have to be sought in the long biblical and exe-getical tradition, the highlights of which I shall briefly outline.

First and foremost, Psalm 140 presents a specific likeness between prayer and incense in a simile concerned with a sense of direction that was to remain a constant element in the exegetic tradition: "Let my prayer be directed to Thee as incense" ("Dirigatur oratio mea sicut incensum in conspectu tuo"). Also in the Apocalypse we find the con-cept of prayer in a syntagmatic union with that of incense: here, after the opening of the seventh seal, an angel came and stopped in front of the altar, holding a censer. Incense was given to him so that he might offer it along with the prayers of all saints: "The angel came and stood in front of the altar, having a golden censer. And there was given to him much incense, that he should offer it with the prayer of all saints. . . . And the smoke of incense ascended up before God out of the angel's hands with the prayer of the saints" ("Angelus venit et stetit ante altare habens turibulum aureum, et data sunt illi incensa multa, ut daret orationibus sanctorum omnium. . . . Et ascendit fumus incensorum de orationibus sanctorum de manu angeli coram Deo" Rev. 8:3–4). Here, as in Psalm 140, the element of the syntagma is evident in the smoke of incense and the prayer of the saints. Smoke becomes almost the viable and *visible* channel of man's communica-tion with God.

In the fourth-century exegetic tradition we find the same concepts in Augustine's commentary on the psalm cited above. He compares the heart of the faithful to a sacred altar: from the heart of man prayer rises in the same way incense rises from the sacred altar. But the commentator goes on to add something extremely important by saying that there is nothing more delectable to God than this fragrance, and therefore, continues Augustine, may all believers be so sweet-scented for God: "Oratio ergo pure directa de corde fideli, tanquam de ara sancta surgit incensum. Nihil est delectabilius odore Domini: sic oleant omnes qui credunt" ("Prayer rises from the faithful's heart in the same way as incense rises from the altar. There is nothing more delectable to God than its fragrance. May all believers be so sweet-scented").[41]

The shift from prayer associated with smoke as a visual aspect (as noted above) to the olfactory characteristic expressed by Augustine—and by Ambrose before him—is a major element that will remain con-stant in patristic exegesis and poetical conceptions down to Dante.

This very pleasant—if I may call it so—olfactory aspect of prayer is strongly reiterated about a century later by Cassiodorus in his commentary on Psalm 140; moreover, he refers to the passage of Revelations quoted above. In his extremely terse prose, Cassiodorus sets up a parallel structure between incense burned by the coals and prayer ignited by the fire of love. In such a setting, he reaffirms the concept already expressed by his predecessors—that the fragrance of incense ascends to the Almighty as the prayers of the blessed *and* that the prayers of the saints are accepted by God as a sweet fragrance.

Incensum est odoriferi pigmenti suavis adustio, quae carbonibus concremata, gratissimum fumum porrigit ad superna, et odorantes se delectabili jucunditate permulcet. Sic beatorum oratio igne charitatis incensa, divinis conspectibus ingeritur, quae magis humilitatis et compunctionis pondere sublevatur. Virtutibus enim Dominus nostris tanquam bonis delectatur odoribus. Nam orationem sanctam velut odorem suavissimum suscipere Dominum et in Apocalypsi legitur, ubi dictum est: "Stetit angelus super aram domini (etc.)."

Incense is the sweet burning of a scented pigment which, fueled by coals, pours forth a very pleasant smoke, filling people with a delightful happiness. In the same way the prayer of the blessed, fueled by the fire of love and lifted by humility and contrition, is brought up in front of God. God enjoys our virtues as much as pleasant smell, and He accepts a holy prayer as sweet fragrance. In fact, in *Revelations* it is written: "The angel came and stood in front of the altar of God (etc.)."[42]

In the biblical and patristic quotations so far presented we have been made quite aware that a similitude was drawn between prayer and smoke, and between prayer and fragrance—what I have called the visual and the olfactory aspects of prayer. With the passing of time, the simile changed, and by the twelfth century it had become a full-fledged metaphor. It must be pointed out, however, that there is evidence for a transformation of the simile into a metaphor even six centuries earlier, during the time of Augustine.

Thus, in a very eloquent and poetic passage from *De Isaac et anima*, Ambrose describes the soul in the desert of this earth choked with the brambles and thorns of our sins. Through prayer she lifts herself up toward God like the shoot of a vine, and like the smoke produced from fire that seeks the heights. Then he likens the fragrance of a pious prayer to the odor of incense. Finally, he interweaves the prayer of the soul and the incense offered to God in a closely knit syntactical structure in which the metaphoric import is made apparent. In this connection, incense does become equivalent to the prayer of the saints, which is, as it were, "fragrant with the sweet ointment of pious prayer, because it had been prepared from prayers for things eternal and invisible, and not for things corporeal. And above all the soul is redolent with incense because she is dead to sin and alive to God."

> Odor autem ille orationis piae redolet suavitatem, quae dirigitur sicut incensum in conspectu Dei. Et in Apocalypsi legimus quod, *Ascendit fumus incensorum de orationibus sanctorum,* quae incensa deferuntur per angelum, sanctorum orationes scilicet, super altare illud aureum quod est ante sedem Dei, et tanquam piae precationis suave fragrat unguentum; quia de aeternorum et invisibilium, non de corporalium petitione compositum est: precipue tamen [anima] redolet et thus, eo quod peccatis mortus sit, et Deo vivat.

> The fragrance of a pious prayer is scented with sweetness and directed, as incense, to God. And in *Revelations* we read that *the smoke of incense ascended up before God from the prayer of the saints.* Incense, that is the saints' prayer, was offered by the angel in front of the golden altar, before God. The fragrance is as sweet-smelling as a pious prayer, because it has been prepared from prayers for things eternal and invisible, and not for things corporeal. And above all, the soul is redolent with incense because she is dead to sin and alive to God.[43]

Throughout the passage, the terms, starting from the physical aspects of their earthly nature, acquire an ever-increasing spirituality. They become, as it were, interiorized and dematerialized to the point that, toward the end of the paragraph, Ambrose feels it necessary to reinforce this process by using an antithetical clause which strongly affirms the spiritual by denying the material ("a prayer for things eternal and invisible, and *not* for things corporeal"). It is, so to speak, the very heart of the physical matter that becomes spiritual and eternal. Throughout the passage Ambrose explicitly conveys to us the metaphoric and allegorical meaning by his use of a semantic solution: the terms lose in physical precision, but they are enriched and gain in spiritual truth. The soul's prayer *is* incense, and therefore she is redolent with its fragrance.

Finally, in one of Alanus's (Alain de Lille) sermons, the full metaphorical meaning is brought out and in fact explained in terms of the simile, which occurs in a speech prepared for the Day of Epiphany. As may be expected, its theme centers on the Magi's offerings. Their gifts are given a trilevel interpretation: "historical" (myrrh), "tropological" (incense), and "anagogical" (gold). Incense is offered by the intellect and, significantly, is placed in the middle of the triad, as an intermediate step on the road from earthly and transitory things (symbolized by myrrh) to celestial and divine contemplation (symbolized by gold). Incense works as a kind of "sursum ductiva" power, a power that lifts up the soul. Through prayer, the door is opened to celestial encounters. Now the same three gifts are offered also by men. Here incense signifies prayer: "Nos autem, fratres karissimi, offeramus Deo tria munera, aureum, thus et mirram. . . . Per thus oratio significatur unde dictum est: *Dirigatur oratio mea sicut incensum in conspectu tuo.*" ("Dearest brothers, let us offer God three gifts: gold, incense, and myrrh. Incense signifies prayer, as it is written, *Let my prayer be directed to Thee as incense*").[44] However, it is in his *Distinctiones* that Alanus makes clear the metaphoric significance of incense. Here the proper meaning of incense is prayer: "*Incensum*, proprie, oratio; unde in Psalmo: Dirigatur, Domine, oratio mea sicut incensum" ("*Incense*, properly speaking, is prayer. Thus in the Psalm is written: *Oh, Lord, may my prayer be directed to Thee as incense*"). The same definition is given for the word *smoke*: "*Fumus*, proprie, oratio vel virtus orationis" ("*Smoke*, properly speaking, is prayer, or the power of prayer"). In this entry we are reminded also of the simile that others had used before him—as smoke drifts toward the heights, so prayer inflamed by the fire of *caritas* ascends upward to God. Finally, one would also expect a similar definition for the entry *odor*. In fact, according to Alanus, fragrance does mean prayer: "*Odor*, proprie, dicitur oratio" ("*Fragrance*, properly speaking, means prayer").[45] The visual and olfactory dimensions of prayer are again in evidence. It must be noted that here the metaphorical meaning almost reabsorbs into itself, so to speak, the proper meaning of the words. The semantic process of enrichment, to which I have alluded above, here reaches its maximum point of development and tension. In Alanus's definition, this uplifting or semantic transfer of the sign (*signum*) from its earthly (literal) significance to celestial meaning is properly called *symbol*. According to a curious etymology given by Alanus ("syn" + "olon"), symbol is a "syntotality," in that the sign comprehends a multiple knowledge of reality. On the surface, the sign sounds literally, but in the interior it becomes understood tropologically and anagogically.[46] As I believe we have sufficiently seen, incense does become the sign of a hidden reality—prayer.

Alain de Lille's biblical reference ("May my prayer, o Lord, be directed to Thee as incense") brings us back to Psalm 140. We have seen that the concept of prayer (laud) as the fragrance rising to God from those who believe is deeply embedded in patristic tradition.[47] And the tradition draws its vital inspiration from the passage of Revelations quoted above as well as from this psalm. It is worth noting that the psalm in question is one of David's, "the humble psalmist," as Dante precisely and pertinently names him in the very episode of the *Purgatorio* under consideration (10.65).

Dante's tercet on the smoke of Purgatory (10.61–63) has sometimes been harshly criticized. It has been felt that here he insists on details to the degree that his expression seems too logical and cannot be justified poetically. Some critics claim that Dante, because of his downshift from the "noble" senses (eyes and ears) to the inferior and material sense of smell (10.59, 62), here becomes forced and unnatural, with the result that the three lines almost appear pedestrian.[48] However, our brief foray into patristic literature, and the discovery and substantiation of the semantic axis (prayer) postulated at the beginning of this section, prevent us from agreeing with that point of view. On the contrary, on the basis of the foregoing analysis, we can say that the tercet not only is totally justified but is also poetically inevitable. In other words, prayer is its vital essence because it is the very basis for its inspiration. Incense as prayer is an essential and eloquent necessity in the profound silence that envelops Dante's purgatorial sculptures.[49] Moreover, the semantic axis justifies, both morally and poetically, the expanded paraphrase of the Lord's Prayer which Dante has the penitent spirits recite at the very beginning of the following canto (11.1–24). As we know, these are the same spirits for whom the sculptures of the "visible speech" were wrought by God as exempla. We may add, then, that the concept of prayer does establish the poetic unity of the first terrace of Purgatory and in fact of the whole *cantica*, which is, as everyone knows, the realm of prayer.

The discovery of this semantic axis is indeed rewarding in other ways, because it helps us to understand more fully other passages in

the *Divina Commedia*. For instance, when Dante finds himself in front
of the superluminous darkness that springs from the river of light—
which transforms itself first into a round sea of light and then into a
celestial rose full of the blessed, a rose full of spiritual *fragrance of
prayer* to the eternal God—the poet does not fail to record it in an
exquisite synaesthetic expression, "The yellow of the unwithering rose
. . . is redolent with the fragrance of praise to the Sun of eternal spring":

> Nel giallo della rosa sempiterna
> che . . . *redole*
> *odor di lode* al sol che sempre verna.[50]
> (*Par.* 30.124–26)

Thus, in these lines, if we were to take the verb *redole* out of context
(an arbitrary act, prohibited even by the strong enjambment that binds
the italicized syntagma) and to consider it as "a rare latinism from
Virgil,"[51] we would certainly lose the full impact of Dante's synaesthesia. The fact is that the verb *redoleo* and its derivatives recur very
frequently in patristic writings in connection with the fragrance of
incense, and bearing the precise meaning I have pointed out above.
From Ambrose and Augustine through Cassiodorus on, all the way up
to the tenth through twelfth centuries, in all corners of Christianity,
even in formulas of incense benediction,[52] the image acquires a specifically profound metaphoric meaning. *Incensum, fumus, odor, oleo,
adoleo, redoleo, suavitas, thus, fragrantia,* and so on become isotopes
of a tightly woven and compact semantic structure, centered around
oratio, prayer. The lines just quoted are the culmination of this long
tradition. In this canto of the *Paradiso,* so close to the end of his
supernatural journey, Dante reaches one of the highest levels of poetic
concentration and condensation.

   With Dante's progression from Purgatory through Paradise, the
motif of a laud in fact becomes first nature to the blessed. There is,
moreover, an increasing association of it with perfume and light, and
the whole is laced around a kinetic element in the form of dance. As
O'Malley has appositely shown, Dante's "intersense metaphor" is of
a philosophical and spiritual nature. In the *Paradiso,* where the concept of "singing and shining and odoriferous lights in the various
spheres tends to dissolve distinctions among senses," we often observe
what O'Malley calls "synaesthetic drift": the synaesthetic images reinforce one another, as in the case of the reflections of song and the

echoing of rainbow splendors at the beginning of canto 12 (1–15). The maximum synaesthetic drift will be reached in the final canto of the *Paradiso* (33.82–90), where Dante beholds, "as though in a simple flame of light, the fusion of all phenomena in a divine unity."[53] Here, of course, we are at the outer limits of sense perception, in a completely spiritual and interiorized sphere. Dante's intense vibrations of pan-aesthetic experiences are here concentrated and condensed into one term—Love. In Love, all sense perceptions are integrated and fused into an all-embracing unity.[54]

Conclusion

In conclusion, I shall recapitulate my argument by saying that the semantic axis, *prayer*, has appeared as a synergetic outcome of the two related terms *fragrance* and *laud*. These terms, however, are offered to us by Dante's translinguistic perception derived from the *smoke of the censers* and from the *chant of the choirs* sculpted on the wall of the purgatorial terrace. By translinguistic perception, I simply mean a perception that does not derive from a linguistic form-order but that may in fact be perfectly equivalent to one and translatable into one.[55] Dante the Poet is the master who provides us with this perfect translation.

The communicative experience that we have tried to grasp from the nonverbal orders of perception in the Dantean "episode" is but a glimpse of a totality composed of verbal and nonverbal elements, unfolding and merging into a continuous *redolent* and *musical panorama* that reaches its ultimate form of poetic expression in the mystical transcendence of Paradise. Beyond that lies the superluminous silence of Dante's aphasia—the Poet's ineffable experience—which of course is, for us, the blank page.

University of Wisconsin-Madison

NOTES

1. Cf. Eckman and Friesen, "Repertoire of Nonverbal Behavior," *Semiotica* 1, no. 1 (1969).

2. See, at least, *Approaches to Semiotics*, ed. T. A. Sebeok, A. S. Hayes, and M. C. Bateson (Paris, 1964). See also A. Ponzio, *La semiotica in Italia* (Bari, 1976), especially 1:2 and 2:2.

3. I have in mind some recent contributions such as the volume by T. Wlassics, *Interpretazioni di prosodia dantesca* (Rome, 1972).

4. See *La Divina Commedia*, commentary by A. Momigliano, *Purgatorio* 21, nn. 103–20.

5. See M. Sansone, "Il canto XXI del *Purgatorio*," *Lectura Dantis Scaligera: Purgatorio* (Florence, 1968), pp. 793–826.

6. Busnelli and Vandelli resolve the expression "de l'occhio" with "con l'occhio." They also quote the following note by M. Barbi: "Il *de* ha, si sa, nell'antico italiano, e generalmente nelle lingue romanze, un uso assai più vario che oggi, per modo da fare anche una grande concorrenza al *cum*" (cf. *Il Convivio*, ed. G. Busnelli and G. Vandelli; 2d ed., A. E. Quaglio, ed. (Florence, 1964), 1:353, n. 9.

7. Canto 18 could be cited to show how the superb craftsman Dante uses various types of communication functionally and structurally to set up a pattern of reciprocal and antithetical relations in order to create unrivaled poetic effects. Here we observe, first, the impossibility of any communication through aphasia (ll. 8–12), then communication through nonverbal elements (13–18), then through verbal expressions (20–21), after which follows nonverbal (22–27), and, again, verbal communication (28–36); and so on.

8. Literary synaesthesia also goes under the name of "intersense analogy." Presumably, this is in order to distinguish it from clinical synaesthesia, which is often associated with abnormal experience. For more details, see G. O'Malley, "Literary Synaesthesia," *Journal of Aesthetic and Art Criticism* 15 (1957): 391–411. However, there may be no need to make such a distinction, since clinical synaesthesia is properly called *synaesthesis* (see P. Dombi Erzsébet, "Synaesthesia and Poetry," *Poetics* 11 [1974]: 23–44).

9. The term was first used by Alexander of Aphrodisias in relation to consciousness of sensation, which accompanies the exercise of man's perceptual powers and is under the control of the common sense (E. Wallace, *Aristotle's Psychology* [New York, 1976], pp. lxxxi–lxxxii and 255; this is a reprint of the 1882 ed., entitled *Peri psychēs*). In the past, many scholars have supposed that synaesthesia is a modern phenomenon that began with Romanticism. Recent investigations, however, have shown that such an assumption is unfounded and incorrect. O'Malley (p. 391) has pointed out that a basic definition of *synaesthesia* as the "metaphor of the senses" is suggested by a remark of Aristotle in *De anima* 2.420a–b (but see also 2.9. 421a–b). In addition, by Aristotle, see also *De sensu et sensato* 4. 440b.30. Cf. also Themistius, *In de anima* 104.

10. G. Cambon, "Synaesthesia in the *Divine Comedy*," *Dante Studies* 88 (1970): 1–16.

11. I am quoting from the Busnelli and Vandelli edition of *Convivio* (above, no. 6), p. 368. However, I am omitting their addition of [*anche*] to the text following "però che" and preceding "altro senso." Such an addition has been correctly labeled *inutile* by M. Simonelli (*Materiali per un'edizione critica del Convivio di Dante* [Rome, 1970], p. 156). For the other addition of [*comuni*] in the same paragraph, see n. 14 below.

12. *De anima* 2.6; 418a 10–20, in Thomas Aquinas, *In Aristotelis Librum de anima*, ed. A. M. Pirotta, O.P. (Turin, 1959), p. 99 (hereafter *In de anima*).

13. "Qaeritur de instrumento sensus communi. Et videtur quod sit aliqua pars cerebri. . . . Sed Philosophus arguit eius organum esse cor velut aliquid simile cordis in non habentibus cor" ("The discussion is about the organ of common sense. It seems to be located in a certain part of the brain. . . . However, Aristotle argues that

it is in the heart, or something similar to the heart in creatures without a heart").
Alexander of Hales *Summa theologica* 1ᵃ. 2ⁱ. 360 (Quaracchi, 2:437–38).

14. Cf. Alexander of Hales, op. cit. The addition of [*comuni*] to "sensibili" in *Convivio* 3.9.6 was first proposed by M. Romani in 1862, who placed it before the noun. In 1874, G. B. Giuliani accepted Romani's addition but placed it after the noun, so as to read "sensibili [comuni]." This addition was also defended by E. Moore in 1896, who has since been credited for it (cf. *Il Convivio*, ed. Busnelli and Vandelli, 1:367–68, n. 5). The addition is now accepted by all editions, since it is claimed that it is necessary for the meaning. Elsewhere in the *Convivio* (4.8.6), Dante in fact does use the expression "sensibili comuni." Thomas Aquinas uses the expressions *sensibilia propria* and *sensibilia communia* as almost constant terms in his works (cf. *In de anima* 2.lect. 13; *Comm. de sensu et sensato*, lect. 2. 28ff.; *S. Th.* 1ᵃ. 78. 3 ad 3; etc.).

15. Thomas Aquinas *In de anima* 3.lect. 3. 609, 613. According to Thomas, the fundamental basis of the organic common sense is to be found in the sense of touch, but *not* intended as a *proper sense*—that is to say, as a touch-sense that can perceive contraries within its range such as hot and cold, moist and dry, and so on (*Summa theologiae* 1ᵃ. 76. 5; see also Alexander of Hales's *Summa theologica* 1ᵃ. 2ⁱ. 355), but insofar as it falls into a more general class of sensation which is the general object of touch (cf. Thomas *Summa theologiae* 1ᵃ. 73. 3 ad 3). As such, the sense of touch is the foundation of all senses, and consequently it is the closest to the "fontal root of all senses," that is, the organic common sense. Thomas's view is made clear also in his commentary to Aristotle's *De anima* (3.lect.3.602): "[Tactus] est primus sensuum et quodammodo radix et fundamentum omnium sensuum. . . . Attribuitur autem ista discretio tactui non secundum quod tactus est sensus proprius, sed secundum quod est fundamentum omnium sensuum et propinquius se habens ad fontalem radicem omnium sensuum, qui est sensus communis" ("[Touch] is the first and in a way the root and foundation of all senses. . . . This power is attributed to the sense of touch not as a proper sense, but because it is the foundation of all senses and the closest to the fontal root of all senses, which is the common sense"). See also n. 23 below.

16. "Attempts to establish it [i.e., synaesthesia] as in itself a sign of illness, degeneration and decadence seem to be inspired largely by prejudice or ignorance" (A. G. Engstrom, "Synaesthesia," *Encyclopaedia of Poetry and Poetics* [Princeton, 1965], p. 840).

17. For a detailed description and in-depth analysis of the Thomistic conception of the soul and its cognitive powers in relation to knowledge, see, among others, L. M. Regis, O.P., *Epistemology* (New York, 1959), pp. 157–308.

18. Cf. *Summa contra gentiles* 2. 75. 1551: "Quae enim coniuncta sunt in re, interdum divisim cognoscuntur: simul enim una res est alba et dulcis: visus tamen cognoscit solam albedinem, et gustum solam dulcedinem" ("Things which are united in the reality are nonetheless perceived separately, as for instance when something is white and sweet; sight perceives only whiteness, and taste only sweetness").

19. Cf. Thomas Aquinas, *In Aristotelis Librum de sensu et sensato* (Taurini, 1949), p. 81, n. 288.

20. Cf. E. Clive-Rouse and A. Baker, "The Wall-Paintings at Longthorpe Tower," *Archaeologia* 96 (1955): 1–57 and plate 17. For a fuller analysis and interpretation of the *Wheel*, see G. Casagrande and Ch. Kleinhenz, "Literary and Philosophical Perspectives on the Wheel of the Five Senses in Longthorpe Tower," *Traditio* 41 (1985): 311–27.

21. It would seem that only four of the animals shown on the rim of the Longthorpe Tower wheel correspond to the animals representing the five senses according to Thomas of Cantimpré. See his *Liber de natura rerum*, ed. H. Boepse (Berlin-New York, 1973), 1, lib. 4, cap. 1, lines 190–94.

22. With the exception of an earlier but differently executed fresco depicting the five senses and found in the Abbazia delle Tre Fontane in Rome. In his study, Carlo Bertelli ("L'enciclopedia delle Tre Fontane," *Paragone* 235 (1969): 24–49) has pointed out the similarities between this fresco and the one in Longthorpe Tower.

23. Thomas Aquinas, *Summa theologiae* 1ª. 73. 3 ad 3, and 1ª. 76. 5; *In de anima* 2.lect. 19. 484; 3.lect. 3. 602; lect. 17. 849; lect. 18. 865. See also Alexander of Hales's *Summa theologica* 1ª. 2ⁱ. 355; and cf. n. 15 above.

24. The synaesthetic process may be further clarified by the diagram below. The dotted lines starting at the terminus of each sensation (at the arrowheads) and intersecting the bands or channels of various senses might be taken to represent the mechanism (scanning and combining) of the common sense. The diagram may be read downward and is self-explanatory.

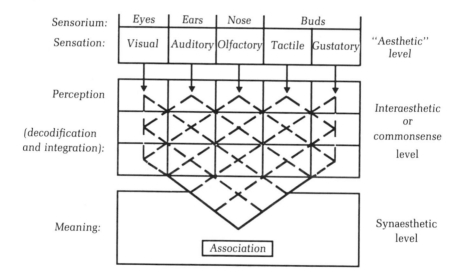

25. "In parte sensitiva invenitur duplex operatio. Una secundum solam *immutationem* et sic perficitur operatio sensus per hoc immutatur a sensibili. Alia operatio est *formatio*, secundum quod vis imaginativa *format sibi aliquod idolum rei absenti, vel etiam nunquam visae.* Et utraque haec operatio coniungitur in intellectu. Nam primo quidem consideratur passio intellectus possibilis secundum quod informatur specie intelligibili. Qua quidem formatus, format secundo vel definitionem vel divisionem vel compositionem, quae per vocem significatur. Unde ratio quam significat nomen, est definitio; et enuntiatio significat compositionem et divisionem intellectus. Non ergo voces significant ipsas species intelligibiles; sed ea quae intellectus sibi format ad iudicandum de rebus exterioribus" ("In the sensitive part two activities take place. One pertains only to *the change* whereby the sense is altered by the objects perceived. The other activity is a *kind of formation* whereby the power of imagination

forms a likeness of something absent, or even of something never seen before. Both activities are connected in the intellect. In the first instance we are dealing with the act of the possible intellect insofar as it gives form to an intelligible image. Once this has taken place, it then forms either a definition, or a division or composition which is articulated by the voice. The meaning of a word is the definition; the enunciation means the composition or division of the intellect. Therefore, utterances do not signify the real intelligible forms, but those that the intellect forms for itself when it gives judgment on exterior things"). Summa theologiae 1ª. 85. 2 ad 3.

26. Cf. In de anima 3,lect. 11, 757–59. Abstractions occur in two ways, one of which is "per modum compositionis et divisionis" ("by way of composition and division") (Summa theologiae 1ª. 85. 1 ad 1). For a detailed analysis of the intellectual faculty of abstraction and composition, as well as composition and division, see B. G. Lonergan, S.J., Verbum: Word and Idea in Aquinas (Notre Dame, Ind., 1967). See also P. T. Durbin, "Unity of Composition in Judgment," The Thomist 31 (1967): 83–120.

27. P. Zumthor, Essai de poétique médiévale (Paris, 1972), chap. 3.

28. O'Malley ("Literary Synaesthesia" [above, n. 8], p. 409) considers the Divina Commedia as one of the best illustrations of "intersense metaphor and synaesthetic conceptions." We must recall here also the article of G. Cambon, cited above (n. 10). With respect to the visual import of "the silent sun" in relation to the synaesthetic attribute that soon afterward Dante uses for Virgil—namely, as "the one who appeared dim for long silence" (1. 63)—see S. Aglianò, s.v. fioco, Enciclopedia dantesca (Rome, 1970), 2:893.

29. A. J. Greimas, Sémantique structurale (Paris, 1966), chap. 1.

30. I avail myself of the example (somewhat modified) used by E. Guidobaldi to exemplify the formula for the semantic axis proposed by A. J. Greimas ("Paradiso XXXIII: Rassegna di ponti semantici analizzati con J. Lacan," Psicoanalisi e strutturalismo di fronte a Dante. II. Letture della "Commedia" (Florence, 1972), pp. 355–437). For the "rapacity" of the wolf a number of authors of bestiaries could be cited. Here is what Thomas of Cantimpré says: "Lupus, ut dicit Iacobus, animal rapacissimum est et fraudolentum" (De rerum natura 4.60). The concept, which was also applied to the Church during medieval times (and of course by Dante himself), is a very ancient one and perhaps stems from Matthew 7:15: "Attendite a falsis prophetis, qui veniunt ad vos in vestimentis ovium: intrinsecus autem sunt lupi rapaces" (cf. B. Rowland, Animals with Human Faces (Knoxville, Tenn., 1973), pp. 162–63).

31. For some pertinent ideas on communication in art, see G. Dorfles, "Communication and Symbol in the Work of Art," Journal of Aesthetic and Art Criticism 15 (1957): 289–97.

32. G. W. Lampe, A Patristic Greek Lexicon (Oxford, 1968), p. 753.

33. G. Fallani, Dante e la cultura figurativa medievale (Bergamo, 1971), p. 73ff.

34. R. Dragonetti, Dante pèlerin de la sainte face (= Romanica Gandensia 11) (Ghent, 1968), pp. 150–51.

35. Fallani, pp. 19–20.

36. Dragonetti, pp. 277–78.

37. Thomas Aquinas, In de anima 3.lect. 1. 581, in Aristotle's De anima, in the Version of William Moerbeke and the Commentary of St. Thomas Aquinas, trans. K. Foster and S. Humphries (New Haven, 1951), p. 355.

38. Thomas Aquinas, respectively, In de anima 2.lect. 13. 395; and Summa theologiae 1ª. 78. 4.

39. Fallani, p. 88 (translation mine).

40. Thomas Aquinas, *In de anima* 2.lect. 13. 395.

41. Augustine, *Enarratio in Psalmum CXL: PL* 37.1818.

42. *Exposition in Psalterium. Psal. CXL: PL* 170. 1000.

43. *De Isaac et anima* 5. 44: *PL* 14.543.

44. Cf. M.-Th. D'Alverny, *Alain de Lille. Textes inédits* (= *Etudes de philosophie médiévale* 52) (Paris, 1956). I follow the "digression" of the Toulouse MS 195, given by d'Alverny on p. 244, n. y.

45. Cf. Alanus *Distinctiones*, s.v. *incensum, fumus, odor: PL* 210.817, 800, 881.

46. Cf. ibid., p. 964. Cf. also *Expositio prosae de angelis*, in D'Alverny, pp. 83–84, 201, and n. 24.

47. Examples could be easily multiplied. For a compact survey on the use of incense among various peoples and cults, see E. Fehrenbach, *Encense, Dictionnaire d'archéologie chrétienne et de liturgie* (Paris, 1922), 5, cols. 2–21.

48. Such is the essence of Momigliano's comment.

49. Along this line—although with reference to a rite in the Eastern church—it may be interesting to quote a passage from the homilies of Narsai in which silence, stillness, prayer, and incense constitute the basic elements of the rite during a pure oblation offered to God: "All the ecclesiastical body now observes silence, and all set themselves to pray earnestly in their hearts. The priests are still and the deacons stand in silence, the whole people is quiet and still, subdued and calm. . . . The mysteries are set in order, the censers are smoking, the lamps are shining. . . . Deep silence and peaceful calm settle on the place: it is filled and overflows with brightness and splendour, beauty and power. . . ." *The Liturgical Homilies of Narsai*, in *Texts and Studies: Contributions to Biblical and Patristic Literature*, ed. J. A. Robinson, vol. 8, no. 1 (Cambridge, 1909), p. 12.

50. Here it is significant to note what may be called another of the several thematic encounters of Dante with Alain de Lille. As is known, the question of similarity between the *Anticlaudianus* and the *Divina Commedia* has been raised by many critics, from E. Bossard to E. Curtius. It is generally accepted among scholars that many points of contact can be established between Alanus and Dante. For a bibliography, see the entry "Alano di Lilla" by C. Vasoli in *Enciclopedia dantesca*, 1:89–91, to which the following must be added: E. Guidobaldi, "Alain de Lille e la scuola di Chartres," *Dante europeo*, vol. 2: *Il Paradiso come universo di luce* (Florence, 1966), pp. 217–36; G. R. Sarolli, *Prolegomena alla Divina Commedia* (Florence, 1971), pp. 96–113: P. Dronke, "Boethius, Alanus and Dante," *Romanische Forschungen* 78 (1966): 119–25: G. Casagrande and Ch. Kleinhenz, "*Inferno*, VII: Cariddi e l'avarizia," *Aevum* 54 (1980): 340–44.

In his interpretation of "Ad celebres rex caelice"—an anonymous *alleluia* composition of the tenth century—Alanus alludes to the same concept expressed by Dante in the lines from the *Paradiso* just quoted. At the end of the *canticum* interpreted by Alanus, there is an invocation to the hierarchical powers and spirits above to join with a newly found humanity in a harmonius expression of jubilation to the Almighty, so that after the day of the final judgment the incense of all, on the golden altar, may be accepted by God:

(16) Vos per ethra
nos per rura, dena
pars electa,
harmonica vota
demus hyperlyrica cythara.

(17) Quo post bella
Michaelis inclita
nostro Deo
sint accepta auream
super aram thymiamata.

Let us all, you up in heaven and we here on earth, let us all give a melodious offering to God with a super-lyric lyre. So that, after the glorious victory of Michael, may the incense on the golden altar be accepted by our God.

The last two lines of each sequence bear closer attention. In the emphasis on the last two lines of sequence 17, Alanus explains that the golden altar on which incense is offered signifies that the souls of men, dwelling in their proper place in the eternal city, offer as incense their mental exultation—precisely the same concept, and even similar terms, used by Dante to describe the Rose Eternal. Cf. "Expositio prosae de angelis," in d'Alverny, *Alain de Lille*, pp. 217, 192.

51. W. Binni, "Il canto XXX del Paradiso," *Lectura Dantis Scaligera* (above, n. 5), 3: 1085.

52. The following formula is of Anglo-Saxon origin and dates to near the end of the tenth century. The entire text is given in Fehrenbach (n. 47), p. 18. I am quoting here only part of the last paragraph: ". . . ubicumque fumus aromatum eius [i.e., of incense] afflaverit, mirabiliter possit atque in odore flagrantissimo tibi, Domine, perpetua suavitate redolere" ("Wherever the savory smoke of incense blows, may it, o Lord, come to you as a very pleasant smell and remain fragrant in perpetual sweetness").

53. O'Malley, "Literary Synaesthesia" (above, n. 8), pp. 409–10.

54. For an extremely suggestive passage describing a perfectly fused process of interiorization of all sensory experiences in relation to divine love, see Augustine's *Confessions* 10. 6, n. 8.

55. Greimas has pointed out that some recent studies, besides stressing—at the level of the substance of the content—the importance of determined categories along the line of *semantic isotopy* (i.e., as categories of gender and number, animate and inanimate, and so on) on the basis of the projection of the morphosyntactic relations of the "énoncé," also "recognize the existence of *semiologic isotopes* by the utilization through poetic communication of organized codes pertaining to various sensory orders, isomorphic to a large extent and translatable into one another (Bachelard; Lévi-Strauss). This means that they confer a structural status upon the ancient metaphysical notion of "correspondences." See A. J. Greimas, *Du sens* (Paris, 1970), p. 291; also B. Uspensky, "Structural Isophormism of Verbal and Visual Art," *Poetics* 5 (1972): 5–39.

The Eunoè or the Recovery of the Lost Good

DINO S. CERVIGNI

Introduction

As the climax of Dante the Pilgrim's purgatorial purification, "the sweet drinking" ("lo dolce ber") from the river Eunoè has rightly caught the attention of Dante critics.[1] Most of them, however, have sought to shed light primarily on the formal aspects of *Purgatorio*'s concluding episode; the few who have glossed the function of the river Eunoè within Dante's purgatorial journey have hardly gone beyond the threefold explanation found in the text: namely, as Matelda first informs the *actor*, the water of Eunoè returns to man's memory all good deeds (*Purg.* 28.129); it revives the soul's faint *virtù* (33.129), as Beatrice states; and, finally, it also remakes Dante new, as new trees are renewed (33.142–45).

According to Dante's text, therefore, the second Edenic river possesses three essential attributes: Eunoè returns to the soul the memory of all good deeds lost because of one's sinfulness, revives the soul's faint *virtù*, and therefore re-creates every creature who drinks from its most holy water.

Hence, one easily understands the importance of the gloss which seeks to explain the function of Eunoè not only in its formal aspects but also in its spiritual purpose so that the final moment of Dante's purgatorial journey may be understood in its totality. The "dolce ber," in fact, is in counterpoint to the drinking from the river Letè, thus bringing to a climax the Pilgrim's purifying experience; most importantly, it also constitutes the ultimate and essential condition that prepares him to ascend to Heaven together with Beatrice.

The Spring and Its Two Rivers

Either explicitly or implicitly, the gloss of the Trecento and Quattrocento commentators almost invariably proposes or suggests that the two purgatorial rivers are a manifestation of the divinity and that the well from which they spring symbolizes God or divine grace.[2] During the following centuries, one witnesses a gradual moving away from this symbolic interpretation in favor of a literal reading of the purgatorial spring, a reading that hardly goes beyond a paraphrase of the Dantean text.[3]

As to the interpretation of the two rivers, throughout the centuries a symbolic reading has understandably prevailed, since Matelda herself proposes it: "Da questa parte con virtù discende / che toglie altrui memoria del peccato; da l'altra d'ogne ben fatto la rende" ("On this side it descends with the virtue of taking away the souls' recollection of sin; on the other side it returns the memory of all good deeds," *Purg.* 28.127–29). In fact, Matelda's explanation constitutes a constant and obviously undisputed motif in all the commentaries I have consulted.[4] After the Cinquecento, however, only the nineteenth and twentieth centuries offer a gloss that goes beyond a simple paraphrase of the Dantean text. Such is, for instance, in the Ottocento, Niccolò Tommaseo's commentary[5] and, much more important, Giovanni Pascoli's elaborate and symbolic reading of the purgatorial rivers, which in his view symbolize the Eucharist.[6] In brief, for Pascoli the two Edenic rivers, both springing from Christ's wounds, delete all sins, save the purifying souls, and perform for them the function which the Eucharist plays in man's earthly pilgrimage toward God.

Pascoli's reading, despite its poetic and esthetic fascination, fails to justify fully the two distinct yet closely interdependent rites that take place around the Letè and Eunoè. In fact, the principal effects of the "dolce ber" from Eunoè, namely, the *renovatio* and the *regeneratio,* find their adequate correspondent not so much in the sacrament of the Eucharist as in that of Penance. The purpose of the Eucharist, in fact, consists in sustaining and augmenting the soul's grace, whereas Penance restores the lost grace, reviving the "tramortita virtù"; the Eucharist augments the merits of the communicant, whereas Penance returns to the penitent the grace and merits lost because of one's sin; finally, the Eucharist brings to maturity the Christian's virtue, whereas Penance renews the tree withered because of sin.[7]

Charles S. Singleton, without focusing on the function of Eunoè but rather on the presence of the two rivers in the Dantean Earthly Paradise vis-à-vis the four rivers of Genesis, presents fundamental conclusions in his "Rivers, Nymphs, and Stars" (Journey to Beatrice, 159–83). According to him, the four rivers of the biblical Eden, which patristic commentators saw as symbols of the four cardinal virtues, are replaced by the four stars the Pilgrim admires in the sky of the Southern Hemisphere. One must point out, however, that Singleton's masterly analysis is concerned first and foremost with the four stars and secondarily with Letè, which Dante, unlike Virgil, can cross. Nothing is said, however, concerning the function of Eunoè, though this Edenic river perforce represents the perfect conclusion of the Exodus theme which Singleton scrutinizes so admirably. In fact, Singleton leaves completely open a fundamental issue. If, on the one hand, the substitution of the four stars, and later the four nymphs, for the four biblical rivers is explained plausibly, on the other hand, short shrift is given to the new meaning that the two Dantean rivers would necessarily assume after losing the meaning of their biblical counterparts.[8]

In sum, whereas the early commentators offer us a richly diversified symbolic gloss of the Edenic spring and rivers, contemporary critics, with the exception of Pascoli and Singleton, limit themselves mostly to paraphrasing the Dantean text.

Dante's Eunoè and Letè: Classical Antecedents and Biblical Tradition

The critics' gloss of the two Dantean rivers, despite its limitations, focuses nevertheless on a fact that, precisely because of their interest, might seem fundamental: namely, whereas the Earthly Paradise of Genesis is irrigated by four rivers, all of them springing from one source, the Dantean Eden is marked by only two, though also issuing from one spring.

Yet one cannot help wondering why Dante commentators have not availed themselves of a different reading of the biblical text that is not at all rare in exegesis and was first brought to the attention of Dante critics, to my knowledge, by Lombardi. In order to explain the difference in number between the biblical and Dantean rivers, he writes: "Ma ben potè il poeta nostro essere del medesimo intendimento di que' sacri interpreti, che affermano essere il Phison, e 'l Gehon una soddivisione dell'Eufrate e del Tigri" ("But our poet could have been of the same opinion as those biblical interpreters who hold Phison and Gihon to be a subdivision of Euphrates and Tigris," *Purg.* 33.113).[9] The same idea was repeated almost verbatim by Raffaele Andreoli in 1863.[10] In 1922, Bruno Nardi also proposed this alternative reading, without, however, quoting Lombardi's or Andreoli's suggestion. Nardi writes:

> The Bible does not say at all that the division in four [rivers] takes place within the Earthly Paradise. On the contrary, some Fathers and exegetes thought that this division took place after the river had come out of Eden. One point saw all medieval interpreters in agreement, namely, that the four biblical rivers, though surfacing in faraway points of the earth, through underground channels derived from the same Edenic spring, as Augustine and Theodoretus wrote. Even more importantly, on the authority of Boethius and Lucan, Dante held that Tigris and Euphrates had one and the same spring here on earth and believed, therefore, that their division took place outside Eden. Before the division into four large rivers—a division which takes place on earth—Dante imagined a prior division into two fresh and clear creeks within the Earthly Paradise. And since he held that the language of Adam had already become extinguished before the tower of Babel, he decided to give them two special names, different from the biblical ones: names which would signify the nature of their waters. (297–98)[11]

Andreoli's and Nardi's suggestions, though unheeded by contemporary Dante commentators, do certainly offer a satisfactory explanation of the question about the difference in the number of the Edenic rivers in the Bible and in the *Commedia*.[12]

Equally constant are certain references to the same classical authors found in Dante commentaries from Pietro Alighieri to our times. The most frequent reference is to *Aeneid* 6.704–51, which describes a vast multitude of souls on the bank of the Lethean river and Anchises' explanation to Virgil that they are destined for rebirth, drinking forgetfulness from the river. Even though Virgil's influence on the Dantean text cannot be summarily dismissed, textual and contextual differences by far outweigh the similarities emerging from the two episodes. First of all, although the *Aeneid* describes the Lethean river, no parallel exists to the Eunoè, which in the *Commedia* brings to fulfillment the function of the first Edenic river. Second, Aeneas inquires about the Lethean river and the souls surrounding it (6.705–12), but he cannot obtain any experience of the river because he still bears his mortal body; conversely, Dante, who also inquires about the two rivers, experiences directly and intimately the spiritual function of Letè and Eunoè by means of his own complete transformation. Last, whereas the purpose of Virgil's Elyseum is to enable the souls to forget, ascend to heaven, and become incarnate in another body, Dante's conception stands in opposition to Virgil's belief, which is later confuted in the *Commedia*. Dante's Christian belief excludes reincarnation; all the purifying souls drink from the two Edenic rivers, and the Christian hero, unlike the pagan wayfarer, drinks from them before ascending to Paradise.

Fluvial Imagery in the Bible

A careful reading of certain fundamental biblical passages, to be viewed from the perspective of patristic commentaries—a reading later to be complemented by theological discussion on the sacrament of Penance—will help us acquire a better understanding of Eunoè.

Since Eunoè returns to the purified soul the memory of the lost good, the implication is that the soul has previously lost that good—a loss caused by sin, namely, by the creature's *aversio a Deo*. Thomas Aquinas explains the effects of sin on the soul through a quotation of the prophet Ezekiel: "Si averterit se iustus a iustitia sua, omnes iustitiae eius quas fecerat, non recordabuntur" ("If a righteous man turns back from his righteous ways, all his righteous deeds which he had done will not be remembered," Ezek. 18:24). The destruction of the good is described by means of *oblivio*, or forgetfulness, which originates in the creator but affects the creature: the good that the creature had accomplished in the state of grace becomes the object of God's oblivion. Memory, therefore, or its opposite, oblivion, creates a dynamic relationship between God and the creature: God first remembers the creature by creating man and woman, who then forget their creator by sinning;[13] consequently, God forgets his own creatures and their past good deeds and remembers their sins so that they may repent and once again acquire their original justice.

Hence the relationship that develops between the divinity and the creature: man's justice brings about the *divinity's* memory of that justice, whereas the creature's *injustice* prompts God's oblivion. Ezekiel most aptly expounds this dynamic relationship:

> Etiamsi dixero iusto quod vita vivat, et confisus in iustitia sua fecerit iniquitatem, omnes iustitiae eius oblivioni tradentur, et in iniquitate sua quam operatus est, in ipsa morietur.

> It may be that, when I tell a righteous man that he will save his life, he presumes on his righteousness and does wrong; then all his righteous acts will be forgotten, and he will die for the wrong he has done. (Ezek. 33:13).

Oblivion, therefore, is followed by a further, more deleterious consequence, the death of the sinner:

> Si autem averterit se iustus a iustitia sua, et fecerit iniquitatem secundum omnes abominationes quas operari solet impius, numquid vivet? Omnes iustitiae eius, quas fecerat, non recordabuntur; in praevaricatione qua praevaricatus est, et in peccato suo quod peccavit, in ipsis morietur.

> If a righteous man turns back from his righteousness and commits every kind of abomination that the wicked practices, shall he live? All the former righteousness which he had done will be forgotten; in his injustices which he has committed and in his sins which he has done, he will die. (Ezek. 18:24)[14]

The sequence of motifs, therefore, proceeds relentlessly: the creature's justice, which is followed by the divinity's remembrance, can be destroyed by the creature's injustice, which prompts God's oblivion as well as the creature's death. At the same time, however, God's judgment is not immutable. In the same way as man can abandon the path of justice and follow injustice, so itinerant man can also return to the right path. This conversion, or Penance, elicits a corresponding turn-about in the divinity, as Ezekiel writes:

> Si autem impius egerit poenitentiam ab omnibus peccatis suis, quae operatus est, et custodierit omnia praecepta mea, et fecerit iudicium et iustitiam, vita vivet et non morietur; omnium iniquitatum eius, quas operatus est, non recordabor; in iustitia sua, quam operatus est, vivet. Numquid voluntatis meae est mors impii? dicit Dominus Deus; et non ut convertatur a viis suis, et vivat?

> If a wicked man does penance for all the sins he has committed, keeps all my laws, and does what is just and right, he shall live and shall not die; I will not remember any of the injustices which he has done; in the righteousness which he does, he shall live. Have I any desire for the death of the wicked man? Would I not rather that he should turn away from his ways and live? (Ezek. 18:21–23)

Schematically, we have: *iustitia creaturae* = *memoria boni; iniustitia creaturae* = *oblivio boni et mors creaturae; poenitentia creaturae* = *vita creaturae et memoria boni*. In the same way as *oblivio boni* corresponds to *mors creaturae*, so the *memoria boni* that follows the soul's regaining of its original justice corresponds to *revivificatio creaturae*.

The soul's first step toward spiritual rebirth is the destruction of sin, which God brings about after the sinner's conversion, an inner transformation which the penitent soul vividly describes in the so-called penitential psalms, primarily in Psalm 50, the *Miserere*. Here we see at work the following motifs: the washing away of sin;[15] its destruction;[16] and God's oblivion of sin and remembrance of previous acts of mercy:

> Reminiscere miserationum tuarum, Domine,
> et misericordiarum tuarum quae a saeculo sunt.
> Delicta iuventutis meae, et ignorantias meas ne memineris.
> Secundum misericordiam tuam memento mei tu
> Propter bonitatem tuam, Domine.

> Remember, O Lord, your mercies, shown from ages past. Do not remember the sins and offenses of my youth. In your mercy remember me because of your kindness, O Lord. (Ps. 24:6–7)

Following the sinner's purification and the sin's destruction, the creature receives a new heart:

Cor mundum crea in me, Deus,
et spiritum rectum innova in visceribus meis.

O Lord, create a new heart in me and renew a righteous spirit within me.
(Ps. 50:12)[17]

Man's inner "re-creation," namely, the sinner's justification, is God's work par excellence, analogous to the act of creation.[18] Therefore, since *creare* includes also the semantic areas expressed by *facere* = *fare*,[19] one can already relate to the same all-powerful act the Dantean *rifatto* ("remade"), which signifies the Pilgrim's renewed condition after he drinks from Eunoè. As one's creation is God's work, so one's re-creation is equally a divine operation, which is brought about time and again during the creature's journey toward the creator.

Theological and Patristic Elaboration

At this moment, in order to explain the concept of *revivificatio*, or bringing back to the penitent all previous good deeds and virtues, we shall turn to Thomas Aquinas and patristic writings. For Thomas, the principal consequence of sin is the loss of all moral and theological virtues,[20] as well as the loss of all the merits previously acquired in the state of grace.[21] Conversely, through Penance man reacquires the friendship of God, through whose mercy he once again obtains the virtues and merits previously lost because of sin. What in Thomas's theological discussion takes place simultaneously through the sacrament of Penance—namely, the destruction of sin and the revival of the virtues and merits—in Dante's Earthly Paradise comes about in two poetically distinct moments. The soul's immersion in Letè is analogous to that aspect of the sacrament of Penance which destroys one's sin, while "lo dolce ber" from Eunoè is analogous to the same sacrament's resuscitation of the soul's previous virtues and merits.

Thomas discusses the *revivificatio* of virtues and merits through Penance in several treatises,[22] but especially in the third part of his *Summa theologiae*, question 89 ("De recuperatione virtutum per poenitentiam," "Of the Recovery of Virtue by Means of Penance"). As a premise to the following discussion, one must bear in mind that, in scholastic theology, man's actions can be morally categorized as follows: *viva, mortificata, mortua, mortifera*. The actions falling within the last two categories cannot be brought back to life, since they lacked the principle of life, or divine grace, from the very beginning. Hence, whenever sin is removed, only those actions can be revived that were originally performed in the state of grace and subsequently "mortified" or "forgotten" because of one's sin. Penance brings about the destruction of sin, in scholastic and patristic writings variously designated as *deletio peccati* or *destructio peccati*, which the Bible, as previously analyzed, designates as *oblivio peccati*. In fact, it is God who destroys or forgets sin, according to a metaphor common to the Bible, scholastic writings, and the Dantean text.[23]

The first effect of Penance, therefore, is the destruction or oblivion of sin operated by God, which corresponds to the Pilgrim's immersion in Letè. However, whereas the Bible attributes the sin's oblivion to God, in the *Commedia* Dante himself is affected by the oblivion of his sinfulness after being submerged in the waters of the first Edenic river.

After the soul's sinfulness is removed, destroyed, or forgotten—in a way, a negative aspect of Penance—the creature is ready to receive divine grace. In the same question 89, Thomas presents the vivifying effects of Penance. The first effect, he expounds in article one, brings about divine grace and all those virtues freely given by God to man. Strictly connected with this issue is the state in which the penitent is reborn after converting and doing Penance. In article two, Thomas proposes an explanation that allows various possibilities:

> Manifestum est autem quod formae quae possunt recipere magis et minus, intenduntur et remittuntur secundum diversam dispositionem subiecti. . . . Et inde est quod, secundum quod motus liberi arbitrii in poenitentia est intensior vel remissior, secundum hoc poenitens consequitur maiorem vel minorem gratiam. Contingit autem intensionem motus poenitentis quandoque proportionatam esse maiori gratiae quam illa a qua cecidit per peccatum, quandoque vero aequali, quandoque vero minori. Et ideo poenitens quandoque resurgit in maiori gratia quam prius habuerat; quandoque autem in aequali; quandoque etiam in minori. Et eadem ratio est de virtutibus, quae ex gratia consequuntur.

But it is evident that forms which admit of receiving more or less, become intense or remiss according to the different dispositions of the subject. . . . Hence in penance, according to the degree of intensity or remissness in the movement of the free will, the penitent receives greater or lesser grace than the one from which he fell by sinning, sometimes an equal grace, sometimes a lesser one. Therefore the penitent sometimes rises to a greater grace than the one he had before, sometimes to an equal one, sometimes to a lesser one. And the same applies to the virtues, which flow from grace.

Reacquiring divine grace, therefore, depends on the Divinity, but the degree of its reception is somewhat determined by the condition of the recipient:[24]

Ad secundum dicendum quod poenitentia, quantum est de se, habet virtutem reparandi omnes defectus ad perfectum, et etiam promovendi in ulteriorem statum: sed hoc quandoque impeditur ex parte hominis, qui remissius movetur in Deum et in detestationem peccati. Sicut etiam in baptismo aliqui adulti consequuntur maiorem vel minorem gratiam secundum quod diversimode se disponunt.

Penance, considered in itself, has the power to bring all defects back to perfection and even to advance man to a higher degree; but this progress is sometimes hindered on the part of man, who moves slowly toward God and in detestation of sin, just as in Baptism adults receive a greater or lesser grace according to the way in which they prepare themselves.

At this juncture, Thomas's discussion focuses on the soul's reacquiring, through penance, what had been lost because of sin—an issue, therefore, closely related to the regenerative function of Eunoè. In article three, "Utrum per poenitentiam restituatur homo in pristinam dignitatem" ("Whether by Penance Man is Restored to His Former Dignity"), Thomas states that the soul obviously cannot reacquire its lost innocence but can nevertheless obtain "aliquid maius" ("something greater"):

Recuperat tamen quandoque aliquid maius. Quia, ut Gregorius dicit, in homilia *De centum ovibus, qui errasse a Deo se considerant, damna praecedentia lucris sequentibus recompensant. Maius ergo gaudium de eis fit in caelo: quia et dux in praelio plus eum militem diligit qui post*

*fugam reversus hostem fortiter premit, quam illum qui nunquam terga
praebuit et nunquam aliquid fortiter fecit.*

At times, however, he recovers something greater. For, as Gregory says
in his homily *On the hundred sheep,* "those who acknowledge to have
strayed away from God make up for their past losses by subsequent
gains. In fact, there is more joy in heaven on their account; even as in
battle the general prefers the soldier who, after running away, returns
and bravely attacks the enemy, over the soldier who has never turned
his back but has never done anything brave."[25]

Not only can the penitent reacquire "aliquid maius," a condition superior to the previous one; in article five Thomas states that the penitent
can also reobtain the good deeds previously accomplished in the state
of grace and subsequently "mortified" because of sin:

> . . . quidam dixerunt quod opera meritoria per peccatum sequens mor-
> tificata non reviviscunt per poenitentiam sequentem, considerantes quod
> opera illa non remanent, ut iterum vivificari possent.[26]
>
> Sed hoc impediri non potest quin vivificentur. Non enim habent vim
> perducendi in vitam aeternam, quod pertinet ad eorum vitam, solum
> secundum quod actu existunt, sed etiam postquam actu esse desinunt,
> secundum quod remanent in acceptatione divina. Sic autem remanent,
> quantum est de se, etiam postquam per peccatum mortificantur: quia
> semper Deus illa opera, prout facta fuerunt, acceptabit. . . . Sed quod isti
> qui ea fecit non sint efficacia ad ducendum ad vitam aeternam, provenit
> ex impedimento peccati supervenientis, per quod ipse redditur indignus
> vita aeterna. Hoc autem impedimentum tollitur per poenitentiam,
> inquantum per eam remittuntur peccata. Unde restat quod opera prius
> mortificata per poenitentiam recuperant efficaciam perducendi eum qui
> fecit ea in vitam aeternam: quod est ea reviviscere. Et ita patet quod
> opera mortificata per poenitentiam reviviscunt.

. . . some have said that meritorious works deadened by subsequent sin
are not revived by the following penance, for they thought that such
works would no longer exist and therefore could not be revived. But this
is no reason why they should not be revived. In fact, they can lead to
eternal life, wherein their life consists, not only as actually existing but
also as abiding in the divine acceptance, after ceasing to exist actually.
So far as they are concerned, they abide thus even after they have been
deadened by sin; in fact, God will always accept those works according
as they were done. . . . That those works cannot bring the man who did

them to eternal life is due to the impediment of the subsequent sin, whereby he is become unworthy of eternal life. But this impediment is removed by penance, whereby sins are taken away. Hence it follows that works previously deadened recover through penance their efficacy in bringing him, who did them, to eternal life; in other words, those works are revived. It is therefore evident that deadened works are revived by penance.

Shortly after (*Ad primum*), Thomas further elucidates this *revivificatio* which is brought about by penance:

> . . . opera ex caritate facta non abolentur a Deo, in cuius acceptatione remanent: sed impedimentum accipiunt ex parte hominis operantis. Et ideo, remoto impedimento quod est ex parte hominis, Deus implet ex parte sua illud quod opera merebantur.

> . . . works done in charity are not destroyed by God, in whose acceptance they abide, but they are hindered on the part of the man who does them. Therefore, if this hindrance on the part of man is removed, God on His side fulfills what those works deserved.[27]

These conclusions of article five, expressed in a metaphoric language that echoes the Dantean text, assume a fundamental importance for the understanding of the function of Eunoè. Our explanation of the recovery of the lost good in the Dantean episode, therefore, is firmly grounded in the Bible and scholastic theology and is further corroborated by patristic commentaries. A few quotations from the church fathers will suffice. John Chrysostom explains through a metaphor the soul's recovery of the lost good:

> Non enim sicut in sensibilibus rebus, ita et hic usu evenit; illic namque is qui ex divitiis in extremam redactus fuerit inopiam, brevi eas reparare nequit; hic autem per misericordiam Dei, si modo condemnare facta nostra, et jam sistere ignaviam voluerimus, poterimus statim ad pristinam abundantiam redire. Talis enim est Dominus noster, tamque magnificus et liberalis. . . .

> In this context things do not take place as in earthly matters; here, in fact, if one loses one's wealth and becomes poor, one cannot regain one's wealth in a short time; in spiritual matters, on the contrary, after condemning our wicked deeds and putting an end to our weakness, we

could immediately return to our previous abundance because of God's mercy. Such is in fact our magnificent and generous Lord. . . .[28]

Whereas in this context of all the books of the Old Testament Ezekiel is usually quoted, in the New Testament two passages from Paul's letters form the constant point of reference for every discussion on the reviving of the good in the repentant soul:

> Non enim iniustus Deus, ut obliviscatur operis vestri, et dilectionis, quam ostendistis in nomine ipsius, qui ministrastis sanctis et ministratis. Cupimus autem unumquemque vestrum eandem ostentare sollicitudinem ad expletionem spei usque in finem. . . .

> For God would not be so unjust as to forget the work you did and the love you showed for the sake of his name, when you rendered service to his saints, as you still do. But we long for every one of you to show the same eager concern until your hope is finally realized. . . . (Heb. 6:10–11)[29]

> O insensati Galatae, qui vos fascinavit non obedire veritati, ante quorum oculos Iesus Christus praescriptus est, in vobis crucifixus? Hoc solum a vobis volo discere: Ex operibus legis Spiritum accepistis, an ex auditu fidei? Sic stulti estis, ut cum Spiritu coeperitis, nunc carne consummemini? Tanta passi estis sine causa? si tamen sine causa.

> You stupid Galatians, who has bewitched you not to obey the truth— you, before whose eyes Jesus Christ was openly manifested upon his cross? Answer me this question: Did you receive the Spirit from the works of the law or from believing? Are you that stupid that, while you began with the Spirit, you now are being consumed by the flesh? Have you suffered so many things without cause? and indeed they would now be in vain. (Gal. 3:1–4)[30]

In conclusion, what in scholastic theology is attributed to penance—which brings about simultaneously the destruction of sin, the infusion of grace, and the revival of the soul's virtues and merits— in Dante's Purgatorio is rendered in two poetically distinct but closely interrelated moments—Letè deletes the soul's sinfulness, while Eunoè brings back to life the good which the soul previously owned and later lost because of sin. Consequently, after crossing and/or drinking from both Edenic rivers, Dante emerges completely renewed.[31]

A corollary emerges from the above discussion. In Dante's *Com-media*, the Earthly Paradise to which the purified souls ascend is, indeed, spatially and really, the same place where "fu innocente l'umana radice" ("mankind's root was innocent," *Purg.* 28.142). How-ever, the spiritual condition that the purified souls regain here cannot possibly be the same which Adam and Eve possessed before their fall—a state of innocence that mankind's primogenitors enjoyed only briefly (*Par.* 26.139–42) and which, once lost, no one can regain. In order to understand what the purified soul can indeed attain, let us briefly return to what Thomas writes about the question: "Utrum per poenitentiam homo restituatur in pristinam dignitatem" ("Whether by Penance Man is Restored to His Former Dignity"). Because of sin, Thomas writes, man loses a twofold dignity before God:

> Unam principalem, qua scilicet computatus erat inter filios Dei per gratiam. Et hanc dignitatem recuperat per poenitentiam. . . . Aliam vero dignitatem amittit secundariam, scilicet innocentiam. . . . Et hanc dig-nitatem poenitens recuperare non potest.—Recuperat tamen quan-doque aliquid maius.

> Man loses a primary dignity, whereby he was previously included among the children of God by virtue of divine grace. Such dignity man recovers through penance. . . . Man loses also a secondary dignity, namely, his innocence. . . . And such dignity man cannot recover. At times, however, he can reacquire something greater. (*S. Th.* 3. Q. 89. a. 3)

In Dante's Earthly Paradise, therefore, the purified soul regains that grace which makes the creature a child of God but never the primordial innocence, which has been lost forever because of the primogenitors' fall and also because of man's own sinfulness. One must, however, underline what Thomas adds. The penitent can re-ceive from God "aliquid maius"—"something greater"—according to the soul's inner disposition.[32] This "aliquid maius" can be obtained by means of the grace made available to mankind through Christ. After Christ, in fact, man can obtain only one state of grace—namely, that won for him through the Redemption.[33]

University of North Carolina

WORKS CITED

Alighieri, Dante. *Commedia di Dante Alighieri con ragionamento e note di Niccolò Tommaseo.* Vol. 2. Milan: F. Pagnoni, 1865.

————. *La Commedia secondo l'antica vulgata.* Edited by G. Petrocchi. 4 vols. Milan: Mondadori, 1966–67.

————. *La Divina Commedia di Dante Alighieri col comento di Raffaele Andreoli.* 2d rev. ed. Naples: Stamperia Nazionale, 1863.

————. *La Divina Commedia di Dante Alighieri nuovamente comentata, spiegata e difesa da F. B. L[ombardi], M.C.* 3 vols. Rome: A. Fulgoni, 1791.

————. *La Divina Commedia.* Commentary by Luigi Pietrobono. Vol. 2. Turin: SEI, 1934.

————. *La Divina Commedia.* Edited and annotated by C. H. Grandgent. Boston: D. C. Heath, 1909.

————. *The Divine Comedy.* Translation and commentary by Ch. S. Singleton. 6 vols. Princeton: Princeton University Press, 1977.

Alighieri, Pietro. *Petri Allegherii super Dantis ipsius genitoris comoediam commentarium nunc primum in lucem editum consilio et sumptibus Bar. G. J. Vernon, curante Vincentio Nannucci.* Florence: Piatti, 1845.

Anonimo. *Commento alla Divina Commedia d'anonimo fiorentino del secolo xiv ora per la prima volta stampato a cura di Pietro Fanfani.* 3 vols. Bologna: Romagnoli, 1866–74.

Benvenuto. *Benevenuti de Rambaldis de Imola comentum super Dantis Aldigherij Comoediam, nunc primum integre in lucem editum sumtibus Guilielmi Warren Vernon, curante Iacopo Philippo Lacaita.* 5 vols. Florence: Barbèra, 1887.

Biblia sacra iuxta vulgatam clementinam. Madrid: BAC, 1982.

Buti. *Commento di Francesco da Buti sopra la Divina Commedia di Dante Alighieri pubblicato per cura di Crescentino Giannini.* 3 vols. Pisa: Nistri, 1858–62.

Cervigni, Dino S. *Dante's Poetry of Dreams.* Biblioteca dell'"Archivum Romanicum," 198. Florence: Olschki, 1986.

Joannis a S. Thoma. *Cursus theologicus.* Vol. 9. Paris: L. Vives, 1886.

Lachance Clément-Marie. *Le Sujet de la grâce et sa guérison selon Saint Thomas: Fonction curative de la grâce. Théologie,* nos. 2–3. Ottawa: Collège Dominicain, 1944.

Lana. *Comedia di Dante degli Allagherii col commento di Jacopo di Giovanni dalla Lana bolognese a cura di Luciano Scarabelli.* Milan: C. Moretti, 1865.

Landino. *Dante con l'espositioni di Christoforo Landino et d'Alessandro Vellutello. Sopra la sua Comedia dell'Inferno, del Purgatorio, e del Paradiso, con tavole, argomenti, e allegorie; e riformato, riveduto, e ridotto alla sua vera lettura, per Francesco Sansovino fiorentino.* Venice: Gio. Battista e Gio. Bernardo Sessa, 1596.

Missale romanum ex decreto sacrosancti concilii tridentini restitutum, sancti Pii V. Pontificis Maximi jussu editum. . . . Baltimore, 1835.

Montano, Rocco. *Storia della poesia di Dante.* Part 3: *La Divina Commedia, Purgatorio.* Naples: Quaderni del Delta, 1963.

Nardi, Bruno. "Intorno al sito del 'Purgatorio' e al mito dantesco dell'Eden." *Il giornale dantesco* 25 (1922): 289–300.

Ottimo. *L'ottimo commento della Divina Commedia.* Unpublished text by a contemporary of the poet, edited by A. Torri. 3 vols. Pisa: Capurro, 1827–29.

Pascoli, Giovanni. *Tutte le opere di G. Pascoli. Prose II.* Intro. A. Vicinelli. 3d ed. 2 vols. Milan: Mondadori, 1971.

Pererius. *R. P. Benedicti Pererii Valentini, e Societate Iesu: Commentariorum et Disputationum in Genesim Tomi Quatuor.* . . . Coloniae Agrippinae: Apud Antonium Hierat, sub Monocerote. 1601.

La Sainte Bible traduite en français sous la direction de l'Ecole Biblique de Jérusalem. Paris: Editions du Cerf, 1956.

Serravalle. *Fratris Iohannis de Serravalle Ord. Min. Episcopi et Principis Firmani translatio et comentum totius libri Dantis Aldigherii, cum textu italico Fratris Bartholomaei a Colle.* Edited by Marcellino da Civezza and Teofilo Domenichelli. Prato: Giachetti, 1891.

Singleton, Charles S. *Commedia: Elements of Structure.* Cambridge, Mass.: Harvard University Press, 1957.

————. *Journey to Beatrice.* Cambridge, Mass.: Harvard University Press, 1958.

Tepe, G. Bernardo. *Institutiones theologicae in usum scholarum.* Vol. 4. Paris: P. Lethielleux, n.d.

Thomas Aquinas. *Summa Theologiae.* 5 vols. Madrid: BAC, 1965–68.

————. *Super epistolas S. Pauli lectura.* Edited by P. Raphaelis Cai. 8th ed. (rev.) 2 vols. Turin: Marietti, 1953.

Tucker, Dunstan. "In Exitu Israel de Aegypto: The *Divine Comedy* in the Light of the Easter Liturgy." *The American Benedictine Review* 11 (1960): 43–61.

Vallone, Aldo. *Dante*. Storia letteraria d'Italia. Milan: Vallardi, 1971.

_____. *Storia della critica dantesca dal XIV al XX secolo*. 2 vols. Storia letteraria d'Italia. Milan: Vallardi, 1981.

Vellutello. See above, Landino.

Virgilius. *Aeneidos*. Book 6, with a commentary by R. G. Austin. Oxford: Clarendon Press, 1977.

_____. *Opera*. Annotated by R. A. B. Mynors. Oxford: Clarendon Press, 1969.

NOTES

1. All quotations of the *Commedia* are from G. Petrocchi's critical edition. All translations of texts originally not in English are by the author.

2. See, for instance, Buti: "esceno d'una fonte, cioè da Dio, che è fonte di tutte le grazie e di tutti li beni" (2.822–23); Anon.: "*Non surge di vena*. Ciò è di stagno, o d'alcuna altra vena terrestre, che sia ristorata da' vapori che 'l ciel converta in acqua— *Ma esce di fontana*. Ciò è dalla grazia di Dio viva" (2.462); Lana: "Non auge, cioè da stagno né da alcuna vena terrestre, o da restoramento, ovvero da scoladura di vene o d'altri vapori" (283); "*Ma esce*, cioè dalla grazia divina di Dio" (284); Benvenuto: the two rivers "oriuntur ab eodem fonte divinae gratiae, qui exit de petra viva, quae est Christus" (4.179); Serravalle: the water "exit de fonte solido et recto, idest a voluntate divina, sic iubente" (756); for Landino the water "procede dalla gratia perficiente, & confirmante, al quale non lascia mancare la fonte" (*Purg.* 28 ad loc.). Concerning the two rivers, Pietro Alighieri comments: "Et licet ista flumina sint et videntur ibi, tamen sub figura accipi possunt" (535); and likewise Lana: "li quali fiumi secondo lo senso istoriale sono da tenere che sieno *realiter*, ma è da sapere ch'elli hanno spirituale significazione" (280).

3. See, for instance, C. H. Grandgent: "The water of this stream comes from a miraculous fount, not from any natural spring fed by condensed aqueous vapor" (ad loc.). Among the most recent translators and commentators, Allen Mandelbaum notes laconically: "But the spring announced in Canto XXVIII (121–23) and encountered here is essentially a remarkable invention by Dante, serving his liturgical, ethical, and cultural fiction" (*Purg.* 33.115–18). Mark Musa adds something very valuable: "The Pilgrim describes his condition after drinking (or being submersed in) the waters of Eunoë and returning to Beatrice in terms of rebirth, new life, resurrection, purity, and freedom to rise—the major motifs of the opening canto of Purgatory" (*Purg.* 33.142–45).

4. Within this general interpretation, one finds several variations. Pietro Alighieri writes: "istud flumen Lethes accipe pro recto proposito firmato ab homine in Deo et virtutibus, adeo quod ejus gustu omnia praeterita in eo sunt oblivione extincta. Nam spiritualis immunditia non potest per aquam corporalem mundari . . ." (521); and

later he adds, about Eunoè: "fons iste Aonius pro prudentiae virtute accipiatur, a qua prudentia omnes aliae virtutes cardinales ut a fonte manant"; "Et hoc est quod poetae figurant in Helicona montanea esse dictum Aonem, et de eo poetae perfecti bibere finguntur, scilicet gustare prudentiam, qua gustata omnium bonorum, quae sunt meritoria, memoriam accipiunt; ut nunc auctor mediante Mathelda fecit, idest activa vita, inductu Beatricis, idest theologiae" (535–36). For Buti, the two rivers signify two virtues: "la prima virtù significa purità e semplicità di mente, la seconda fervore e carità di Dio" (2.687); and later, "l'una [grazia] a diminticare [sic] lo male e lo suo fomite e lo suo incentivo, e l'altra d'arricordarsi del bene e del suo amore, che esceno d'una fonte" (2.822–23). And for Lana, the river Letè "è fiume d'oblivione e dismenticanza d'ogni viziosa concupiscenzia; l'altro a nome Eunoe, il quale è fiume d'ogni buona memoria, e siccome lo primo è di privazione d'ogni vizio, così lo secondo è d'ogni abito di virtude. Li quali due fiumi hanno per allegoria . . . a denotare la immobilitade dell'anime slave" (305); "Letè . . . è fiume d'oblivione delli malvagi atti. . . . Eunoè . . . rammemora ogni buono e virtudioso esercizio" (284). Giovanni da Serravalle: "Eunoè, qui habet reducere ad memoriam omnia bona: nam purgatis omnibus vitiis, introductis virtutibus, homo pervenit ad statum felicitatis" (813). Landino develops a moralistic reading: "Lethe da sinistra è oblivione de' vitij. Il che significa perfettione, laquale fa, che noi, non dico resistiamo a' vitij, come nell'altre virtù, ma tutti gli dimentichiamo, perché è sommerso, & al tutto estinto ogni appetito irrationale. Dalla destra di questa fonte nasce Eunoè, che significa buona mente. & questo è ardentissimo fervor di carità, & volontà immensa nelle virtuose operationi. Et non adopra, non fa vero prò questa fonte, se non è gustata quinci, & quindi, cioè, se non gustiamo, & di Lethe, & d'Eunoè insieme; perché non può esser l'animo perfetto, se non ha dimenticato ogni perturbatione, & non è tutto acceso dell'amor della virtù" (Purg. 28, ad loc.); in his gloss to canto 33, Landino adds: "Questi fiumi pon la Bibia in questo paradiso . . . ma il Poeta per servir alla sua allegoria, gli chiama Lethe, del qual di sopra ha fatto mentione, & Eunoè escon d'un fonte, perché danno ciascuno gratia non mediocre, perché Lethe ci fa dimenticar il vitio, & ogni suo fomite, & incentivo, & Eunoè, che in Greco significa buona mente, c'induce a ricordarci delle virtù, & c'infiamma dell'amore" (Purg. 33 ad loc.).

5. "Dante . . . faceva di costà scaturire le due simboliche fonti; l'una che toglie all'anima la memoria del peccato commesso; l'altra che gli rende quella del bene operato. Intendeva non già che l'anima rivivente alla Grazia perda la ricordanza del male, ma si libera dal rimorso e dalla tentazione di quello, e tanto l'ha innanzi a sé quanto giova a nutrirle la riconoscenza e l'amore; intendeva che il bene fatto da lei, misto al male, a lei, rinnovata, apparisce nella sua purità, e la consola insegnandole come negli errori stessi lo spirito umano conservi l'istinto del retto, e come l'obbedire, tuttoché imperfettamente, a siffatto istinto sia merito e cagione a speranza" (2.502).

6. "Dante nel suo Letè fonde le due idee di S. Bernardo: le due idee del fiume che dalla ferita di Gesù morto è sgorgato a farci salvi, e del fonte di misericordia, nel quale ci laviamo dai nostri peccati. Tuttavia egli ha continuato a leggere il sermone: 'Ma non solo questo è l'uso delle acque; né soltanto esse lavano le macchie, ma e la sete estinguono.' Ora nel paradiso terrestre Dante pone anche un altro fiume, l'Eunoè. In questo Dante non è tuffato, ma vi beve. . . . Gli altri fonti di S. Bernardo versano acque di 'discrezione' . . . di 'devozione'. . . di 'emulazione'. . . . Che tutti questi concetti Dante assommi nello Eunoè, vedesi nel fatto che a Eunoè beve, che il bere è dolce e ravviva le virtù, e più da ciò che colui che beve ritorna dall'onda come se fosse stato irrigato . . ." (Giovanni Pascoli, L'altro viaggio, in Sotto il velame, 576).

7. Dunstan Tucker and Rocco Montano have also proposed to view Eunoè as the symbol of the Eucharist. Montano writes: "I due fiumi operano solo se si beve l'acqua di entrambi. Sono in sostanza *la confessione o remissio peccati* e la comunione" (*Storia della poesia di Dante*, 3.241 ad loc.); Tucker: Eunoè "belongs to the Christian dispensation, and for it there is no parallel in the Old Testament writings. It symbolizes the Eucharist" (61). For Thomas, the Eucharist also brings forgiveness of sins, especially venial but even mortal, at least in certain situations; see 3.79.3 and 4.

8. An additional objection to Singleton's reading derives from the evidence I shall propose momentarily. If it is true that Dante has followed the biblical exegetes' division of the fountain into two rivers inside Eden and into four outside the garden, Singleton's thesis—it would seem—might lose some of its interpretive appeal.

9. Pererius discusses the question of the Edenic rivers in *Commentariorum et Disputationum in Genesim, Tomi Quatuor* 145–52. Almost all the authors quoted by Pererius have Phison and Gihon derive from Tigris and Euphrates; at the same time, however, one must not neglect the fact that Pererius and several medieval authors favor a different interpretation: ". . . cum Tigrim et Euphratem liquido constet ex diversis fontibus oriri, quod Moses inquit eos dimanare ex uno eo flumine quo rigabatur Paradisus, non aliter videtur posse intelligi, quam ut per unum illud flumen significetur locus ille, in quo Tigris & Euphrates mistis aquis simul coëunt, & aliquantisper unius fluminis instar habent. Postea facto aquarum divortio, rursus in proprios alveos separantur: ne solum ipsi, sed etiam duo alia flumina Phison & Gihon indidem derivantur. Quamobrem valde fit verisimile, circa locum ille, quo Tigris & Euphrates confusis aquis specie unius fluminis decurrunt, consitum fuisse paradisum" (152). Pererius also quotes all those classical authors usually mentioned in Dante commentaries in relation to the Tigris and Euphrates: Plinius, Strabo, Joseph, Theodoretus, Isidorus, Lucan, and Philostratus, in addition to the usual Christian commentators.

10. "ma forse Dante fu dell'avviso di quegli interpreti che fanno questi due secondi fiumi [Phison e Gihon] derivare da' primi. Vedi Pererius, *Gen.*, Lib. 3, De Parad. c. 2" (Purg. 33.112–13).

11. Nardi quotes, in notes 1–5: (1) Pererii *In Genesim* (Rome, 1589), bk. 3: *De quatuor fluminibus Paradisi*; P. D. Huetii, *De situ Paradisi terrestris*, in *Thesaur. Antiqu. Sacrarum* (Venice, 1747), vol. 7, chap. 5, n. 1; (2) Augustine *De genesi ad litteram* 8.7; (3) Teodoreto, cited by Pererius (n. 10 above) *de primo flumine Phison*; (4) Boethius *De consolatione philosophiae* 5.1; (5) Lucan *Pharsalia* 3.256–58.

12. Concerning the origin of the two rivers (Purg. 33.113, "uscir d'una fontana"), Singleton quotes Roger Bacon, who allegedly opposes the common origin of Tigris and Euphrates ("that the Tigris and Euphrates spring from the same source is contested by Roger Bacon"). Singleton's reading of Bacon's quoted passage, however, is not convincing. In reality, Bacon offers *different explanations* of the common origin of the two rivers. Singleton also adds that Bacon's reference to Sallust cannot be found in any of his extant works. Also, Benvenuto refers to Sallust and Plinius "et alii multi" (4.283). H. Gmelin's commentary (ad loc.) refers to Solinus, without any further indication (probably, G. C. Solinus, third century A.D., author of a compendium of Plinius's *Historia naturalis*), and also to Brunetto Latini ("Et le milieu est la fontaine ki trestot l'arouse, et nest en IV fleuves," *Trésor* 1.122–23).

13. One cannot help but think of Dante's condition at the beginning of the *Commedia*: "Io non so ben ridir com'i' v'intrai, / tant'era pien di sonno a quel punto / che la verace via abbandonai" (*Inf.* 1.10–12).

14. See also Ezek. 14:9–23; 33:9.

15. "Amplius lava me ab iniquitate mea, et a peccato meo munda me" (v. 4); "Asperges me hyssopo, et mundabor; lavabis me, et super nivem dealbabor" (v. 9).

16. "Miserere mei, Deus, secundum magnam misericordiam tuam; et secundum multitudinem miserationum tuarum, dele iniquitatem meam" (v. 3); "Averte faciem tuam a peccatis meis, et omnes iniquitates meas dele" (v. 11).

17. See also Ecclus. 6:37: "Et ipse dabit tibi cor"; Ezek. 11:18–19: "Et ingredientur illuc, et auferent omnes offensiones, cunctasque abominationes eius de illa. Et dabo eis cor unum, et spiritum novum tribuam in visceribus eorum; et auferam cor lapideum de carne eorum, et dabo eis cor carneum"; Ezek. 36:26: "Et dabo vobis cor novum, Et spiritum novum ponam in medio vestri; et auferam cor lapideum de carne vestra, Et dabo vobis cor carneum"; Eph. 4:20–24: "Vos autem non ita didicistis Christum, Si tamen illum audistis, et in ipso edocti estis, sicut est veritas in Iesu: deponere vos secundum pristinam conversationem veterem hominem, qui corrumpitur secundum desideria erroris. Renovamini autem spiritu mentis vestrae, qui secundum Deum creatus est in iustitia, et sanctitate veritatis."

18. "La justification du pécheur est l'oeuvre divine par excellence, analogue à l'acte créateur" (Bible de Jérusalem, 702 n. e). In the same note we also read that the verb creare can be attributed only to God and designates something new and wonderful: "In principio creavit Deus caelum et terram" (Gen. 1:1); "Ecce enim ego creo caelos novos, et terram novam" (Isa. 65:17); "quia creavit Dominus novum super terram" (Gen. 31:22).

19. Gen. 1:7: "Et fecit Deus firmamentum . . ."; Gen. 1:16: "Fecitque Deus duo luminaria magna . . ."; Gen. 1:25: "Et fecit Deus bestias terrae iuxta species suas . . ."; Gen. 1:26–27: "Faciamus hominem ad imaginem et similitudinem nostram, et praesit piscibus maris, et volatilibus caeli, et bestiis, universaeque terrae, omnique reptili, quod movetur in terra. Et creavit Deus hominem ad imaginem tuam. . . ."

20. Faith is lost as a theological virtue, though it remains as an intellectual assent. For this issue, see S. Th. 2, Q. 4, a. 4–5. (I owe this note to my colleague Joseph Wawrykow at the Department of Theology, University of Notre Dame.)

21. Thomas, S. Th. 1, Q. 89, a. 4, considers the question "Utrum opera virtutum in caritate facta mortificari possint." The answer is affirmative: ". . . res viva per mortem perdit operationem vitae: unde per quandam similitudinem dicuntur res mortificari quando impediuntur a proprio suo effectu vel operatione. Effectus autem operum virtuosorum quae in caritate fiunt, est perducere ad vitam aeternam. Quod quidem impeditur per peccatum mortale sequens, quod gratiam tollit. Et secundum hoc, opera in caritate facta dicuntur mortificari per sequens peccatum mortale."

22. Thomas: In IIIum Sent., distinctio 36, a. 5, at 1; In IVum Sent., dist. 14. Q. 2, at 2 and 5; dist. 21, Q. 1, a. 1, p. 1, at 3; dist. 22, Q. 1, a. 1, at 6; In ep. ad Thessalonicenses, c. 3, lect. 1; In ep. ad Heb. c. 6, lect. 1 and 3.

23. "opera mortua [= mortifera] non vivificantur per poenitentiam, sed magis abolentur. . . . impossibile est quod opera mortua iterum fiant viva per poenitentiam" (3, Q. 89, a. 6); "omne peccatum in hac vita per poenitentiam deleri potest" (3, Q. 86, a. 1).

24. Joseph Wawrykow has pointed out to me that Thomas, in the treatise on penance, presupposes our familiarity with the discussion in 1–2, Q. 112, for God in fact works this preparation for grace which decides the amount of grace received by the person.

25. In note: In Evang. 1.2 homil. 34: ML, 76, 1248.

26. In note: "Hugo de S. Victore, De sacram 1.2 p.14 c.4: ML, 176, 558."

27. Wawrykow thus commented on this issue: "Repentance restores the power to merit to our earlier performed good acts and causes God to accept our good acts as meritorious; Dante has in fact 'telescoped' these two into the simple statement that the person 'remembers his merits.' "

28. John Chrysostom, in cap. 1 *Genes. Homil.* 6. *PG*, 53, cols. 55–56. See also Bruno: "Innovare dicit, non quantum ad essentiae spiritus renovationem, cum immutabilis sit: sed quantum ad bonorum operum reparationem, quae in eo defecerant: quasi diceret: *Redde mihi spiritum rectum*, per cujus inhabitantem gratiam renoventur in anima affectiones bonae, quae defecerunt . . . ;" *PL*, 152, "Expositio in Psalmos. Ps. L," col. 865. See also the following references in Q. 89 by Thomas, analyzed above: Gregory, *ML*, 76, col. 1248; Isidore, *ML*, 83, 890; Augustine, *ML*, 33, 812. Jerome thus writes, in commenting on Paul's Epistle to the Galatians: "Quas [persecutiones] frustra arguuntur fuisse perpessi, si a gratia Christi recedant, propter quam tanta perpessi sunt. Simul et illa spes, quod quicumque ob Christi fidem laboraverit, et postea lapsus fuerit in peccatum, sicut priora sine causa dicitur passus fuisse dum peccat, sic rursum non perdat ea, si ad pristinam fidem et ad antiquum studium revertatur" (*PL*, 26, "S. Eusebii Hieronymi Commentarium in epistolam ad Galatas Lib. I, cap. III," Gal. 3:1–4; quoted by Tepe G. Bernardo, *Institutiones theologicae in usum scholarum* 4.511, where additional patristic sources can be found [508–20]).

29. See also Heb. 10:32–34: "Rememoramini autem pristinos dies, in quibus illuminati, magnum certamen sustinuistis passionum: et in altero quidem opprobriis et tribulationibus spectaculum facti: in altero autem socii taliter conversantium effecti. Nam et vinctis compassi estis, et rapinam bonorum vestrorum cum gaudio suscepistis, cognoscentes vos habere meliorem et manentem substantiam."

30. Tepe G. Bernardo: "Ad rem S. Hieronymus in hunc locum: 'Quicumque ob fidem Christi laboraverit et postea lapsus fuerit in peccatum, sicut priora sine causa dicitur passus fuisse, dum peccat, sic rursus non perdit ea, si ad pristinam fidem et ad antiquum studium revertatur.' Et S. Chrysostomus (in cap. 3 epist. ad Gal. comment. n. 2): 'Omnium, inquit (Apostolus), illorum, quae sustinuistis, isti (pseudapostoli) jacturam vos facere volunt, et coronam vobis student intervertere. Mox, ne concuteret illorum animos nervosque dissolveret . . . subtexuit: Si tamen frustra. Si volueritis, inquit, expergisci ac revocare vos ipsos, non frustra passi fueritis ' Similia habet alibi e.g. in cap. 1 Gen. homil. 6. n. 2. . . . Et ad Theod. laps. 1. 1. n. 7: 'Hic (filius prodigus) non alienus erat, imo filius . . . is in improbitiem lapsus est non vulgarem, sed in ipsum, ut ita dicam, malorum extremum: dives, liber, nobilis famulis, extraneis mercenariisque miserior effectus est. Attamen pristinum in statum rediit amissamque gloriam recuperavit. . . . Quia resipuit nec desperavit, post tantam corruptionem, eumdem ipsum assecutus fortunae splendorem; pulcherrimo induitur amictu et majoribus fruitur bonis, quam frater non lapsus. . . . Tanta est virtus poenitentiae' " (Tepe G. Bernardo, 511–12).

31. "In iustificatione impii sunt duo termini, scilicet a quo, qui est remissio culpae, et haec est renovatio, et ad quem, qui est infusio gratiae, et hoc ad regenerationem pertinet" ("Ad Titum," c. 3, lect. 1, v. 7, n. 94).

32. This concept is often developed in the liturgy of the Mass, for instance, in the Offertory: "Deus, qui humanae substantiae dignitatem mirabiliter condidisti et mirabilius reformasti: da nobis, per hujus aquae et vini mysterium, ejus divinitatis esse consortes, qui humanitatis nostrae fieri dignatus est particeps, Jesus Christus Filius tuus Dominus noster" (*Missale romanum*, 185–86).

33. The Dantean episode requires further analyses on equally essential elements, primarily, the intertextual connections among the three rivers: namely, the Pilgrim's

crossing of Acheron, Letè, and Eunoè; the Pilgrim's fainting along the banks of Acheron and Letè vis-à-vis his experience of Eunoè while fully aware; his regaining of consciousness along the inner bank of Acheron but in the middle of Letè; and, finally, the tree metaphor ("Io ritornai da la santissima onda / rifatto sì come piante novelle / rinovellate di novella fronda"—"I returned from the holiest water / remade as new trees / are renewed with new foliage," Purg. 33.142–44), which finds its full explanation within a complex contextual analysis of arboreal images and which leads, therefore, to a complete understanding of Purgatorio's last line, "puro e disposto a salire a le stelle" ("pure and prepared to ascend to the stars").

The Sins of the Blind Father: The Statian Source for Dante's Presentation of Ugolino in *Inferno* 32 and 33

CARON ANN CIOFFI

Few characters in the *Commedia* are more perversely compelling than Count Ugolino, the political traitor locked forever with his betrayer, Archbishop Ruggieri, in an icy hole in Antenora. His episode, which begins and ends with the "bestial sign" (*Inf.* 32.133) of gnawing on his enemy's skull, is carved in a space of history that no chronicle could ever tell: the dreams and private thoughts of a dying man forced to watch his children die before him. Ugolino's chilling narration, given as a gloss on his infernal hate, revolves around the motifs of treachery, paternity, the sacrifice of the children, and hunger. In particular, the ambiguous final line of his oration—"then fasting had more power than grief"—raises the possibility that, overwhelmed by starvation, Ugolino had resorted to technophagy.

Given these themes, critics have proposed various sources and parallels for *Inferno* 32 and 33. Marianne Shapiro has argued that Dante modeled his episode on the Old French *Amis et Amiles*, a *chanson de geste* in which Amis, stricken with leprosy and told by an angel that the cure consists of bathing in the blood of the children of his best friend, Amiles, moves the father to infanticide. Amis is cured, the sons are miraculously restored, and Amiles gives a feast to celebrate the victory over illness and death.[1] More recently, critics such as John Freccero[2] and Ronald Herzman[3] have delineated the story of Ugolino

81

using the Christological model. They link the children's suffering with that of the Savior who, like them, called for paternal aid and was a victim of betrayal, and they view the implied cannibalism as a parody of the Eucharistic feast.

It is my contention that Dante had at his disposal a different source—classical, epic, and relentlessly focused on the motifs of paternal and fraternal strife, political treachery, youthful sacrifice, and cannibalism. I refer to the *Thebaid* of Statius, to which Dante himself draws attention by comparing the gnawing of Ruggieri's head by Ugolino to the mutilation of Menalippus by Tydeus in book 8 (751–66) of the Latin text. Dante immediately establishes a complex grid of parallels and contrasts between Tydeus and Ugolino, and Menalippus and Ruggieri, the overarching function of which seems to be to prevent any possible sympathy on the part of the reader for the count and the archbishop.

In the *Thebaid*, Menalippus is a coward who tries to hide and who is fearful ("trepidum," 8.720) when he realizes he has speared Tydeus. With his remaining strength, Tydeus strikes his assailant back, and this *ardor* (8.728) is so tenacious that it holds off death for a bit—long enough for the Calydonian warrior to utter his final request. What is interesting here is the way that self-loathing is channeled into hatred of the enemy: "I hate my limbs and my body so frail and useless, deserter of the soul within it. Thy head, thy head, O Menalippus, could one but bring me that!" (8.738–40).

With unconscious irony, Tydeus then asks the assistance of Hippomedon, reminding him that the blood of Atreus runs in his veins. The reference to Atreus, who repeated with variation the crime of his grandfather Tantalus by killing the children of his brother Thyestes and feeding them to their father, foreshadows Tydeus's own act of cannibalism. The fact that it is Capaneus, the despiser of the gods later killed by Jove for his impiety, who carries out the request highlights its obscene nature. When Tydeus receives the severed head, he gazes into the "lumina torva" ("wrathful eyes," 8.756) and is himself inflamed ("gliscit," 8.755) to see his enemy still warm in life. This moment of perverse identification gives way to the final unholy act, prompted by the Fury Tisiphone and witnessed by Pallas, who had come to bestow immortal honors ("decus immortale," 8.759) on Tydeus. The goddess sees him befouled with brains ("cerebri," 8.760) and living blood ("vivo sanguine," 8.761) and abruptly averts her face, using the Gorgon on her shield atropopaically.

At the opening of book 9, Tydeus's own men condemn him as mad ("rabies," 9.1), because he broke the lawful bounds of hate. Eteocles also denounces the cannibalism and claims that the Greeks are beasts rather than men, tigers or lions who "with hooked fangs bite us" ("morsibus uncis," 9.13). Mocking the Greeks' astonishment at the earthquake that swallowed their priest, Amphiaraus, Eteocles asks, "Would even their own earth bear them?" (9.23–24). His speech instills *furor* into the Thebans, who immediately set about desecrating Tydeus's corpse.

Dante utilizes several elements of the Statian episode. The "lumina torva" of Menalippus become the "occhi torti" ("eyes askance," 33.76) of Ugolino when, after his oration, he again bites into Ruggieri's skull. Dante substitutes for the explicit mention of brains and gore in Statius the more oblique phrase, "fiero pasto" ("savage meal," 33.1). The effect is to heighten our horror in imagining what exactly must be wiped from Ugolino's mouth. Just as Tydeus had gazed into the face of Menalippus, a face that reflected back to him his own anger and his own mortality, so Ugolino had gazed into the faces of his children and discerned in them his own look (33.47–48, 56–57) of hunger and certain death.

Although Ugolino is blind to the truth, the readers perceive that he and Ruggieri are also mirror images of each other, defined by the same sin of treachery, just as death leveled Tydeus and Menalippus. Dante understood political betrayal (much as Statius had) as an attack on the clarity of the categories by which communal life is ordered.[4] When the distinctions between good and evil, father and son, man and beast, break down, violence inevitably results. As René Girard astutely notes in his own discussion of the Oedipus story, social order depends on hierarchical differences.[5] When those differences are effaced, as in the case of Oedipus, who literally returns to the womb of his begetting ("revolutus in ortus," 1.235) and becomes both father and brother to his sons, chaos prevails and conflict perpetuates itself.[6] In the *Thebaid*, Oedipus's own moral confusion leads inevitably to "fraternas acies" (1.1); the impiety of the father to his own father, Laius, whom he mockingly calls "the trembling dotard" (1.65–66), is perpetuated in the impious behavior of Eteocles and Polynices, who have mocked Oedipus's blindness and shunned him. In retaliation, Oedipus invokes

Tisiphone to further his unnatural wish ("perversa vota," 1.59) that all ties of kinship between the sons be dissolved and replaced by hate.

Certainly, by the end of the poem, the conflict of Eteocles and Polynices culminates in a violent mimesis. Statius is quite clear about this. The horses of the two men fall simultaneously, and the bridles and weapons "miscentur" ("are mixed together," 11.518–20). Both brothers are consumed by hate, each seeking the other's blood even as his own is flowing (11.536–40). Not even a spatial distinction between them is made: no ground divides them as they lock arms (11.527–29). The image of the one dying on top of the other makes of them a horrid single entity, and the poet himself reduces both to "savage souls" ("truces animae," 11.574). Not even death ends the conflict, for Eteocles and Polynices continue to feud as ghosts upon the same pyre, forming a single flame with a double head (12.431–32).

The Oedipus story, as Statius tells it, shows how patricide, incest, and fraternal revenge abolish all family differences.[7] In larger terms, the Thebaid also demonstrates the tragic nature of such familial dissolution when that family happens to be the ruling one in a community. The violence in such a royal household inevitably engulfs the entire social body; the personal vendettas of Oedipus and his sons initiate a chain reaction that puts society itself in jeopardy. Such is the nature of vengeance, which professes to be an act of reprisal but really amounts to violence indefinitely repeated; for every reprisal calls for yet another reprisal.[8]

Dante undoubtedly understood and shared Statius's view that revenge is endless, cyclical bloodshed, and that betrayer and betrayed are to a large extent indistinguishable. Drawing on the sameness of Eteocles and Polynices, and of Tydeus and Menalippus, he presents Ugolino and Ruggieri as suffering a contrapasso in which they form a "terrible mirror":[9] "two frozen in one hole so close that the head of one was a hood for the other; and as bread is devoured for hunger, so the upper one set his teeth upon the other where the brain joins with the nape" (32.125–29). The two men who should have been allies are now literally bound to one another, not in a spirit of communitas but in one of hate and destruction. When Ugolino calls himself "such a neighbor" ("tal vicino," 33.15) to the archbishop, that ironic phrase reveals the two as a parody of friendship, of social ties, that bind the body politic. As with Tydeus and Menalippus, and Eteocles and Polynices, spatial closeness is actually a measure of the distance between two characters caught in a tangle of mutual loathing. The physical expression of that hatred takes the form of cannibalism meted out by Ugolino to Ruggieri. But in the political economy, wherein both sinners belonged to the same body politic,[10] anthropophagy is always a self-eating. Thus, it comes as no surprise to us that Ugolino bites his own hands (33.58) when he sees the hungry faces of his children: the violence he has done to others in his political intrigues boomerangs and is revealed as what it truly is—namely, self-destruction. Whether or not he actually eats his sons is less important than the idea that this act, too, reduces to self-eating, since their flesh, as they themselves remind him, is his own: "Thou didst clothe us with this wretched flesh and do thou strip us of it" (33.62–63).

Just as Tydeus's horrific act was compared by Statius to that of a beast, so Dante views Ugolino's eating as bestial (33.133). This is apparent from the reference to his teeth, "strong on the bone like a dog's" (33.78). More subtly, Dante uses the prophetic dream of Ugolino to show how political treason reduces men to animals tearing apart other animals. Just as Eteocles had referred to the sharp fangs of the Greeks that rent his men, so Ugolino dreams that he is a wolf, his children the whelps, which are torn by the "sharp fangs" ("l'agute scane," 33.35) of hounds under command of the Ghibelline families who turned against him. Ruggieri, reduced in Hell to an object, a skull ("teschio," 33.77), appeared in the dream as the "master and lord" (33.28) who organized the hunt. As the running tires the wolf and cubs, they are called "father and sons" (33.35), an expression that reveals Ugolino's psychological identification with the trapped dreambeast and also the poet's artistic identification of the two. Ugolino has, by virtue of his treachery, become a wolf, the emblem of the Guelf party somehow literalized into an animal which, though here victimized, is also capable of great ferocity. The metamorphosis of man to wolf and then back to man at the moment of destruction by the dogs provides the key to the imagery of the infernal *contrapasso*. The lupine victim on earth becomes the canine victimizer in Hell, chewing not on a nobleman but on a bone.

The reference to Tydeus, who spoke no further word after his impious wish, coupled with the action of gnawing, leads us to expect either mute silence from Ugolino or an animal sound. But he returns to the sphere of the human, as it were, by wiping his mouth:[11] "That sinner lifted his mouth from the savage meal, wiping it on the hair of the head he had wasted behind" (33.1–3). The fact that, with a blood-ied mouth that must resemble a gaping wound, Ugolino still pays lip service (if I may pun) to human etiquette shocks us.

Although no such grotesque gesture is found in the Tydeus-Men-alippus episode, there is a parallel moment in the *Thebaid* (2.675–81). There Tydeus has just finished slaughtering all but one of the fifty warriors sent by Eteocles to ambush him. Statius compares him to a lion who, with hunger sated in abundance of blood, and with neck and mane congealed with gore, stands with open mouth amid the sheep carcasses: "gone is his savage fury, he only snaps in the air his empty jaws, and with hanging tongue licks them clean of the soft wool" (680–81). Like Tydeus's *furor*, Ugolino's wrath toward the enemy takes on the appearance of hunger, the difference being that in the simile the cleaning of the lion's mouth is done after the violence of killing and eating the sheep is over. For Ugolino, wrath is unending and will never be satisfied. If Dante did have this Statian passage in mind, it would underscore the point that even beasts utilize oral hygiene.

The final point about the Tydeus episode concerns Eteocles' state-ment that the Greeks are so savage and lawless that their own earth would swallow them up, as it has already done to Amphiaraus. Ugo-lino himself had longed for just such an earthquake: "Ah, hard earth, why didst thou not open?" (33.66). Though often interpreted as a ref-erence to the earthquake at the Crucifixion, this line may instead refer to the moment when a "gaping chasm" ("ore profundo," 7.816) engulfed the still-living augur of Apollo and hurled him down to the Underworld.

In the *Thebaid*, Amphiaraus is a pious figure who foresees the horror of the war and the deaths of all the Seven against Thebes, but who is powerless to stop any of these events. In his final moments in the upper world, Amphiaraus learns from Apollo that his end has come but that the god will spare him the horrors of dying. The priest stoically accepts his fate and asks the god to look after his "betrayed home" ("deceptum larem," 787), inhabited by his abominable wife and the son who will avenge her wickedness. We recall that Eriphyle betrayed her husband's life out of her desire to possess the necklace of Harmonia. Her deception is recalled again in the Underworld, when Amphiaraus pacifies Dis, the Lord of Erebus, by stressing his innocence and blaming his unnatural wife ("nefanda coniunx," 8.120–21) for prompting him to war.

Dante's recalling of this episode serves two functions. First, it illuminates the craftiness of Ugolino, who obliquely compares his victimization by Ruggieri to that of Amphiaraus by Eriphyle. But Dante never lets us forget that this parallel is drawn by a man who desperately craves sympathy (33.40–41) and who refuses to accuse himself of any wrongdoing. Like Amphiaraus, Ugolino was a victim of betrayal. But, unlike the seer, Ugolino is guilty of the same offense that he rails against. It is as if the "ore profundo," literally the "boundless mouth," that swallows Amphiaraus has become, in *Inferno* 33, "la bocca" (1), "the mouth of darkness" as Pézard called it,[12] that engulfs the archbishop, who had rendered those once-living jaws stationary through lack of food. Amphiaraus wins his case and goes unpunished by Dis; Ugolino is similarly eloquent but wins no pity for himself from Dante or God. In fact, Ugolino's narrative focuses, as he himself lets slip, on how cruel was *his* death (33.20), and the repetition of the personal pronoun "io" in the account (46, 47, 49, 52, 56, 59, 71, 72) reveals his solipsism. Obsessed by his own pain, he offers no words of comfort to his children, only calling out to them when it is too late, when they are dead. Dante sees through Ugolino's rhetorical ploy, for in his invective against Pisa he excuses only the children and not their father (33.85–87).

Second, the Statian Underworld scene provides an important link between Hell and earth, a link that Dante, too, makes at the end of the canto when he reveals that the souls of the betrayers of guests plummet straight to Hell at the moment of their treachery, while their bodies are left on earth to be controlled by devils until the time of actual death (33.122–47). Statius's Underworld is ruled by the same dark world of violence that characterizes the earth. Dis appears like Eteocles, a tyrant surrounded by his henchmen and outraged at the thought of a live intruder disturbing his realm. In fact, he mistakes the descent of the seer for an act of civil war. Dis immediately cries out, "Which of my brothers thus makes war on me?" (8.36), and then accuses Jove of divine espionage. Although ultimately convinced that Amphiaraus has no ulterior motives, Dis nonetheless avenges Apollo's assault on his prerogatives by sending Tisiphone to incite men to acts offensive to the supernal deities—acts which include the cannibalism of Tydeus, the duel of Eteocles and Polynices, the refusal of burial rights by Creon, and the madness of Capaneus, who challenges Jove directly. All these events are the work of Hell, and go beyond what even Oedipus had willed.[13]

Similarly, Dante is intent on demonstrating the possibility of infernal evil on earth.[14] The betrayers of guests are so wicked that when devils take over their bodies no one notices. Dante himself can hardly believe that Frate Alberigo and Branca d'Oria are not still on earth (33.121, 139–41). This vision of death-in-life is shocking both in itself and because it contradicts the orthodox theological notion, dramatized in *Purgatorio* 5, that a man can repent even at the last moment of his earthly existence. The heinousness of Ugolino and Ruggieri, two humans who mirror each other as beasts, can only be topped by the terrifying equation of man and demon. As in the Amphiaraus episode, the world of eternity intersects with the world of time, and the reality of Hell pollutes that of earth.

Dante makes the final connection between Ugolino and the *Thebaid* when the count describes how, for six days, he watched his sons starve but could not bring himself to cry or speak (33.49, 52–54, 65). When all four are dead, Ugolino tells us, "I gave myself, now blind, to groping over each and for two days called on them after they were dead" (33.72–74). Here Dante forges a precise parallel between Ugolino and his children and Oedipus and his sons. The source for this description is *Thebaid* 11 (594–626), where the blind Oedipus is led by Antigone to the corpses of his sons and he flings himself, speechless, upon them. I quote the relevant passage in full:

> nec vox ulla seni: iacet immugitque cruentis
> vulneribus, nec verba diu temptata sequuntur.
> dum tractat galeas atque ora latentia quaerit,
> tandem muta diu genitor suspiria solvit:
> "tarda meam, pietas, longo post tempore
>   mentem
> percutis? estne sub hoc hominis clementia
>   corde?
> vincis io miserum, vincis, Natura, parentem!
> en habeo gemitus lacrimaeque per arida
>   serpunt
> volnera et in molles sequitur manus impia
>   planctus.
> accipite infandae iusta exsequialia mortis,
> crudeles, nimiumque mei! nec noscere natos

adloquiumque aptare licet; dic, virgo, precanti,
quem teneo? quo nunc vestras ego saevus
   honore
prosequar inferias? o si fodienda redirent
lumina et in voltus saevire ex more potestas!
heu dolor, heu iusto magis exaudita parentis
vota malaeque preces! quisnam fuit ille
   deorum,
qui stetit orantem iuxta praereptaque verba
dictavit Fatis? furor illa et movit Erinys
et pater et genetrix et regna oculique cadentes;
nil ego!" (11.601–21)

The old man [speaks] no utterance; he throws himself down and bellows on the bloody wounds, nor do long-attempted words follow. While he gropes and searches for the faces hidden beneath the helmets, the father at length releases his long-silent sighs: "Late, after so long a time, piety, do you pierce my feelings? Is there mercy in this human heart? Oh! You have conquered, Nature, conquered this wretched parent. I have groans and tears that creep over these dry wounds, and this impious hand follows in effeminate beating [of my breast]. Receive these just obsequies of your unnatural deaths, cruel ones, too truly mine! I cannot recognize my sons, nor make my speech appropriate. Tell me, virgin, I beg, which am I holding? With what honors now can one as cruel as I attend to your rites? Oh, if my dug-out eyes could be restored so that I could wreak revenge upon my face as I once did. Ah, pain, ah, for a parent's prayers and curses granted too completely! What god was it who stood by and snatched up my words and told them to the Fates? It was madness that set in motion those [ills] and the Fury and my father and my mother and my kingdom and my falling eyes—not I!"

The correspondences with Ugolino here are striking: he, too, is a blind and beaten father who crawls over the sons he cannot recognize, dead sons who cannot respond to his long-overdue words. Just as Oedipus employs his hands in a futile gesture of flagellation, so Ugolino had bitten his own impious hands. Yet Dante withholds from Ugolino the elements that make us pity Oedipus: the count's lack of tears is noted twice, and he accepts no responsibility for the sins that damned his children to torment. In contrast, Oedipus's guilt is so intense that he wishes to repeat the act of self-destruction he committed after learning of his patricide and incest. He does what Ugolino still cannot bring himself to do: Oedipus repents the curses he issued upon his sons; then, because of the enormity of the admission, he rationalizes his crimes by blaming his parents, Tisiphone, Thebes itself, his derangement, and the "falling eyes" upon which the sons had trod (*Thebaid* 1.238–39). This psychological projection of guilt onto others becomes, in Ugolino's case, a total release from wrongdoing. It was, he tells Dante, the "evil devices" of Ruggieri (33.16) that caused the tragedy. Oedipus, true to his bent for self-knowledge, understands that he has channeled his own pain and anger outward, toward Eteocles and Polynices, the spawn of his incest. At last he sees himself in the dual role of victim and instrument of Fate. But Ugolino stubbornly denies that his own intrigues brought about his children's deaths. He directs his own volatile mix of *dolor* (33.5) and *disdegno* (32.131) solely toward Ruggieri and away from himself.

The comparison with Oedipus invites us to interpret Ugolino's silence in the face of his children's suffering as a refusal to admit to them his own treachery, the real reason for their imprisonment. Their suffering is more pitiable than that of Eteocles and Polynices, who themselves were guilty of tyranny, vengeance, and envy. Oedipus's sons were, as their father himself points out, "crudeles" ("cruel ones"), but Ugolino's children were "innocenti" (33.88). (We recall the Latin etymology of this adjective, from *in nocere*, "unable to harm.") Ugolino's children have hurt no one: in fact, they try to save their father's life by offering him their own: "Father, it will be far less pain for us if thou eat of us" (33.61, 62). The sons' sacrifice poignantly provides Ugolino with the opportunity to meditate on his own faults; but he does not. He *is* "turned to stone within" (33.49), and this metaphor has all the connotations of hardness, coldness, and obduracy in sin[15] that summarize his spiritual and emotional state.

It is a harsh message indeed that Dante intends by the analogy with Oedipus: he contrasts a classical father who was fated by the gods to sin and who, despite his sons' impieties, nonetheless conquers his unnatural hardheartedness toward them in the end, to a modern father who has freely chosen to act basely and who, despite his sons' loving self-sacrifice, remains incapable of paternal tears. The only fatality in Ugolino's story is that of nature itself, which dictates that without food men must die. Just as Pisa is a "novella Tebe" (33.89), renewing all the vices of its classical antecedent, so Ugolino is a new Oedipus, renewing and even surpassing the evils of his counterpart. Oedipus's weeping orbs signal an instance of regained *pietas*, but Ugolino's eyes remain blind in life to his crimes, and whatever tears he may weep in Hell are immediately frozen into ice (32.46–48).

Dante's subtle references to Tydeus, Amphiaraus, and Oedipus and his sons in *Inferno* 32 and 33 are part of a larger network of Theban allusions in the final cantos of this canticle. These references include: the pride of Capaneus on the walls of Thebes in the canto of the thieves (*Inf.* 25.13–15); the pyre of Eteocles and Polynices in the canto of the false counselors (*Inf.* 26.52–54); and Juno's hatred of the Theban household, particularly of Semele and Athamas and Ino, in the canto of the falsifiers (*Inf.* 30.1–12). As the sins increase in gravity, so do the Theban allusions, reaching a crescendo in canto 32. Here we find the reference to Amphion's building of the walls of Thebes (32.10–12). Here, too, Dante calls the betrayers "the wretched weary brothers" (32.21), a term that evokes Eteocles and Polynices ("diros fratres," 12.85). Here the infernal punishment consists of pain locked up in the eyes (32.38–39), which recalls Oedipus's self-mutilation. Finally, Dante refers to the Alberti brothers, who are buried together in the ice, as having issued "d'un corpo" ("from one womb," 32.58), the exact phrase used by Statius to describe Oedipus's sons just before their final duel ("unius ingens bellum uteri," "the monstrous conflict of one womb," 11.407–8). The parallel is clear: the Alberti brothers, one a Guelf, the other a Chibelline, disputed their inheritance and killed each other. Like Eteocles and Polynices, they share a single bier that mocks the ideal of fraternity.

The extraordinary density of Statian allusions in the last two cantos suggests that lower Dis, like Thebes, is the ultimate *disutopia*.[16] The sinners of the ninth circle have, like the negative figures in the *Thebaid*, rejected *pietas*, understood as the justice owed to one's gods, one's homeland, and one's family. Yet Thebes is also the model of cities like Pisa, Pistoia, and Florence, and hence an emblem of the chaos of earthly politics.[17] For Dante, all secular history is characterized by fraud, betrayal, violence, and familial discord, and it always uses gratuitous scapegoats for its cohesion.

Statius knew this only too well. In his epic, the true victims are the innocent. We have already mentioned Amphiaraus. But here too we must include Opheltes, the baby who is accidentally killed by a sacred serpent when his nurse, Hypsipyle, abandons him in order to lead the parched Greek army to water (*Theb.* 4.739–96; 5.499–753).

Not coincidentally, another serpent, which was sacred to Mars and killed by Cadmus, demands another act of violence: to placate the god of war, Creon's young son, Menoeceus, must be killed (10.610–15). In an act of extraordinary *pietas* toward the gods and his country, Menoeceus impales himself with his sword on the walls of Thebes (10.756–82). He is a scapegoat whose function, as Girard notes, is to absorb the violence of society and dispose of it, thereby preventing reciprocal bloodshed.[18] In the *Thebaid*, Amphiaraus, Opheltes, and Menoeceus are deified after death, and their funeral rites momentarily interrupt the flow of the war. But violence resumes and the evil of man remains unpurified by sacrifice.

Dante's political vision is even bleaker than that of Statius: the pagan characters in the *Thebaid* had no central numinous exemplar of communal atonement, but as a Christian, Ugolino knows the lesson of the Crucifixion, a lesson poignantly recalled by Dante's own anger at the Pisans for having put the children "a tal *croce*" ("to such a cross," 33.87). Dante outdoes Statius, as he had surpassed Ovid and Lucan in *Inferno* 25 (94–99), by presenting a stark picture of an unregenerate man, who had at his disposal an infinite source of grace, the Christological sacrifice performed to enlighten his heart of darkness, but who chose instead, as Statius had said of Oedipus, "to sink his guilty shame in eternal night" ("merserat damnatum pudorem aeterna nocte," 1.47).[19]

NOTES

1. Marianne Shapiro, "An Old French Source for Ugolino?" *Dante Studies* 92 (1974): 129–47. The idea was first suggested by Gianfranco Contini, in "Filologia ed esegesi dantesca," in *Atti dell'Accademia Nazionale dei Lincei, Rendiconti delle Adunanze Solenni*, anno 362, vol. 7 (1965): 24–27; reprinted in English in *Dante Studies* 87 (1969): 15–16.

2. John Freccero, "Bestial Sign and Bread of Angels (*Inferno* 32–33)," *Yale Italian Studies* 1 (1977): 53–66, reprinted in *Dante: The Poetics of Conversion* (Cambridge: Harvard Univ. Press, 1986), pp. 152–66.

3. Ronald Herzman, "Cannibalism and Communion in *Inferno* XXXIII," *Dante Studies* 98 (1980): 53–78.

4. Leonard Barkan, *The Gods Made Flesh: Metamorphoses and the Pursuit of Paganism* (New Haven: Yale Univ. Press, 1986), p. 147.

5. René Girard, *Violence and the Sacred*, trans. Patrick Gregory (Baltimore: Johns Hopkins Univ. Press, 1977), pp. 47–51.

6. Ibid., p. 51.

7. Ibid., p. 74.

8. Ibid., p. 14

9. Barkan, p. 148.

10. On Dante's conception of the body politic, see Ernst Kantorowicz, *The King's Two Bodies: A Study in Medieval Political Theology* (Princeton, N.J.: Princeton Univ. Press, 1957), pp. 451–95, esp. pp. 467–68; Nicholas Havely, "The Self-Consuming City: Florence as Body Politic in Dante's *Commedia*," *Deutsches Dante Jahrbuch* 61 (1986): 99–113.

11. Emilio Pasquini, "Il canto XXXIII dell'*Inferno*," *Letture Classensi* 10 (1980): 191–216.

12. André Pézard, "Le Chant XXXIII de l'Enfer," *Letture dell'Inferno* of the *Lectura Dantis internazionale* (Milan, 1963), pp. 343–96.

13. David Vessey, *Statius and the 'Thebaid'* (Cambridge: Cambridge Univ. Press, 1973), p. 264.

14. Herzman, p. 70.

15. For the link between Ugolino's stoniness and his lack of spiritual understanding, see Freccero, *Dante: The Poetics of Conversion*, p. 158.

16. Jeffrey Schnapp, *The Transfiguration of History at the Center of Dante's 'Paradise'* (Princeton, N.J.: Princeton Univ. Press, 1986), p. 18.

17. Freccero, *Dante: The Poetics of Conversion*, p. 154.

18. Girard, p. 109.

19. I would also like to mention that the *Thebaid* makes recurrent use of the themes of infanticide and cannibalism that plagued the Theban royal line. Often, the two crimes are linked. For example, the myth of Tantalus, who killed his son Pelops and boiled him as a feast for the gods, is mentioned many times (*Theb.* 1.246–47; 2.436; 4.576; 4.590; 6.122–23; 6.283–84; 7.94–96; 7.207; 7.248; 7.422; 10.785; 11.127–28; 12.540). At least three references are made to the story of Atreus, the grandson of Tantalus who killed his brother Thyestes' sons and fed them to their father (*Theb.* 4.307–8; 8.742; 11.129). Statius demonstrates that Cadmus's lineage is saturated with child-killings and that this tragic pattern continues in his descendants. He refers to Semele, Cadmus's daughter, whose child, Bacchus, was nearly destroyed by his father Jove when he came to Semele as a thunderbolt (*Theb.* 2.71–73; 4.564; 4.673–76; 7.156–60; 7.178–80; 7.666–67; 8.234; 9.424–25; 10.67; 10.903; 11.215–16). He recalls Athamas and Ino, the latter Semele's sister, who are driven by madness to kill their children (*Theb.* 1.12–15; 3.190; 4.59; 4.565–69; 7.421; 10.425), and to Niobe, the daughter of Tantalus and wife of Amphion of Thebes, who boasted of her fourteen children and was punished by their all being slain by Apollo and Artemis (*Theb.* 1.711; 3.191–94; 4.575–78; 6.124–25; 12.131). Finally, Statius mentions Autonoe, daughter of Cadmus, whose son Actaeon was torn apart by his own dogs after Diana changed him into a stag (*Theb.* 4.562; 572–74), and Agave, another daughter who killed her son Pentheus in a bacchic frenzy (7.211–14). Thus, Dante need not have relied solely on the descriptions of cannibalism and infanticide in the Thyestean banquet found in Horace's *Ars poetica* (89–91) and Seneca's *Thyestes* (1006–1100), as Gianfranco Contini (above, n. 1, pp. 13–14) has suggested. Technophagy is the most radical example of the loss of distinction. Like infanticide, it reverses the temporal hierarchy by forcing the parents to survive the children. But it goes a step further: the father who consumes his own offspring totally destroys the distinction between himself and them by literally taking them into his own body.

The "Canto of the Word" (*Inferno* 2)[1]

ROBERT HOLLANDER

The opening canto of the *Commedia* sweeps us into the perilous situation of its protagonist. No matter how artificial its action may seem, it is nonetheless intense, focusing our attention on events and their consequences. Canto 2, in comparison, is more distant and discursive. In the first canto we were most involved in sharing Dante's sense of his own vulnerability to sin and were most aware of him as a threatened and mortal being, one who shares our own mortal plight. As the second canto opens, we inferentially become aware that he is a being altogether different from us, a poet:

> Lo giorno se n'andava, e l'aere bruno
>   toglieva li animai che sono in terra
>   de le fatiche loro; e io sol uno
> m'apparecchiava a sostener la guerra
>   sì del cammino e sì de la pietate,
>   che ritrarrà la mente che non erra.

> Daylight was fading, and the darkening air
> Released all living things that are on earth
> From their labors; and I, lone among men,
> Was readying myself to face the struggle
> Both of the way itself and of the pity,
> Which memory, unerring, will retrace.

The passage, which prepares for an action—the descent into Hell—draws our attention to the poetic nature of that descent, first by virtue of being in itself a Virgilian borrowing, second by insisting on the intervention of our poet's *mente*, or memory, between the events recorded and our reception of them. The Virgilian provenance of Dante's vigil in the growing darkness of evening was noted by many of the early commentators, even though opinions varied (and continue to do so) as to exactly which Virgilian text lies behind Dante's (see Mazzoni [1967], p. 165: *Aeneid* 3.147; 4.522–28; 8.26–27; 9.224–25).

As for the second matter, Singleton (1970), who has been instrumental in reshaping our understanding of Dante's troubling claim that his poem is not a fiction, offers the following gloss to the sixth verse: "Memory will now faithfully retrace the real event of the journey, exactly as it took place. This most extraordinary journey through the three realms of the afterlife is represented, never as dreamed or experienced in vision, but as a real happening. . . . Here, then, and in the following invocation, the poet's voice is heard for the first time as it speaks of his task as poet."

Thus do the first six verses put us in mind of poetry, first with their reminiscence of Virgil, not as some generalized representative of "Reason," as the insistent allegorizer has contrived to make us believe through the centuries,[2] but as that most particular poet who wrote the *Aeneid*. As he enters the poem in its first canto, Virgil is addressed first by name (79), then as "de li altri poeti onore e lume" (82) and as "maestro e . . . autore" (85), finally as "poeta" (130). Dante's first spoken word in canto 2, in addressing Virgil, is again "poeta" (10). By the end of the canto the guide's title will refer more to his present functions in the journey: "duca, segnore, maestro" (140); indeed, these denominations will henceforth be used more often than any others (see Gmelin [1954], pp. 59–60). Yet at the outset the titles which Dante confers upon Virgil would clearly imply that his having been a poet was the single most important qualification for his astonishing role as guide in this Christian poem. And that fact itself would not be without surprise.

If the first canto of *Inferno* is the "canto of fear," as is often asserted (see Mazzoni [1967], p. 49, with recognition of F. D'Ovidio and C. Ballerini), the second is the "canto of the word." The substantive *parola* occurs five times, more than in any other canto in the poem (43, 67, 111, 135, 137),[3] as though to mirror the insistent presence of *paura* in the preceding canto, where that phonically similar word also occurs five times (and similarly, more often there than in any other

canto). Still more indicative of the significance lodged in the word
parola in the second canto is the fact that only one other canto of
Inferno includes a higher percentage of poetic space allocated to direct
discourse. The eleventh, as it is primarily devoted to Virgil's verbal
diagram of Hell, opens with nine lines of description but is subsequently given over entirely to dialogue; thus 106 of its 115 verses (92
percent) are spoken. The second canto follows hard upon; a total of
118 of its 142 verses (83 percent) are spoken, either by Dante or by
Virgil. No other canto of the *Inferno* except the eleventh is so filled
with spoken words.[4]

It has become a commonplace to assert that the first canto serves
as preface to the entire *Commedia*, the second as prologue to *Inferno*
(Pagliaro [1967], p. 17, cites Conrad of Hirsau: "*Proemium prefacio est
operis, prologus quedam ante sermonem prelocutio*"). This schema is
perhaps acceptable; yet the fact that both *Purgatorio* 1 and 2 as well
as *Paradiso* 1 and 2 constitute similar introductory units may eventually erode its distinction. Nonetheless, by postponing his invocation
to the second canto Dante would clearly seem to be calling our attention to a structural principle of $1 + 33 + 33 + 33 = 100$. In this
respect the separateness of the first two cantos from one another is
underlined, since invocations occur in each of the first cantos of the
succeeding *cantiche*. At the same time, their structural similarity tends
to make them a unit:

	Inferno 1		Inferno 2
1–27	Dante's peril	1–42	Dante's uncertainty
	simile (22–27)		simile (37–40)
28–60	Three beasts	43–126	Three blessed ladies
	simile (55–58)		simile (127–130)
61–136	Virgil's assurances	127–142	Dante's will firmed

The three segments of narrated action and reported speech, separated
by similes, are evidently parallel. And the last verse of the second
canto, "intrai per lo cammino alto e silvestro," clearly echoes, as many
a commentator has noticed, words that began the first canto: *cammin*
(1), *selva* (2), not to mention *intrai* (10) and *alto* (16). Dante thus suc-
ceeds in giving his two proemial cantos distinct purposes while combining them into an introductory unit.

Since Homer, poets have taken trouble to establish their authority.
What are Dante's qualifications as teller of this tale? His invocation

does not make them immediately clear. It is one of the most vexed passages in the canto (7–9):

> O Muse, o alto ingegno, or m'aiutate;
>   o mente che scrivesti ciò ch'io vidi,
>   qui si parrà la tua nobilitate.
> O Muses, O lofty genius, now sustain me.
> O memory, that recorded what I saw,
> Here shall your true worth be made apparent.

From three lines the commentary tradition has inherited three major problems, although only the first two are widely recognized:

1. Why are pagan muses invoked in a Christian poem?
2. What is (and to what power belongs) "alto ingegno"?
3. Is the invocation double or triple? That is, are we to take memory as being invoked along with the first two powers or not?

My own responses to these questions are as follows.

1. Either Dante is invoking the pagan muses for aid in composing, by human art, the poetic artifact that will make his direct experience of God's universe available to mankind, or he is speaking of "Muses" as veiled metaphoric equivalences of the inspiration granted by the Holy Spirit. Most commentators unhesitatingly choose the former and certainly more comfortable alternative. Yet if muse and alto ingegno are to be taken as synonymous, as many commentators believe (for example, Mazzoni [1967], pp. 175–76), we are faced with a considerable difficulty, as the ensuing discussion of the second of these powers will attempt to show. In my view, the two powers invoked are indeed of different orders, muse representing what humans may learn of art, ingegno, on the other hand, being the power of conceiving things which are true. Dante's four subsequent couplings of the words ingegno and arte in the Commedia (Purg. 9.125, 27.130; Par. 10.43, 14.117) respect this significant distinction—namely, that between conceptualization and articulation. If this is the case, then muse here represents the source which grants to the poet—any poet, whether Christian or pagan—the human power to express what he has conceived. Dante's own gloss on his invocation to Apollo (Par. 1) in the Epistola a Cangrande (18 [47]) is of help here.[5] Distinguishing between the proemial gestures made by rhetoricians and poets, he notes that, whereas both need to prepare their readers, only poets must make invocation, "since they must seek from higher entities [superioribus substantiis] that which resides not in the common human

measure, something like a divine gift [*quasi divinum quoddam munus*]." If even in the *Epistola* Dante is careful not to make his claims for divine inspiration more than cautiously, his doubly hedged remark nonetheless points the way to a theological and Christian interpretation of the "good Apollo" invoked in *Paradiso* 1.13. The final invocations in the *Commedia* (*Par.* 30.97–99; 33.67–75) are overt appeals to God himself; they may lead us to suspect that others in the *Commedia* are more veiled appeals to the same power (for recognition of the fact that there are nine invocations in the poem, see Hollander [1980], pp. 31–38). It seems to me far more likely that *alto ingegno* is the element in this first invocation which has the higher and veiled meaning, while the Muses retain their traditional role as grantors of more usual artistic gifts.

2. It is difficult to believe, given Dante's many high claims for the revealed truth of his *poema sacro*, that he would say he sought his ultimate inspiration from any source other than God. Yet few commentators have been open to this disturbing possibility (for the radical views of Castelvetro, Dionisi, and Bennassuti, see Mazzoni [1967], p. 176; and, for the first, see n. 7, below). The majority of commentators remain wedded to the unlikely view that the *ingegno* in question is Dante's own. For the poet to have invoked his own "genius" would not only have been in the poorest taste but would involve a catastrophic error in logic. How can one invoke one's own genius for genius? Whatever the agency invoked, it must be external to Dante. That much should be clear, as some commentators between Pietro di Dante (1340) and Mazzoni (1967; pp. 173–77), reminding us of the model to be found in *Aeneid* 6.264–67, have taught us. What remains at issue is whether *muse* and *ingegno* are synonymous or, as I believe is far more likely, differentiated. I would propose that Dante first invokes the human skills of poetic expression from more traditional sources and then the power of the highest conceptualization from its sole and very source. The raw daring of such a claim, which the poet of necessity must contrive to keep as tacit as he can, has undoubtedly kept our following wit at a nervous distance. (For circumstantial evidence that helps to confirm this hypothesis, see *De vulgari eloquentia* 2.4.9–10, where Dante quotes *Aeneid* 6.125–31, to the effect that only those, like Aeneas beloved of God ["dilectos Dei," from Virgil's "quos aequus amavit Iuppiter"] may be "sublimatos ad ethera" ("raised to heaven"). Not only is Dante here discussing the qualifications of the poet, but the passage represents the sole locus in the work in which he refers both to *ingenium* and to

ars.[6] It was likely to have been on his mind as he composed the first invocation of the *Commedia.*

3. *Mente,* or "memory," is nearly universally understood as being the final element in a trinitarian invocation (see Pietro di Dante [1340]: "nam est in anima similitudo Trinitatis, scilicet mens, notitia et amor"). It is not. *Muse* and *alto ingegno* are sought outside the poet, the first learned, the second granted. *Mente* is put forward as the power within him that recorded what *alto ingegno* made available to it. It is not invoked.[7] Surely it would have been as absurd for Dante to have *invoked* a capacity that he already possessed (and had acknowledged as his "source" a mere three verses earlier) as for him to *invoke* his own genius, as his own son seems to have acknowledged.[8] We should long ago have come to grasp the distinctions that Dante here insists upon and that are made patent by the very language of this tercet, in which the first two entities apostrophized are indeed asked for aid ("O muse, o alto ingegno, or m'aiutate"), while the third merely has a claim made concerning its worthiness ("o mente . . . qui si parrà la tua nobilitate").

With the conclusion of the proem of this prolusory canto, its dialogues begin. Excepting only two intervening similes, the first expressing the protagonist's lack of will to begin the journey, the second, his willingness,[9] everything between the invocation and the concluding two verses of the canto is presented as direct discourse. The pattern observable in the order of the speakers is interesting:

1. Dante (10–36)
    2. Virgil (43–57)
        3. Beatrice (58–74)
            4. Virgil (75–84)
        5. Beatrice (85–114)
    6. Virgil (115–26)
7. Dante (133–40)

We must surely agree that the symmetry of this chiastic pattern is not the result of chance. The extended and symmetrical series of speeches (exchanged between Dante and Virgil on earth, between Virgil and Beatrice in Limbo, between Mary and Lucy, then Beatrice and Lucy in Heaven) allows us to perceive that what is crucially at stake in

Inferno 2 is the question of *auctoritas*. To whom may it be said to belong? We should remember the opening six verses, where we find Dante the pilgrim alone despite the company of Virgil (see n. 2, below), as the poet thought Aeneas had been alone despite the company of the Sibyl: "quando esso Enea sostenette solo con Sibilla a intrare ne lo Inferno" (*Convivio* 4.26.9), and as we recognize that Dante was "alone" in fact as he began to write the poem. The shade of Virgil, the presence of the Sibyl, the text of the *Aeneid*—all of these—may bring a hero or a poet to a certain readiness; however, since only he can change or be changed in the subsequent action or vision or composition, he is perforce alone, though he be in company.

We know in fact that, in this poem, the activities of journeying and writing are one and the same, except in the poem's given that the event of writing is separate from the events written about. Yet when we accept that pretext, which we must do or be condemned to let Dante's words be only self-referential, we find ourselves contemplating the shade of Virgil, present here on earth, serving in the evidently authoritative role as guide. At this point in the text we have just read an invocation, the single poetic act which most directly confronts the question of *auctoritas*. To what may be our surprise, since we have been witnesses to the outburst of enthusiasm with which Dante welcomes Virgil's first appearance in the poem, the entirety of what follows in this second canto is dedicated to a confirmation of Dante's—but not Virgil's—poetic authority. And while it is undoubtedly true in fact and on the testimony of the first canto that the *Commedia* simply could not have existed in anything like its actual form without the *Aeneid*, it is at the same time disquietingly evident that the second canto has among its primary tasks that of placing Virgil, who is bathed in such effulgence in the first, in a less glorious light. It does so precisely by limiting his poetic authority.

> Io cominciai: "Poeta che mi guidi,
>   guarda la mia virtù s'ell' è possente,
>   prima ch'a l'alto passo tu mi fidi.
> Tu dici che di Silvïo il parente,
>   corruttibile ancora, ad immortale
>   secolo andò, a fu sensibilmente.
> Però, se l'avversario d'ogne male
>   cortese i fu, pensando l'alto effetto

ch'uscir dovea di lui, e 'l chi e 'l quale
non pare indegno ad omo d'intelletto;
   ch'e' fu de l'alma Roma e di suo impero
   ne l'empireo ciel per padre eletto:
la quale e 'l quale, a voler dir lo vero,
   fu stabilita per lo loco santo
   u' siede il successor del maggior Piero.
Per quest' andata onde li dai tu vanto,
   intese cose che furon cagione
   di sua vittoria e del papale ammanto.
Andovvi poi lo Vas d'elezïone,
   per recarne conforto a quella fede
   ch'è principio a la via di salvazione.
Ma io, perché venirvi? o chi 'l concede?
   Io non Enëa, io non Paulo sono;
   me degno a ciò né io né altri 'l crede.
Per che, se del venire io m'abbandono,
   temo che la venuta non sia folle.
   Se' savio; intendi me' ch'i' non ragiono."

I began: "Poet, O you who lead me,
Assess my powers, whether they be sufficient,
Before you commit me to the lofty crossing.
You yourself say that Silvius's father,
Still subject to decay, went to the deathless
Realm, and was there in his own body.
But that the adversary of every evil
So favored him, considering what high sequel
Would spring from him, and who and what he was,
Seems not unjust to a man of understanding;
For he was chosen in empyrean heaven
To be father of holy Rome and of her empire:
The one and the other, if we tell the truth,
Were established in the sacred place
Where the successor of greatest Peter sits.
From this journey, with which you credit him,
He learnt of things ordained to be the cause
Of his own victory, and of the papal mantle.
There, later, the Chosen Vessel went,
Thence to return with comfort for that faith
Which begins the journey toward salvation.
But I, why should I go there? Who permits it?

I am no Aeneas, I am no Saint Paul.
Not I, not any one, thinks me worthy of it.
Therefore, if I resign myself to coming,
I fear it may be madness. You are wise,
You understand things better than I can say them."

Dante's first speech (10–36). While the protagonist Dante of the first canto is filled with humble enthusiasm in his initial response to Virgil (1.79–87), the poet who speaks in these lines has assumed the role of seasoned Christian commentator of the *Aeneid*: "Tu dici che di Silvïo il parente, / corruttibile ancora, ad immortale / secolo andò, e fu sensibilmente" (13–15). The reference to the *Aeneid* (6.763–66) is periphrastic on purpose—to remind us not only of the divine line of Roman kings to descend from Aeneas but also of the familiarity with the details of the text which the scholarly speaker expects of his reader. That reader, if he is a pagan, will be surprised to learn that Aeneas's descent to the Underworld, which in a moment will be compared to Paul's ascent to Heaven, is regarded as being specifically sanctioned by God (16–21). In Dante's bold reinterpretation of *Aeneid* 6, God chose Aeneas to found Rome so that it might become a seat of empire *and* church—a meaning decidedly absent from Virgil's poem. We shall never know whether Dante believed absolutely in the objective truth of this voluntaristic doctrine; we must grant that, within his poem, the "fact" is accorded every bit as much credence as it might have elicited had it been discovered in Scripture. Virgil, however, is himself presented as a more questionable reporter of event: "Tu dici . . ." ("You say . . .") that Aeneas went to the Underworld, a journey later (25) referred to as the "andata onde li dai tu vanto" (literally, "the journey over which you give him vaunt"). These formulations do not withhold credence from Aeneas's journey so much as they imbue the speaker's acceptance of the veracity of Virgil's account of that journey with a certain feeling of dubiety.[10] "Per quest' andata onde li dai tu vanto" is rhetorically parallel to the opening line of the following tercet, which describes Paul's journey to Heaven (but not to Hell, despite Dante's almost certain knowledge of the *Visio Pauli*; see Mazzoni [1967], pp. 223–31): "Andovvi poi lo Vas d'elezïone" (28). The quotation of Acts 9:15, *vas electionis*, like the phrase "di Silvïo il parente," refers its reader to a source, this time the Bible. It does so without any concomitant qualifications concerning authority. How can we fail to see that a comparison of the two structurally balanced passages is to Virgil's disadvantage? The poetical quality, the fictiveness, of the *Aeneid* is what Dante calls to our attention, at least when we consider the relative claims for literal truth that may be allowed the inscribers of these two texts. Yet such a tactic decidedly puts Dante's own poem in similar jeopardy. "Tu dici che . . ." indeed! Dante seems to invite our challenge on the very ground on which we are asked to question Virgil. Do we not wonder about the supposed veracity of the journey of this new Aeneas and new Paul, especially after its author has made us aware of the relative imaginative invention of the *Aeneid* when it is placed alongside Scripture? Where shall we place Dante's poem, with Virgil's or with the Bible? He has taken a terrible chance with his reader. He will take the same chance in still more breathtaking fashion when he swears that he saw the obviously fictive Geryon (*Inf.* 16.124–36). Allowing himself the claim of a Bible-like historicity, Dante treats Virgil's epic as authoritative at only a second remove: the story it tells is based in history; its teller did not understand its full significance. It is in this spirit that Dante will allow himself the various intentional misreadings of the *Aeneid* that have so long troubled his readers (for example, *Inf.* 20.52–102; *Purg.* 22.40–42; see Hollander [1980, pp. 169–218; 1983, passim]).

> E qual è quei che disvuol ciò che volle
>   e per novi pensier cangia proposta,
>   sì che dal cominciar tutto si tolle,
> tal mi fec' ïo 'n quella oscura costa,
>   perché, pensando, consumai la 'mpresa
>   che fu nel cominciar cotanto tosta.
> "S'i' ho ben la parola tua intesa,"
>   rispuose del magnanimo quell' ombra,
>   "l'anima tua è da viltade offesa;
> la qual molte fïate l'omo ingombra
>   sì che d'onrata impresa lo rivolve,
>   come falso veder bestia quand' ombra.
> Da questa tema a ciò che tu ti solve,
>   dirotti perch' io venni e quel ch'io 'ntesi
>   nel primo punto che di te mi dolve.
> Io era tra color che son sospesi,
>   e donna mi chiamò beata e bella,
>   tal che di comandare io la richiesi.

Lucevan li occhi suoi più che la stella;
    e cominciommi a dir soave e piana,
    con angelica voce, in sua favella. . . ."

And, like one who unwishes what he wished for
And changes his intent on second thoughts
So that he quite gives over what he'd started,
Such I myself became on that dark slope,
For, by thinking, I sapped the undertaking
Which had been so prompt in its inception.
"If I have understood your words aright,"
Replied the shade of that great-hearted one,
"Your spirit is impaired by cowardice,
A thing which often so impedes a man
That it turns him from some noble enterprise
As a beast sees false and shies away from shadow.
That you may be delivered from this fear
I will tell you why I came, and what I heard
At the first instant I felt pity for you.
I was one of those who are suspended,
When a lady called me, one so beautiful,
So blessèd, that I begged her to command me.
Her eyes shone forth more brightly than the star,
And sweetly, softly, she began to speak
With the voice of an angel, in her native tongue. . . ."

Virgil's first speech (43–57). We understandably tend to see Virgil, since Dante's earlier accolades have indeed been enthusiastic, as possessing greater authority than the text in fact grants him. Just as Aeneas's mission is found to have been sanctioned in a Christian Heaven, so is Virgil's to Dante. In this remarkable invention, Beatrice has descended to Limbo (for her resemblance to Christ harrowing Hell, see Iannucci [1979]) in order to send Virgil to Dante in his travail on earth, whence he will lead our protagonist back into the netherworld and eventually to Eden. Beatrice's descent gives Virgil motive and cause; without her intervention he would have known nothing (the damned, we learn at *Inferno* 10.100–108, do not know the present state of things on earth), done nothing. Virgil's actions are thus so circumscribed that we can hardly miss Dante's point. It is Beatrice in Heaven, not Virgil in Limbo, who is first aware of Dante's plight (49–51). And the burden of Virgil's words here is to give testimony to the power and glory of Beatrice, to whose charge he immediately consigns himself (53–54). It is she, not he, who initiates the action of the *Commedia*, something we did not know a canto ago.[11]

> " 'O anima cortese mantoana,
>   di cui la fama ancor nel mondo dura,
>   e durerà quanto 'l mondo lontana,
> l'amico mio, e non de la ventura,
>   ne la diserta piaggia è impedito
>   sì nel cammin, che vòlt' è per paura;
> e temo che non sia già sì smarrito,
>   ch'io mi sia tardi al soccorso levata,
>   per quel ch'i' ho di lui nel cielo udito.
> Or movi, e con la tua parola ornata
>   e con ciò c'ha mestieri al suo campare,
>   l'aiuta sì ch'i' ne sia consolata.
> I' son Beatrice che ti faccio andare;
>   vegno del loco ove tornar disio;
>   amor mi mosse, che mi fa parlare.
> Quando sarò dinanzi al segnor mio,
>   di te mi loderò sovente a lui.' "

> " 'O courteous Mantuan spirit,
> Whose glory still continues in the world
> And will continue while the world endures,
> A friend of mine, who is no friend to Fortune,
> Upon the desolate slope is so impeded
> On his way, that he has turned back in terror.
> Judging from what I have heard of him in heaven,
> I fear he is already so far astray
> That I may have risen too late to be of help.
> Go now, and with your polished speech
> And whatever else is needed for his safety
> Come to his aid, that I may be consoled.
> I, who send you forth, am Beatrice.
> I come from a place where I would fain return.
> Love it was that moved me, that makes me speak.
> When I am once again before my Lord
> Often will I speak to Him in praise of you.' "

Beatrice's first speech (58–74). Her utterance, which Daniello (1568) compared to Juno's words to Aeolus in *Aeneid* 1, is described by Virgil as being "soave e piana" (56). She will, in her turn, refer to Virgil's "parola ornata" (67). The two adjectives *piana* and *ornata* should remind us immediately of a major distinction, found among the medieval categorizations of rhetorical styles, between the plain (*umile*) and the ornate (*alto*). Benvenuto da Imola (1373) was the first to point it out, glossing "soave e piana" as follows: "divine speech is sweet and humble, not elevated and proud, as is that of Virgil and the poets."[12] Thus Virgil's description of Beatrice's words corresponds antithetically to hers of his; her speech, we may reflect, represents the sublimely humble style valorized by the *Commedia*, while his recalls the high style that marked pagan eloquence. Dante's stylistic distinctions mirror his religious opinions, which put Beatrice in Heaven, Virgil in Hell. In this scene, for all her humility and modesty, it is Beatrice who is distinctly in charge: "I' son Beatrice che ti faccio andare" (70). Virgil, a posthumous Christian, is only pleased to be so commanded.

> "Tacette allora, e poi comincia' io:
> 'O donna di virtù sola per cui
>   l'umana spezie eccede ogne contento
>   di quel ciel c'ha minor li cerchi sui,
> tanto m'aggrada il tuo comandamento,
>   che l'ubidir, se già fosse, m'è tardi;
>   più non t'è uo' ch'aprirmi il tuo talento.
> Ma dimmi la cagion che non ti guardi
>   de lo scender qua giuso in questo centro
>   de l'ampio loco ove tornar tu ardi.' "

> "Then she fell silent; and then I began:
> 'O lady by whose virtue and nought else
> The human race surpasses all that lies
> Within the smallest compass of the heavens,
> Your commandment is so pleasing to me
> That, were it done already, it would seem late.
> You have only to express your wishes to me.
> But tell me the reason why you are not wary
> Of descending here, into this center,
> From the spacious place you are burning to return to.' "

Virgil's question (75–84). Virgil's response (76–81) to Beatrice is as filled with awe as was Dante's to his appearance in canto 1 (79–90).

It is followed (82–84) by a question that has met with displeasure among the many commentators who find Virgil's wonderment at Beatrice's lack of fear at entering Hell both unnecessary and aesthetically pallid. Yet, if we consider that Virgil owes his presence in Hell precisely to his lack of faith in the coming of Christ (he himself has informed us that he had been a rebel to God's law at 1.125) and then recall that he will shortly make it clear that he has seen Christ harrow Hell, at 4.52 – 63, we better understand the justice of his condemnation. For, even in his posthumous state, Virgil does not understand that the blessed fear no evil (for examples of other limits on Virgil's understanding, see Ryan [1982]). The question he poses is indeed an awkward one, emphasizing once again Virgil's inadequacy in matters of faith. It leads to Beatrice's triumphant rejoinder; it is surely not a lapse on Dante's part.

> " 'Da che tu vuo' saver cotanto a dentro,
>   dirotti brievemente,' mi rispuose,
>   'perch' i' non temo di venir qua entro.
> Temer si dee di sole quelle cose
>   c'hanno potenza di fare altrui male;
>   de l'altre no, ché non son paurose.
> I' son fatta da Dio, sua mercé, tale,
>   che la vostra miseria non mi tange,
>   né fiamma d'esto 'ncendio non m'assale.
> Donna è gentil nel ciel che si compiange
>   di questo 'mpedimento ov' io ti mando,
>   sì che duro giudicio là sù frange.
> Questa chiese Lucia in suo dimando
>   e disse: "Or ha bisogno il tuo fedele
>   di te, e io a te lo raccomando."
> Lucia, nimica di ciascun crudele,
>   si mosse, e venne al loco dov' i' era,
>   che mi sedea con l'antica Rachele.
> Disse: "Beatrice, loda di Dio vera,
>   ché non soccorri quei che t'amò tanto,
>   ch'uscì per te de la volgare schiera?
> Non odi tu la pietà del suo pianto,
>   non vedi tu la morte che 'l combatte
>   su la fiumana ove 'l mar non ha vanto?"
> Al mondo non fur mai persone ratte
>   a far lor pro o a fuggir lor danno,

com' io, dopo cotai parole fatte,
venni qua giù del mio beato scanno,
    fidandomi del tuo parlare onesto,
    ch'onora te e quei ch'udito l'hanno.' "

" 'Since you so desire to learn the cause,'
She said in answer, 'I will tell you briefly
Why I am not afraid of entering here.
One has to be afraid of those things only
Which possess the power to do one harm;
Of others not, for they give no cause for fear.
I, of His mercy, have been made by God
Such that your wretchedness does not affect me,
Nor in this great fire does one flame assail me.
In heaven a gracious lady feels such pity
At this hindrance for which I send you out
That she is breaking a strict law on high.
This lady summoned Lucy to her bidding
And said: "One faithful to you now has need
Of you; and I entrust him to your care."
Lucy, the enemy of all things cruel,
Arose and came to the place in which I was,
Where I was seated with venerable Rachel.
"Beatrice," she said, "true praise of God,
Why do you not help him who loved you so
That for your sake he left the common herd?
Can you not hear the pity of his tears?
Can you not see the death contending with him
On the swollen river the sea itself can't best?"
Never were people in the world so prompt
To seek their profit or eschew their harm
As was I, after those words were spoken.
Down here I hurried from my blessèd seat,
Placing my faith in your fit and noble speech,
That honors you and all who have heeded it.' "

Beatrice's answer (85–114). Since Hell cannot harm the blessed, these do not remain absent from Hell out of fear (as Virgil's question had assumed), but only because it is the harsh law of Heaven ("duro giudicio," 96) that the blessed may not show the damned any form of compassion, such as their very presence might seem to confer. It is mercy for lost Dante, not pity for damned Virgil, which has initiated this heavenly relay of intercession (which has a literary antecedent in the similar "relay" in *Aeneid* 1.223–304; see Hollander [1969], pp. 91–92). We have hitherto heard the voices of Dante and Virgil, then Beatrice's voice in Virgil's, now Mary's in Beatrice's as reported by Virgil. Mary, whom we shall see seated in glory in *Paradiso* 32 (after our first vision of her in *Paradiso* 23), is thus a presence both in the second and the penultimate cantos of the *Commedia*. *Inferno* 2.94–99, attains—offstage, as it were—the highest point of Heaven that we as readers shall confront before *Paradiso* 32.1. Her *misericordia* is, chronologically speaking, the first evidence of grace directed toward Dante that is recorded in the poem. In Mary's enterprise Lucy and Beatrice are quickly enrolled.[13]

Lucy's question has greater relevance to the canto's concern for the question of the truthfulness of poetry than is generally supposed. She describes Dante to Beatrice as one who "uscì per te de la volgare schiera" (105), a formulation which is variously glossed by the early commentators, but generally in the sense that Dante cut himself off from more usual human pursuits in order to study theology (a tradition that began with Guido da Pisa [1327], p. 52). I am fully in accord with Mazzoni's (1967) interpretation (pp. 288–93) that the verse points to Dante's having left behind the "herd" of other vernacular poets in order to set off on his own to write poems in praise of Beatrice's true (and theologized) nature, a reading confirmed, in Mazzoni's eyes and mine, by *Purgatorio* 24.49–51, where Bonagiunta marks the turning point in Dante's career as being the first poem he wrote in the "dolce stil novo," "Donne ch'avete intelletto d'amore." The Beatrice whom he praised then is now to be understood, in Lucy's words, as "loda di Dio vera" (103). She is asked to look down on Dante's piteous condition in the place where we saw him losing the battle against sin and which is now described as "la fiumana ove 'l mar non ha vanto" (108).

Perhaps no verse of the canto has had so tortured a history in the commentaries. Not only is there a continuing debate about whether the river is to be construed literally (from the Ottimo [1333] to Pagliaro [1967], pp. 39–42) or figuratively (from Jacopo Alighieri [1322] to Mazzoni [1967], pp. 302–3), but there is no final consensus in either camp as to what the noun and its related clause mean (see Mazzoni [1967], pp. 296–303, for a detailed review of earlier interpretations). While it may seem that the very locution of the phrase tends to support those who find only a metaphorical sense operative here (Jacopo's "la viziosa e ignorante operazione del mondo" is still to the point), we should perhaps entertain the possibility suggested by a more historical reading—namely, that this river is Dante's "Jordan." If the actions of the first two cantos may be understood as being linked to successive stages in the progress of salvation history,[14] have we come, in the poem's analogous if recondite record of these events, to Jordan? Filippo Villani (ca. 1400), in his commentary to this verse, was the first to propose as much: "su la rivera [scilicet Jordanis fluminis, qui ponitur pro Sacramento baptismatis . . ."]). And we might want to consider some of the later reasons for this interpretation offered by A. Belloni (cited by Mazzoni [1967], p. 297), for whom the Jordan is not a tributary of a mare, but of the Dead Sea, a lacus.[15] Were this admittedly venturesome reading to find favor, Virgil would then come as John the Baptist, a view of his role in the Commedia which I support (see n. 18, below). Beatrice, hearing the parole of Lucy, departs for Limbo to seek the aid of Virgil's "parlare onesto" (113) in order to help Dante begin the process that will lead to his baptism at the hands of Virgil in Purgatorio 1, then under the supervision of the Christ-like Beatrice in Purgatorio 31 and 33, and finally in the river of light in Paradiso 30.

> "Poscia che m'ebbe ragionato questo,
>   li occhi lucenti lagrimando volse,
>   per che mi fece del venir più presto.
> E venni a te così com' ella volse:
>   d'inanzi a quella fiera ti levai
>   che del bel monte il corto andar ti tolse.
> Dunque: che è? perché, perché restai,
>   perché tanta viltà nel core allette,
>   perché ardire e franchezza non hai,
> poscia che tai tre donne benedette
>   curan di te ne la corte del cielo,
>   e 'l mio parlar tanto ben ti promette?"

"When she had spoken to me to this effect
She turned her weeping, shining eyes aside,
So that I hastened all the more to come;
And I came to you, as she had asked me to:
I saved you from the beast that cut you off
From the short route up the lovely mountain.
So then, what is it? Why are you standing there?
Why harbor so much cowardice in your heart?

Why do you not have courage and conviction,
Seeing that three such blessèd ladies plead
In your favor in the high court of heaven
And my own words assure you of so much good?"

Virgil's questions (115–26). Moved still more by Beatrice's tears of compassion, Virgil intercedes for Dante. He has completed his description (115–20) of the "prologue in Heaven and Hell" that occurred before the action which concludes the first canto. The rest of his final speech peppers Dante with four rapid questions (the word *perché* occurs four times in three lines, as Fallani [1967], p. 44, observes). One can sense the exasperation of the condemned pagan, wondering at the *viltà* of a Christian soul possessed of such potent friends and who yet lingers.

Quali fioretti dal notturno gelo
    chinati e chiusi, poi che 'l sol li 'mbianca,
    si drizzan tutti aperti in loro stelo,
tal mi fec' io di mia virtude stanca,
    e tanto buono ardire al cor mi corse,
    ch'i' cominciai come persona franca:
"Oh pietosa colei che mi soccorse!
    e te cortese ch'ubidisti tosto
    a le vere parole che ti porse!
Tu m'hai con disiderio il cor disposto
    sì al venir con le parole tue,
    ch'i' son tornato nel primo proposto.
Or va, ch'un sol volere è d'ambedue:
    tu duca, tu segnore e tu maestro."
    Così li dissi; e poi che mosso fue,
intrai per lo cammino alto e silvestro.

As little flowers, by the frost of night
Bent down and closed, when the sun brightens them,
All straighten up and open on their stems,
So did I likewise with my flagging powers;
So much good ardor rushed into my heart
That I began, like a man set free:
"Compassionate was she who came to aid me!
Courteous were you, to have obeyed so swiftly
Those words of truth which she addressed to you!

With your own words you have so prepared my heart
With such desire to come
That I have now returned to my first resolve.
Go now, for a sole will is in us both:
You are my lord, my leader, and my teacher."
Thus I spoke to him; and when he set out
I started on the deep, wild way.

Dante's response (133–40). Virgil's message from Heaven is the sun which, in simile, straightens up the drooping flowers: Dante is finally ready to set out. The agency of his readiness is Virgil's voice: "le tue vere parole" (137); yet his words are so significant precisely because they contain verbatim reports of the words of others who are his betters—Mary, Lucy, and Beatrice—which enfranchise his *parola ornata* (67). Virgil's role as guide in the *Commedia* is sanctioned by a favoring Heaven which he is quick to obey (134). Although Dante does not forget his debt to the greatest of the pagan poets, Virgil must pay a not inconsiderable registration fee to approach, even on a temporary basis, the Heaven which has been denied him.

In such ways, disturbing and surprising given the usual desire to read Dante's Virgil in a prehumanistic vein, does Dante employ the seven symmetrically arranged speeches of *Inferno* 2 to explore the limitations and the power of the word. His *Commedia*, more than any other poem save possibly Milton's, would have us believe that it purveys the Word.

This brief discussion of Dante's conflicting loyalties—one to God and one to Virgil—has attempted to show that what we shall witness later in the *Inferno*, the poet's surprisingly patronizing view of his pagan predecessor's intellectual credentials, is established early in the program of the poem.[16] At the close of *Inferno* 1, despite his own disclaimers (as when Virgil informs Dante that he cannot enter Heaven because he had been a "rebel to God's law," 124–26), or perhaps because of them and in light of Dante's enthusiastic encomia of Virgil (79–90),[17] we probably, and with cause, believe that our poet will portray Virgil only in a positive light. Indeed, in the first canto Virgil has been granted, if in ways that are not immediately obvious, the role of John the Baptist to Beatrice's "Christ."[18] To earlier perceptions of this relation between the *Commedia*'s first two guides I would like to add the following.

At verse 122 Virgil refers to Beatrice as "anima . . . più di me degna." So far as I have been able to ascertain, no one has heard the echo of John 1:27 in that verse: "Ipse est qui post me venturus est, qui ante me factus est: *cuius ego non sum dignus* ut solvam eius corrigiam calceamenti" ("He it is, who coming after me, who was made before me, whose shoe's latchet *I am not worthy* to unloose"; italics added). The words of the Baptist, deferring to Jesus in John's gospel, are likely to irradiate Virgil's words here. The abject insistence on his unworthiness on the part of the one who was, for Dante, the greatest pagan poet would surely seem to indicate that Virgil's conduct as character in his poem will proceed with nothing less than total approbation on Dante's part, and that his works will be received in Dante's text only with good will. If that is what the first canto leads us to expect, it is surely what nearly all of Dante's readers have found when they continued their consideration of the text. It is my contention that, beginning with the second canto, Dante sets about the task of downgrading the authority of Virgil overtly, if with delicacy.[19] The phrase "Tu dici . . ." (13) is thus the first clear sign, one that requires only good sense to recognize that Dante has begun to distance himself from his own so very remarkable resuscitation of Virgil. He has come not only to praise Virgil, but to bury him. As unfair as this element in Dante's treatment of Virgil may seem to us, a clearer perception reveals its necessity in this poem which is striving to convince us of its accord with a higher truth than Virgil had managed to come to know.

Princeton University

SELECTED BIBLIOGRAPHY

The existence of the commentary on *Inferno* 2 by Francesco Mazzoni, perhaps the finest commentator Dante has ever had, makes the task of one who would speak of this canto both easier and more difficult, a remark intended as a compliment. It is to Mazzoni's work, more than anyone else's, that I have turned, as will be clear at a glance. The following list of works cited is only that. For fuller bibliographical information, see note 1, below. Some of the early commentators (who

are not listed here) are cited from La "Divina Commedia" nella figu-
razione artistica e nel secolare commento, ed. Guido Biagi (Turin:
UTET, 1924). Dates and bibliographical information for these commentators may be found in my "A Checklist of Commentators on the
Commedia (1322–1982)," Dante Studies 101 (1983): 181–92. Several
of these dates are subject to debate; I have in general been content to
reproduce those found in the apposite entries of the Enciclopedia
dantesca.

Albert, Henri. "Trois types de composition dans l'Inferno." In Studi
in onore di Angelo Monteverdi, 1: 323–26. Modena: STEM, 1959.

Auerbach, Erich. "Sermo Humilis." In Literary Language and Its Public
in Late Latin Antiquity and in the Middle Ages, trans. Ralph Man-
heim, pp. 25–66. Princeton, N.J.: Princeton University Press, 1965.

Ball, Robert. "Theological Semantics: Virgil's Pietas and Dante's
pietà." Stanford Italian Review 2 (1981): 59–71.

Bernardo, Aldo S. "The Three Beasts and Perspective in the Divine
Comedy." PMLA 78 (1963): 14–24.

Carroll, John S. Exiles of Eternity. London: Hodder and Stoughton,
1904. Reprint Port Washington, N.Y. and London: Kennikat, 1971.

Chimenz, Siro A. "Canto II." In Nuova Lectura Dantis, ed. S. A. Chimenz. Rome: A. Signorelli, 1950.

Fallani, Giovanni. "Canto II." In Lectura Dantis Scaligera, pp. 25–45.
Florence: Le Monnier, 1967.

Freccero, John. "The River of Death: Inferno II, 108." In The World of
Dante, ed. S. B. Chandler and J. A. Molinaro, pp. 25–42. Toronto:
University of Toronto Press, 1966. Reprinted in Dante: The Po-
etics of Conversion, ed. Rachel Jacoff. Cambridge, Mass.: Harvard
University Press, 1986.

Giglio, Raffaele. "Il prologo alla Divina Commedia." Critica letteraria
1 (1973): 131–59.

Gmelin, Hermann. Kommentar. Vol. 1. Stuttgart: Klett, 1966.

Guido da Pisa. Expositiones et Glose super Comediam Dantis, ed.
Vincenzo Cioffari. Albany: SUNY Press, 1974.

Hollander, Robert. Allegory in Dante's "Commedia." Princeton, N.J.:
Princeton University Press, 1969.

————. Studies in Dante. Ravenna: Longo, 1980.

————. Il Virgilio dantesco. Florence: Olschki, 1983.

————. "Dante's Pagan Past." Stanford Italian Review 5, no. 1 (1985):
23–36.

Iannucci, Amilcare A. "Beatrice in Limbo: A Metaphoric Harrowing of Hell." *Dante Studies* 97 (1979): 23–45.

Lansing, Richard H. *From Image to Idea: A Study of the Simile in Dante's "Commedia."* Ravenna: Longo, 1977.

Mazzoni, Francesco. "Inferno II." In his *Saggio di un nuovo commento alla "Divina Commedia,"* pp. 149–313. Florence: Sansoni, 1967.

————. *La Divina Commedia, con i commenti di T. Casini, S. A. Barbi e di A. Momigliano: Inferno. Introduzione e aggiornamento bibliografico-critico di Francesco Mazzoni.* Florence: Sansoni, 1972.

Mazzotta, Giuseppe. *Dante, Poet of the Desert.* Princeton, N.J.: Princeton University Press, 1979.

Padoan, Giorgio. "Il canto II dell' *Inferno.*" *Letture classensi* 5 (1976): 41–56.

Pagliaro, Antonino. *Ulisse.* Messina-Florence: G. D'Anna, 1967.

Pasquazi, Silvio. "Il canto II dell' *Inferno.*" In *"Inferno": Letture degli anni 1973–76,* ed. S. Zennaro, Casa di Dante in Roma, pp. 35–65. Rome: Bonacci, 1977.

Pézard, André. *Dante sous la pluie de feu.* Paris: Vrin, 1950.

Porcelli, Bruno. " 'Chi per lungo silenzio parea fioco' e il valore della parola nella *Commedia.*" *Ausonia* 19, no. 5 (1964): 32–38.

Ricci Battaglia, Lucia. "Polisemanticità e struttura della *Commedia.*" *Giornale storico della letteratura italiana* 152 (1975): 161–98.

Ryan, Christopher J. "Virgil's Wisdom in the *Divina Commedia.*" *Medievalia et Humanistica* 11 (1982): 1–38.

Singleton, Charles S. "Sulla fiumana ove 'l mar non ha vanto." *Romanic Review* 39 (1948): 269–77.

————. "Virgil Recognizes Beatrice." *74th Annual Report of the Dante Society* (1956), pp. 29–38.

————. *"Inferno" 2: Commentary.* Princeton, N.J.: Princeton University Press, 1970.

Villani, Filippo. *Comento al primo canto dell' "Inferno,"* ed. G. Cugnoni. Città di Castello: Lapi, 1896.

NOTES

1. For an essential bibliography of readings of *Inferno* 2, see Mazzoni (1967), pp. 158–59, updated in Mazzoni (1972), pp. 39–40. A full treatment of the canto, with a considerable bibliographical apparatus, has recently been completed by Rachel

Jacoff and William Stephany for the *Lectura Dantis Americana*, an enterprise undertaken with the backing of the Dante Society of America. The first two volumes in the
series were published by the University of Pennsylvania Press in 1989. The Italian
text of the *Commedia* cited above is that established by Giorgio Petrocchi, *La Commedia secondo l'antica vulgata* (Milan: Mondadori, 1966); the English translation is
by Patrick Creagh and Robert Hollander, first published in the second volume of the
Lectura Dantis Americana and reprinted here with the kind permission of the University of Pennsylvania Press.

I would like to insist that the treatment of the canto presented here is neither a
commentary nor a full-scale *lectura*. It was written in somewhat shorter form early
in 1982, for inclusion in the *California Lectura Dantis*, ed. Allen Mandelbaum and
Anthony Oldcorn, to be published by the University of California Press, and is printed
here with the kind permission of the press and the editors.

2. Let one commentator's ingenuity stand for the similar efforts of many. Confronting the puzzling fact (about which I shall say more below) that Dante, in verse 3,
says that he was "alone" as he prepared to make his infernal journey when in fact
he is accompanied by Virgil, Buti (1385) was pleased to find confirmation of the usual
allegorical interpretation that equates Virgil with "Reason": "si deve intendere che
Virgilio non era con Dante se non quanto alla lettera, per seguitamento che Dante
seguiva la sua poesia, et allegoricamente s'intende la ragione umana . . . che non era
altro che Dante." This misleading notion—that Virgil exists in the *Commedia* entirely
(or even mainly) as an internalized rational capacity of the protagonist—lies at the
heart of one of the most persistent basic misreadings of the text confronting students
of the poem. In this particular, it should be clear that Dante intended to be understood
as being "alone" morally, despite Virgil's presence. Only *he* will or can experience
Hell in a fully meaningful way, as his salvation is not yet achieved (despite the many
promises offered throughout the poem of its likelihood). He is *in via*. The fate of his
guide has already been determined; there is no "guerra / sì del cammin e sì de la
pietate" for him.

3. This is to overlook the three uses of the verb *parlare* in the canto (72, 113,
126), the last two times as a verbal noun.

4. *Inf.* 20 is the closest challenger: 103 of 130 verses (79 percent), followed
closely by 27 (104 of 136, 76 percent); 33 (117 of 157, 75 percent); 15 (84 of 124, 68
percent); 13 (100 of 151, 66 percent); 10 (90 of 136, 66 percent); 26 (88 of 142, 62
percent) 5 and 14 (83 of 142, 58 percent). As a "control," we may consider 25—so
full of narrated action: only 17 of 125 verses (14 percent) are spoken, and by a total
of six laconic speakers. It is worth considering that Dante's most talkative sinners are
precisely those who tend to draw the most compassion from his modern readers and/
or the most pitying reactions from the protagonist.

5. Since I first wrote this essay, those who would question the authenticity of
the Epistle have again come forward. See Peter Dronke, *Dante and Medieval Latin
Traditions* (Cambridge: Cambridge Univ. Press, 1986), and Henry A. Kelly, "Dating
the Accessus Section of the Pseudo-Dantean *Epistle to Cangrande*," *Lectura Dantis
[Virginiana]* 2 (1988): 93–102. While a proper rejoinder is beyond the scope of a
footnote, I would like to go on record as saying that I find neither of these arguments
convincing.

6. "Et ideo confutetur eorum stultitia, qui, *arte* scientiaque immunes, de solo
ingenio confidentes, ad summa summe canenda prorumpunt." That these harsh
words are aimed at those who should desist from poetic activity implies a better pair

of sources, at least from the vantage point of the new poem, from which a true poet might draw his craft and conceptualization as he sings of the highest things sublimely.

7. Castelvetro (1570) glosses the terzina in what seems to me a satisfying way, even though he is not quite willing to do more than suggest exactly what he thought Dante meant the higher power represented by alto ingegno in fact to represent: "Ora chiama le muse acciocchè l'aiutino . . . solamente a far versi, per cagion della favella e non per cagion della materia o perchè gli ricordino o rivelino cosa niuna. O alto ingegno: più alto che non è l'umano o il mio. O mente. Quinci appare che non vuole l'aiuto delle Muse quanto è alla materia, ma si confida nella sua memoria."

8. Pietro's gloss insists that Dante "invocat altum ingenium in generali et abstracto; quod ingenium est extentio intellectus in incognitorum cognitionem." If Pietro's thoughts do not fly up as high as Castelvetro's or my own, he does resist the notion, common to so many of the early commentators and those who followed them, that Dante is calling upon his own genius in these lines.

9. For discussion of the movement from fear to hope and from hope to fear in the chiastically related two pairs of similes in the first two cantos, see Lansing (1977), pp. 128–31.

10. Here I strongly disagree with Padoan (1976), p. 45, who sees these phrases precisely as conferring auctoritas upon Virgil's words. My position is in basic accord with that of Chimenz (1950), pp. 7–8, Mazzoni (1967), pp. 154, 186, and Singleton (1970), p. 25.

11. For an appreciation of Virgil's limited understanding of Beatrice, see Singleton (1956), pp. 32–33.

12. ". . . sermo divinus est suavis et planus, non altus et superbus sicut sermo Virgilii et poetarum"; see Auerbach (1958), pp. 65–66; Mazzotta (1979), pp. 157–58; Hollander (1980), pp. 217–18. And for consideration of the later undercutting of the honor accorded Virgil's "parola ornata" effected by the use of the phrase "parole ornate" to describe Jason's deceptively seductive words to Hypsipyle at Inf. 18.91, see Hollander (1983), p. 153, and (1985), pp. 30–31.

13. The modern commentary tradition, not accepting earlier formulations that associate each lady with a separate category of divine grace, tends to take these three ladies as representing charity, hope, and faith, respectively: see Giglio (1973), pp. 156–57; Pasquazi (1977), p. 40. The whole question of Dante's devotion to Lucy remains a problem. An important recent contribution is to be found in Pasquazi, pp. 40–60; and now we will soon have the lengthy discussion devoted to Lucy in Jacoff and Stephany (see above, n. 1), pp. 29–38.

14. See Freccero (1966). For views which hold that the reflection of this progression in the poem should be seen to mirror, first of all, Adam's postlapsarian condition outside Eden, see: Villani (ca. 1400), p. 99; Bennassuti (1864), pp. 52–54; Bernardo (1963), p. 16; Mazzoni (1967), p. 4; and Hollander (1969), p. 80.

15. For a discussion of Isidore of Seville's distinction between the two terms in Etym. 13.19, see the discussion in Hollander (1969), pp. 262–63, also adverting to Freccero's (1966) arguments for Jordan, which develop an earlier interpretation of the verse by Singleton (1948). For a similar interpretation, see Ricci Battaglia (1975), p. 194n.

16. For a venturesome exploration of the distinctions inherent for Dante in his appropriation of a Virgilian moral vocabulary, see Ball (1981).

17. For a discussion of the structurally parallel but stylistically very different speeches of Virgil and Dante in Inf. 1.67–78, 79–90, see Albert (1959).

18. Partial recognitions perhaps begin with Carroll (1904), p. 27. See also Pézard (1950), p. 343. Porcelli (1964), pp. 34–36, moved the argument forward considerably. My own attempts to establish this vital connection may be found in Hollander (1969), pp. 261–63; (1980), pp. 86–87, 193n; and (1983), pp. 69–77.

19. But see Hollander (1983), pp. 69–77, for a reading of *Inf.* 1.63, "chi per lungo silenzio parea fioco," which finds that even at his first appearance in the poem Virgil is presented (tacitly) by Dante as one who failed to speak the Word. It was only after I had returned the final proofs of that book to the publisher that I was apprised of Giorgio Brugnoli's article on *Inf.* 1.63 in *Letteratura comparata: problemi e metodo: Studi in onore di Ettore Paratore* (Bologna: Pàtron, 1981), 3:1169–82. Although we do not agree on this particular, our two treatments of the verse have many points in common.

When the Sky Was Paper: Dante's Cranes and Reading as Migration

KENNETH J. KNOESPEL

In a little-known paper entitled "Und wenn der Himmel war Papier," the late-nineteenth-century German philologist Reinhold Köhler marked the fascination of patterns formed by birds against the sky as they fly and noticed how they have provided a symbol for writing itself.[1] Whether one considers Homer's *épea pteróenta*, or "wingéd-words," or the richly developed topos of *Zugvögel*, or migratory birds in nineteenth-century German poetry, many poets have discovered compelling patterns in bird formations. Not surprisingly, Heidegger, Gadamer, and Derrida also use such figures to reveal the way the graphic representation of speech comes to engender and encase meaning.[2] Their amplification of such topoi is not as unique as sometimes appears when viewed by students whose reading horizon extends little beyond the nineteenth and twentieth centuries. As Heidegger, Gadamer, and Derrida would readily acknowledge, their work extends inquiries begun centuries ago. Within the early Christian tradition, it is Augustine in particular who challenges readers to discover in the flight of birds divine writing spread across the heavens, as over an expansive parchment.[3] The medieval poet who most fully employs such a topos, and whose strategies pose vital questions for modern hermeneutics as well, is Dante.

As the Pilgrim enters the orbit of Jupiter in *Paradiso* 15, he notices that spiritual creatures are flying among its holy scintillations in such

121

a way that they form patterns he can recognize as the Latin language. As a conscientious celestial traveler, the Pilgrim tries to comprehend the unique scene before him by comparing it to earthly experience.[4]

> Io vidi in quella giovïal facella
>   lo sfavillar dell'amor che lì era
>   segnare a li occhi miei nostra favella.
> E come augelli surti di rivera
>   quasi congratulando a lor pasture,
>   fanno di sé or tonda or altra schiera,
> sì dentro ai lumi sante creature
>   volitando cantavano, e faciensi
>   or D, or I, or L in sue figure.
>
> (Par. 18.70–78)

I saw in that torch of Jove the sparking of the love that was there to trace out our speech to my eyes; and as birds risen from a river-bank, as if rejoicing together over their pasture, make of themselves, now a round flock, now another shape, so within the lights holy creatures were singing as they flew and made themselves, in the figures they formed, now D, now I, now L.

Although the passage does not identify these "augelli," late medieval and Renaissance commentators on Dante suggest that we may think of them as cranes with confidence. Jacopo della Lana, L'Ottimo, Benvenuto Rambaldi da Imola, Francesco di Buti, and Cristoforo Landino all mention cranes in their gloss of the passage.[5] That they should so identify the birds is not surprising, for Dante's description alludes to a long tradition that found in the flight of cranes a metaphor for writing and reading. The gloss is even less strange when we recall that it occurs within a sequence of references to cranes placed carefully throughout the *Commedia*. After considering all these facts, we learn that these references delineate aspects of language and the difficulties of its interpretation. In Inferno 5.46–49, Dante signals the vigilance associated with the crane and entwines the exemplary function of the bird with the careful attention required by the act of reading. In *Purgatorio* 14.64–69 and 26.43–49, cranes are again linked with letters. Here, however, it is not the reading but the writing of letters which is of concern, especially within literary communities. In *Paradiso* 18.73– 78, cranes make another appearance and again are linked with writing, but rather than being expressions of secular writing, here they depict God's Word, the political message that it bears, and the manner in which this message should be read.

Ernst Curtius has reminded us that we should approach such tropes with more than an impulse to classify them within rhetorical tradition.[6] While gleaning references to such tropes provides an instructive field in which to examine particular examples, it should not dominate research. Tropes are more than ready-made figures waiting for installation in narratives; they afford the reader an opportunity to understand the inherent structure of the text. In particular cases, tropes might even be thought of as narrative ligatures that tell us a considerable amount about the way Dante expected his reader to assimilate his story. Every time the trope appears, the field of the metaphor expands. So, by following the progression of the trope, we discover an implicit acknowledgment of the reader's progress through the text as he or she configures its evolving significance. Indeed, as we shall see in the case of the crane topos, the reader is challenged not simply to configure but to refigure the trope in such a way that it becomes an indication of the way in which readers were expected to recreate the text as they read. After briefly noting the extensive use of the figure in classical and medieval culture, I shall follow Dante's use of it in the *Commedia*. Finally, I shall argue that Dante's figure quite literally works to instruct readers how, exerting vigilance and diligence, they should negotiate their way through the narrative. As we shall see, Dante's cranes challenge readers to view the very process of their reading as a migration toward illumination.

I

A long tradition of classical and medieval commentary sought to explain the habits of cranes and draw from their flight and behavior on the ground meanings that could enhance human life.[7] For the early naturalist, cranes exhibited two habits that were of special interest: (1) they flew in patterns that suggested letters and (2) they appeared to live in disciplined communities with a system of revolving leadership. Aristotle emphasized the unusual intelligence of cranes and recorded his observations about their abilities to fly at great heights, forecast weather, and maintain air and ground patrols.[8] Pliny inquired into cranes' nocturnal habits and found that "they have sentries who hold a stone in their claws which, if drowsiness makes them drop it, falls and convicts them of slackness."⁹ Virgil, Statius, and Lucan found a metaphor for military organization in the flight of cranes. In the *Aeneid*, Virgil compares a shower of arrows and the cries that accompany it to a flock of cranes. Statius compares them to a column of marching soldiers, and Lucan to an orderly naval flight fighting the wind.¹⁰

> Sed nox saeva modum venti velique tenorem
> Eripuit nautis excussitque ordine puppes.
> Strymona sic gelidum bruma pallente relinquunt
> Poturae te, Nile, grues, primoque volatu
> Effingunt varias casu monstrante figuras;
> Mox, ubi percussit tensas Notus altior alas,
> Confusos temere inmixtae glomerantur in orbes,
> Et turbata perit dispersis littera pinnis.
>
> (5.709–16)

But night, proving unkind, robbed the sailors of steady wind, stopped even the progress of the sails, and threw the ships out of station. Thus, when cranes are driven by winter from the frozen Strymon to drink the water of the Nile, at the beginning of their flight they describe various chance taught figures; but later, when a loftier wind beats on their outspread wings, they combine at random and form disordered packs, until the letter is broken and disappears as the birds are scattered.

By comparing the orderly flight patterns of cranes to the formation of letters, Lucan also alludes to a considerable mythological tradition that associated the invention of the Greek alphabet to the figures cranes form in flight.¹¹ Classical allusions that stressed cranes' intelligence, ability to live in orderly groups, and the vigilant and magnanimous behavior of the lead crane, and that saw letters in their ordered flight patterns, provided fertile matter for medieval commentary.

Vigilance, seen in their nocturnal behavior and ordered flight patterns and applied to civil and monastic life, unifies all medieval commentary on cranes.¹² For Ambrose (333–97), cranes become a justification for an elaborate discourse on government and an exemplum for those brothers who would run to the refectory to grab a place.[13] For Rabanus Maurus (780–856), the way cranes followed a single leader provided a model for cloister life in general and offered an exemplary description of how brothers should follow a leader while singing psalms.[14] By the twelfth century, the stone described by Pliny had become a symbol for Christ, the bird community was compared at length with monastic life, and the lesson of the crane was condensed into the virtue of vigilance.[15]

Isidore of Seville (560?–636) was the first to draw attention to the "lettered" flight of cranes. "Hae autem dum properant, unam sequuntur ordine litterato. De quibus Lucanus: Et turbata perit dispersis littera pennis" (*PL* 82.460–61) ("While they hastily move along together they follow a lettered order. About this Lucan says the following: 'The letter is broken and disappears as the birds are scattered' "). Isidore was also the first medieval commentator to emphasize that the lead crane orders the pattern of flight with its voice: "Castigat autem voce quae cogit agmen. At ubi raucescit, succedit alia" (*PL* 82.460–61) ("The crane who compels the procession forward calls out with its voice. But when it grows hoarse it is replaced by another"). The most extensive elaboration of "litterato ordine" appears in Hugh of St. Victor (1097–1141):

Grues cum de loco ad locum transvolant, ordinem procedendi volando servant. Illos autem significant, qui ad hoc student, ut ordinate vivant. Grues enim ordine litterato volantes designant ordinate viventes. Cum autem ordinate volando procedunt, ex se litteras in volatu fingunt. Illos autem designant, qui in se praecepta Scripturae bene vivendo formant. Una earum reliquas antecedit, quae clamore non desinit, quias praelatus, qui primum locum regiminis obtinet, suos sequaeces moribus et vita praeire debvet, ita tamen ut semper clamet, et viam bonae operationis sequacibus suis praedicando demonstret. Quae autem alias antecedit, si raucas facta fuerit, tunc alia succedit, quia; praelatus si verbum Dei subjectis non praedicet, vel praedicare nesciat, cum raucus fuit, necesse est utalius succedat. (*PL* 177.40–41)

When they fly from one place to the next, cranes protect their order by flying one after the other. Indeed, they signify to those who examine this subject that they may live with order. Surely cranes, with their lettered order, point out living with order. As they proceed in flying order they fabricate from themselves letters in flight. They signify those who living justly formulate in themselves the precepts of Scripture. One of them precedes the others, one who does not cease to cry out because going in front, he who holds the first position of the column, ought to go before his followers with his life and habits so that he always calls out and exemplifies the life of good works by preaching to those following him. If he who precedes the others becomes hoarse then another would take his place because if he who goes before does not preach the Word of God to those subject to him, or neither know not how to preach because he is hoarse, it is necessary that he be replaced by another.

Hugh's commentary—which probably draws on Isidore and others—is significant for its extension of the disciplined order of cranes beyond the mechanics of Christian communities exhibited in the refectory, or at watch, or in singing. It finds in the lettered order of cranes a way to represent the lettered order of a Christian who follows scriptural precepts. Rather than simply emphasizing physical order, Hugh identifies the divine force that has inscribed itself in scripture, in human community, and in nature. For Hugh, and as we shall see for Dante too, the crane topos offers a means for joining two books: the book of scripture and the book of nature.

Although the reception of cranes in the Middle Ages could be elaborated further, we now have a sufficient matrix of connotations before us to understand what riches the image of cranes could offer to a medieval poet. With these miniature narratives in mind, I would like to return to the *Commedia*—not, however, to the configuration of spirits in the celestial sky, but to the progression of references that precede them.

II

Vigilantia   When the Pilgrim descends into the circle of carnal sinners in *Inferno* 5, he first hears the wailing of souls whose reason was overwhelmed by carnal desire. Their appearance is conveyed by two similes. What first appears as the nervous, disordered flight of starlings is qualified by the more ordered flight of cranes.

> E come li stornei ne portan l'ali
>   nel freddo tempo, a schiera larga e piena,
>   così quel fiato li spiriti mali
> di qua, di là, di giù, di sù li mena;

nulla speranza li conforta mai,
non che di posa, ma di minor pena.
E come i gru van cantando lor lai,
faccendo in aere di sé lunga riga,
così vid' io venir, traendo guai,
ombre portate de la detta briga;

(*Inf.* 5.40–49)

As in the cold season their wings bear the starlings along in a broad,
dense flock, so does that blast the wicked spirits. Hither, thither, downward, upward, it drives them; no hope ever comforts them, not to say
of rest, but of less pain. And as the cranes go chanting their lays, making
of themselves a long line in the air, so I saw approach with long-drawn
wailings shades borne on these battling winds.

The double simile depicts the visual resolution of a chaotic swarm into
a more ordered entity. The two-step simile, used frequently by Dante—
another example would be his ordering of the falling-leaf image in
Inferno 3.112–17—describes a process through which the imagination
seeks to define or resolve something that at first appears indistinct or
unknown, by associating it with a series of known things. The
sequence of similes literally renders the windblown spirits intelligible
to Virgil and the Pilgrim. After first appearing noisy and indistinct in
the rushing wind, they fall into a long line, "lunga riga," that permits
Virgil to identify them as they pass overhead. More precisely, the
"riga" which appears in the sky invites us to think that Dante has
represented Virgil in the act of reading.

This assumption is based on the medieval meaning of *riga*, the
subject of the canto—the cranes lead to the Pilgrim's interview with
Paolo and Francesca—and of the crane figure itself. DuCange notices
that *riga* comes to refer to the "fulcus literarum" a common metaphoric
representation of writing as a furrowed field in which seeds are
planted.[16] Here the furrowed field becomes transformed into aeronau-
tical *sententiae* that may be reviewed by teacher and student alike.
Virgil's role as teacher is specified—"il mio dottore" (70). The context
also supports the link between *riga* and reading. As they pass overhead
in their airborne lines, the spirits are chanting poetry or lays: "E come
i gru van cantando lor lai, / faccendo in aere di sé lunga riga" (46–47).
And who are the spirits Virgil reads in the sky? The figures include

Semiramis, Dido, Cleopatra, Helen of Troy, Achilles, Paris, and Tristan, and more than a thousand others ("più di mille," 67)—all men or women about whom Dante would have read. In the case of Semiramis, identified as a woman "di cui si legge" this is even overtly stated. By describing all of them singing lays, Dante further emphasizes an association with secular poetry. It is hardly coincidental that this long line of romantically corrupted figures leads the Pilgrim to his interview with Francesca and the revelation that she and Paolo were led into adultery by reading the romance of Lancelot (127–28).

The crane simile reinforces the meditation on reading. I have already mentioned how "the order of letters" ("ordine litterato") was found in crane formations by church fathers like Isidore. It is, however, not simply a graphic link between the flight of birds and writing that Dante would have us notice, but the attribute that permits such an ordered pattern to be generated. Like Isidore, Rabanus Maurus, and others, Dante finds in the flight of cranes an emblem for vigilance, above all demonstrated by the calling voice of the lead crane. "One of them precedes the others, one who does not cease to cry out; he who holds the first position in the column, should go before his followers with his life and habits so that he always cries out and demonstrates the life of good works to those following him" ("Una earum reliquas antecedit, quae clamore non desinit, quias praelatus, qui primum locum regiminis obtinet, suos sequaces moribus et vita praeire debet, ita tamen ut semper clamet, et viam bonae operationis sequacibus suis praedicando demonstret," PL 177.40). The crucial responsibility attributed to the vigilant leader in Hugh's twelfth-century commentary must next be considered within the canto's own configuration.

By joining a symbol of vigilance to a seemingly unending line of misdirected figures, Dante shows how a single book, wrongly perceived as a guide, can lead many to error. For Paolo and Francesca, naive faith in one book's authority resulted in misinterpretation—and adultery. Above I drew attention to the double simile (starlings/cranes) and now want to note how it creates what is only an illusion of order. As a rhetorical figure, the crane simile renders what is disordered legible. Here the perception of order is only artifice. The figures in the sky are like cranes so that they can be read and finally understood as leaderless and eternally condemned to chaos. Viewed in such a way, the crane figures require critical analysis. Like the Pilgrim's sympathetic reaction to Francesca's story, which at first appears so logical, our reaction to the writing that moves before us must be guarded.

Recognized as a symbol for vigilance, the cranes complement the central motif of the canto. Finally, the "lunga riga" refers not only to the line of spirits in the infernal sky but marks out the very lines that Dante has placed before his reader. Just as the Pilgrim must learn to interpret figures for himself, so Dante's reader must learn to decipher the "lunga riga" or "ordine litterato" that moves before him on the page. Virgil acts as a teacher for Pilgrim and reader alike. But for the reader the text's own referential structure also works as a teacher. As he proceeds, the reader recognizes in encounters with rhetorical figures like the cranes that there are features in the text which can only be intended for his own education. In fact, the very placement of *vedi* in the lines invites the reader to discover a **graphic V that reinforces the** importance given to vigilance. Three times in succession Virgil uses the word *vedi* to direct the Pilgrim's attention to the spirits passing above in the "lunga riga." By linking them, we can see they form a large wedge that literally points in the direction of our reading.

> Elena *vedi*, per cui tanto reo
>> tempo si volse, e *vedi* 'l grande Achille,
>> che con amore al fine comatteo.
> Vedi Parìs, Tristano; e più di mille
>> ombre mostrommi e nominommi a dito,
>> ch'amor di nostra via dispartille.
>>>> (*Inf.* 5.64–69; italics mine)

See Helen, for whose sake so many years of ill revolved; and see the great Achilles, who fought at the last with love; see Paris, Tristan—and he showed me more than a thousand shades, naming them as he pointed, whom love parted from our life.

The graphic pattern is emphasized not only by the repetition of *vedi* but through the juxtaposition of *mostrommi* and *nominommi*, words that literally call attention to the patterns before the Pilgrim. Gian Roberto Sarolli has shown that textual symbolism such as this is not extraordinary in the *Commedia*.[17]

Another nuance is here as well. By comparing the figures to birds known for travel, Dante reminds us that his own words, physically transmitted by the scribe, are leading the reader or listener on a migratory flight. The words not only move beneath the reader's eyes but quite literally sustain his movement or progression through the text. The lesson of the canto's skywriting comes when we realize that true migration can happen only when one is certain of the direction in which one is going. Certainty, however, is not an individual decision alone but becomes bound up with the movement of the group one is part of.

Communitas While the association of cranes with vigilance marks a particular emphasis of *Inferno* 5, it is the exemplary nature of cranes' cooperation and communal life that draws our attention in *Purgatorio*. Having provided the ancient Romans with a metaphor for military organization, and the patristic fathers with a model for monastic obedience, the ordered groups of cranes become for Dante a model for politicians and poets as well. In both *Purgatorio* 24 and 26, where Dante looks back upon his own poetic enterprise, we discover the crane metaphor used as an image of faithful cooperation and moderation.

After bunching together to look at the Pilgrim's shape in *Purgatorio* 24, the spirits resume their ordered movement along the terrace.

> Come li augei che vernan lungo 'l Nilo,
> alcuna volta in aere fanno schiera,
> poi volan più a fretta e vanno in filo,
> così tutta la gente che lì era,
> volgendo 'l viso, raffrettò suo passo,
> e per magrezza e per voler leggera.
> (Purg. 24.64–69)

As birds that winter along the Nile sometimes make a troop in the air, then fly with more speed and go in file, so all the people that were there, facing round, quickened their steps, being light both with leanness and desire.

The simile describes a visual resolution similar to that found in the transformation of the disordered swarm of starlings into the "lunga riga" of the cranes. Here, however, the simile bears no ironic meaning. Rather than forming a "riga" as they did previously, the cranes' bunched flock, or "schiera," is resolved into a single line, or "filo," which encourages the reader to think of a military line or file. Statius, whose literal presence in the canto now guides the Pilgrim, provided Dante with the model. Having described the way troops are marshaled for a long march, the Latin poet compares their disciplined ranks to birds in migration.[18] The Latin passage, which also anticipates the journey's end, reminds us that a similar argument is implicit in Dante's comparison. By virtue of their disciplined ranks, the souls of Purgatory will one day reach Paradise.

Dante's allusion to cranes is sustained much further. Immediately following the crane reference, Forese, the executed leader of the Blacks, appears:

> E come l'uom che di trottare è lasso,
>   lascia andar li compagni, e si passeggia
>   fin che si sfoghi l'affollar del casso,
> si lasciò traspassar la santa greggia
>   Forese, e dietro meco sen veniva,
>   dicendo: "Quando fia ch'io ti riveggia?"
>   (Purg. 24.70–75)

And as one tired with running lets his companions go on and then walks till the heaving of his chest is relieved, so Forese let the holy flock pass and came on with me behind, saying: "How long will it be till I see thee again?"

Forese's actions model another quality attributed to cranes, one described most vividly by Latini in his Tesoro. When a lead crane grows weary, he may be helped to renew his strength by being held aloft by his compatriots.[19]

E quando questa ch' è capitano è stanca di guardarle, che la sua boce è arantolata e roca, non si vergogna, che un'altra ne genga in suo luogo, ed ella torna a schiera, e vola con le altre. E quando v'è alcuna che sia stanca, che non possa volare con l'altre, elli l'entrano allora sotto, e tanto la portano in questo modo, ch'ella ricovera sua forza, tanto che la vola con l'altre.

And when the one who is the captain becomes tired of holding watch, because his voice is dry and worn, without disgrace another takes his place, and he returns to the flock and flies with the others. But if he is so exhausted that it is impossible for him to fly with the others, they fly under him and support him until he regains his strength and can fly with them.

Like a tired crane being supported by the flock, Forese appears to have momentarily fallen back to regain his strength. The crane metaphor takes on another nuance as well. By raising questions about the political leadership of Florence, Forese and the Pilgrim also specify the issue of leadership conveyed by the crane metaphor. When he departs to rejoin the migratory group now ahead of him, Forese appears refreshed and ready to resume his journey. The description of him surging forward like a rider that has separated himself from a cavalry band also recalls Latini's account of the cavalry-like cranes:"Grue sono una generazione d'uccelli che vanno a schiera, come i cavalieri che vanno a battaglia, e sempre vanno l'uno dopo l'altro, si come i cavalieri in guerra (185)" ("Cranes are a kind of bird who travel in groups like cavalry troops riding into battle, and always travel one after the other like cavalry troops in battle"). The idea of rest does not pertain to Forese alone. Just as Forese is a member of a band that seeks renewal, so the Pilgrim desires renewal in his journey—renewal that comes from acknowledging his position as a follower.

The theme of leadership and renewal shifts from Forese to the Pilgrim himself as the canto progresses. As he moves forward behind Virgil and Statius, Dante is suddenly recognized as the innovator of "le nove rime." "Ma di s'i' veggio qui colui che fore / trasse le nove rime, cominciando / 'Donne ch'avete intelletto d'amore' " ("But tell me if I see here him who brought forth the new rhymes, beginning with 'Ladies that have intelligence of love,' " 49–50). Bonagiunta's remark, which quotes the first line of the Vita nuova, makes it evident that he looks to the Pilgrim as one who goes before the others. The Pilgrim's response, however, qualifies Bonagiunta's idea of leadership by reverently reminding him that he follows another spiritual leader.

> E io a lui: "I' mi son un che, quando
> Amor mi spira, noto, e a quel modo
> ch'e' ditta dentro vo significando."
>
> (Purg. 24.52–54)

And I said to him: "I am one who, when love breathes in me, takes note, and in that manner which he dictates within go on to set it forth."

The corrective response once more enlarges the crane topos. Rather than following a leader whose acts and words are physically manifest, the Pilgrim diligently follows the inspiration of another leader. The comparison is amplified in Bonagiunta's confession that his love of style (*stilo*) had impeded his capacity to comprehend spiritual authority.

> Io veggio ben come le vostre penne
>> di retro al dittator sen vanno strette,
>> che delle nostre certo non avvenne;
> e qual più a gradire oltre si mette
>> non vede più dall'uno all'altro stilo.
>
> (Purg. 24.58–62)

I see well how your pens follow close behind the dictator which assuredly did not happen with ours, and he that sets himself to examine further sees nothing else between the one style and the other.

The reference to cranes follows immediately, formally linking the discourse on political and poetic leaders. Here, as in *Inferno* 5, discussion of poetic models is reinforced by the allusion to cranes. In fact, three rhyming words, *stilo*, *Nilo*, and *filo* weave the comments on composition with the cranes and encourage the reader to explore the relation between the literary discussion and the symbolic use of cranes. Once again, the reference to cranes is supported by tradition. Just as the lead crane determines the formation of an "ordine litterato" and signifies persons who shape themselves upon God's Word, so the Pilgrim affirms that he shapes his own words upon divine inspiration. In both cases, divine dictates are metaphorically linked to the lead crane whose cry provides guidance to those following.

Dante alerts readers both to the vigilance needed for interpretation and to the watchfulness important for a community where members may be spiritually nourished and replenished. In *Purgatorio* 26, cranes appear once more in a setting that helps to define the idea of poetry and leadership. Just as the Pilgrim is about to identify himself to his beloved teacher and previous leader Guido Guinizzelli, he is distracted by a strange sight. At the appearance of a new troop of souls, Guido's group and the one that has just arrived rush toward each other to exchange greetings and information. As they separate, each group seeks to outshout the other with slogans proclaiming their sins. Their subsequent departure is compared to the flight of cranes.

> Poi, come grue ch'a le montagne Rife
> volasser parte e parte inver' l'arene,
> queste del gel, quelle del sole schife,
> l'una gente sen va, l'altra sen vene;
> e tornan, lacrimando, a' primi canti
> e al gridar che più lor si convene;
> (Purg. 26.43–48)

Then, like cranes flying, some towards the Riphean Mountains and some towards the sands, these shunning the frost and those the sun, the one crowd goes and the other comes on and they return with tears to their former chants and to the cry that most befits them.

The simultaneous northerly and southerly flight of cranes described here is impossible, as the subjunctive *volasser* attests. The reason for this implausible phenomenon—at least in general—is not difficult to understand. The unnatural description of cranes's behavior corresponds to the varied ways in which penance must be sought by those who have followed unnatural sexual habits or habits contrary to God's law. The Sodomites, for example, move in the "wrong" direction here to undo the impulsive direction they had followed in life. Just as cranes follow God's law in seeking a warmer climate, so the souls must follow the way of purification appropriate to them.

As before, the crane simile helps to order the references to writing and poetry. The shouts of repentant souls, like the calls of cranes, are warnings that urge vigilance. The Pilgrim's reaction to what he has witnessed shows that he would read and learn from the reactions of these new cranelike souls. Seeing the crowd of souls streaming behind Guido, the Pilgrim is prepared to have their meaning dictated to him.

The situation is reminiscent of Virgil's identification of the "riga" of spirits in *Inferno* 5. But there is a critical difference: early in his journey the Pilgrim's impulse was to react to the pathos of the figures before him rather than to try to fathom God's justice. Now he is better prepared to listen and learn, showing that he is ready to follow the warning given by Virgil at the beginning of the canto: "Guarda: giovi ch'io ti scaltro" (3) ("Watch, take heed of my warning").

In *Purgatorio* 24 Bonagiunta testified to the Pilgrim's prominence as the innovator of the "dolce stilo." Now, in his conversation with Guido Guinezzelli, the Pilgrim testifies to the model he found in his teacher. Their exchange becomes modulated, not by a facile attention to rank and order as in the case of Bonagiunta, but by an appreciation that poets belong to a community that changes over time. The first thing Guido observes when he sees Dante is that he follows others: "O tu che vai, non per esser più tardo / ma forse reverente, a li altri dopo" (*Purg.* 26.16) ("Oh thou who goes behind the others, not from tardiness but perhaps from reverence"). Guido now recognizes the Pilgrim's secondary position, a ranking the Pilgrim himself acknowledged in *Purgatorio* 24 as he followed his "gran mareschalchi." Here, Guido's observation affirms the importance of such a position and anticipates his own humble deference to Arnault Daniel. Humility characterizes Guido. Even the way he takes his leave of the Pilgrim emphasizes his willingness, like the lead crane, to retire so that another may occupy his place: "Poi, forse per dar luogo altrui secondo / che presso avea, disparve per lo foco, come per l'acqua il pesce andando al fondo" (*Purg.* 26. 133–35) ("Then, perhaps to give place to others who were near him, he disappeared through the fire as through the water a fish goes to the bottom").

The relationship Dante depicts between Guido and the Pilgrim is even more complex. At the same time as Guido has inspired the Pilgrim's own verse, his invention has led to his own corruption. Love poetry, for Guido, became not a vehicle for purification but for venery. Consequently, Guido and the Pilgrim illustrate the contrary impulses evoked by the "dolce stilo." The anxious movement of the line of cranes—movement of which Guido is part—graphically portrays the different ways in which poetry may be taken. When the Pilgrim meets his teacher and lovingly acknowledges the importance of Guido's "rime" for his own verse, he is responding to the spirit of love he found in the rhymes themselves rather than to the sexual fantasies Guido came to enact.

By presenting the problem of contrary responses to poetry, the canto returns to the interpretive issues raised in *Inferno* 5. Now, however, the question of response is more sophisticated. While the canto warns that love poetry should not incite sexual play, it raises questions about interpretation and authorial intention. I have already said that Dante's own generous response to his teacher must be regarded as a reaction to Guido's spiritual influence. But this is not all. In contrast to the warmth the Pilgrim shows toward Guido, one cannot help but notice his cool response to Arnaut. Even though Guido specifically concedes that Arnaut should go first because he is the "miglior fabbro" (117), there is reason to wonder whether Dante is not more sympathetic to Guido's spirit than to Arnaut's artifice. By having Arnaut describe himself as one "que plor e vau cantan" (142), Dante recalls the volatile figures of *Inferno* 5 who "van cantando lor lai" (46). The echo carries an implicit warning that readers must practice vigilance when looking at Arnaut's "verse d'amore e prose de romanzi" (118). The fact that Arnaut now appears at the head of the phalanx of poets and inspires others makes it even more crucial not to mistake his voice.

Illuminatio   Dante's thorough incorporation of the crane topos in the first two canticles of the *Commedia* allows him both to represent the problem of reading and writing his text and to draw attention to the reader's own assimilation of the work. When we return to the passage from the *Paradiso* mentioned at the beginning of this essay, acts of reading become more articulated.

The reading metaphor associated with cranes becomes explicit in *Paradiso* 18 when cranelike spirits spell out against the heavens the first verse of the Book of Wisdom: DILIGITE IUSTITIAM / QUI IUDICATIS TERRAM ("You who judge the earth / love justice"). Only after the Pilgrim has carefully examined and synthesized letters does he perceive a message in the flight of the holy creatures. At first he is only conscious that the "figure" (78) being formed appears letterlike. Then, like a child who can recognize letters but cannot yet make out words, the Pilgrim seeks instruction.

> O diva Pegasëa che li 'ngegni
>   fai gloriosi e rendili longevi,
>   ed esse teco le cittadi e' regni,

> illustrami di te, sì ch'io rilevi
> le lor figure com'io l'ho concette:
> paia tua possa in questi versi brevi!
> (*Par.* 18.82–87)

O divine Pegasean that givest glory and long life to genius, as it does through thee to cities and kingdoms, illumine me with thyself that I may set forth their shapes as I deciphered them. Let thy power appear in these brief lines!

The invocation prepares us for the Pilgrim's interpretation and anticipates that the meaning to be revealed is not restricted to an individual witness but is extended to "cities and kingdoms." The message created by a congregation of spirits will speak not to one but to many.

The Pilgrim's actions following the invocation show that the meaning does not come easily. Counting vowels and consonants, finding words in the letters, identifying verb, object, and relative clause, he vigilantly construes the signs that appear before him. For a moment the process recalls a grammar class and the steps a student is expected to take in elementary reading. Only after all thirty-five figures are formulated is the Pilgrim able to arrange them grammatically into individual words and construe those words into a particular meaning. The sequence asks the reader to consider a process implicit in the construing of every line in the *Commedia*. Previously, Dante has signaled the rhetorical function of figures; but nowhere has he described so carefully the steps involved in reading. Numerical symbolism affirms the significance of the experience. As the number of letters that appear in the heavens is identical to the year of perfection mentioned in the *Convivio* (4.24) and marks the very origin of the poem, "[il] mezzo del cammin di nostra vita," the experience acknowledges that the Pilgrim has finally approached the frontier of higher illumination.[20] Once again, it is implicit that illumination is a process intimately bound up with reading and writing.

Ordinary language as depicted by Dante is a collection of figures that must be arranged and correctly set forth before meaning is achieved. Should a single figure be misrepresented, understanding would be led astray. The setting closely resembles the textual metaphor operative in Martial's epigram on cranes: "You will disturb the lines, and the letter will not fly entire if you destroy one single bird of

Palamedes" (13.75).[21] The caution suggested by the invocation to the muse is also present as the Pilgrim describes what he has seen. Three times the nature of his experience is noted, and each time with greater clarity. Seeing letters, he qualifies their appearance: "come mi parver dette" (90) ("what they seemed to me to mean"). When the heavenly creatures maintain their order in the shape of the M in TERRAM he compares the new figure to an ornamental capital: "Poscia ne l'emme del vocabol quinto / rimasero ordinate; sì che Giove / pareva argento lì d'oro distinto" (94–96) ("Then in the M of the fifth word they kept their order, so that Jupiter seemed there silver pricked out with gold"). Finally, watching and listening to the figures descend on the summit of the M, he believes, "credo" (99), that what they sang concerned "il ben ch'a se le move" (99) ("the good that draws them to itself"). "Credo" does not simply mean that the Pilgrim "thinks" this is what they sang but joins his perception to an act of belief. Faith is a prerequisite to the vision unfolding before him, just as it is manifest in the spirits that conform to divine inspiration.

The faithfulness of the Pilgrim's transcription is heightened when the reader is reminded that false interpretation is still possible. As the sparkling creatures disperse from the M they have joined to create, Dante compares them to the shower of sparks that fly upward when burning logs are struck. But then, as if to call into question his own simile, he warns that such earthly sparks cause foolish interpreters to hunt in vain for meaning in empty things that fly up from earth. The verb augurarsi—which refers to "divination by consulting the behavior of birds"—directs our attention back to the scriptural formations made in the heavenly sky and affirms that they stand forth with authority.[22]

Early in the canto, Beatrice appears as "quella donna ch'a Dio si menava" (4), followed by Cacciaguida's presentation of the holy military leaders (28–51). But as the Pilgrim seeks guidance from both, it is also evident that they are only instruments to reveal the presence of a more absolute guide. In the letters that shape themselves against the celestial sky the Pilgrim recognizes the force that needs no guide.

Quei chi dipinge lì, non ha chi 'l guidi;
ma esso guida, e da lui si rammenta
quella virtù ch'e forma per l'nidi.
(Par. 18.109–11)

He that designs there has none to guide Him. He Himself guides, even
as we recognize to be from Him that power which is form for the nests.

The lines acknowledge the power of God's guiding inspiration inherent
in the heavenly configuration of scripture. They also affirm such guidance by inviting the reader to think of God as the illuminator of His
holy text. God is described, not only as the inspiration for the biblical
text, but as the artist or illuminator who completes an ornate manuscript book. The lines literally appeal to the greater freedom custom-
arily granted to the medieval illuminator.[23] While the scribe would be
expected to copy a text line by line, following the ruled page before
him, the responsibility for illumination would be saved for a more
experienced and trusted artist. By alluding to the process of medieval
book manufacture, Dante plays with the evolving structure of his own
book. While the material of the earlier canticles may be thought of as
more mundane and crude, the subject matter of *Paradiso* warrants
artistic elaboration. It is as though one's progression through the *Commedia* takes one from a common manuscript to one that is richly orna-
mented because it is finished in Heaven.

   The lines appeal to another progression as well. By comparing
God's guiding inspiration to the nesting instinct of birds, Dante also
appeals to the force inherent in his earlier description of the migratory
flight of cranes. Dante's own words set before us since the first line of
the *Inferno* comprise a migratory progression. By following the pattern
of those words, readers may think of themselves as part of a body of
spirits borne through stages of evolving illumination. Through vigilance and the affirmation that all personal action bears responsibility
to the community, the reader's mind is finally drawn to the heavens.
Words, like birds, will find their ultimate force in the power of God's
spirit.

III

The crane topos not only tells us much about the evolving structure
of the *Commedia* but comprises an example of Dante's hermeneutical
practice. While the figure of the crane is used as a component in the
work, its incorporation also indicates how Dante approached writing

as a form of interpretation. In his recent work on narrative, Paul Ricoeur describes reading as a process that involves prefiguration, configuration, and refiguration.[24] Each time we encounter Dante's cranes we prefigure their significance through our own experience and our knowledge of the trope. In each case such prefiguration also becomes adjusted as we adapt our projected meaning to the particular context. Eventually, the way we configure the meaning of the cranes at a particular moment brings about a refiguration of the text's evolving meaning. In effect, Ricoeur's formulation describes the hermeneutical circle in which projected meaning is tested and augmented by our ongoing experience of the text.

I want to emphasize the active force of the trope by briefly comparing its use in the *Commedia* to a reference to migratory birds in a recent consideration of language in a phenomenological setting. In response to a paper that had surveyed Heidegger's examination of references to animals in early Greek philosophy and their bearing on "human" language, Derrida asked the author David Krell about the appearance of *Zugvögel*—or migratory birds—in Heidegger's writing (49). Playing on Heidegger's use of *Zug* (drift or pull) to describe the human tendency to become preoccupied by the inessential,[25] Derrida's question momentarily opens another possibility that has a bearing on our discussion. Migratory birds, or *Zugvögel*, when used to represent writing, do not only have a negative connotation but may also describe the capacity of words to pull or draw the reader into previously unimagined meanings. Krell's response indicates such a dual significance. Referring to Heidegger's lectures on Parmenides, he noticed that here "birds fly into and show us the open, *das Offene* and in singing they call us and make announcements; it also says that the bird ensnares us in the open or the bird is itself ensnared—*seira*, the origin of the word *sirena*. Sirens are those who ensnare" (47).

It is not an exaggeration to compare Dante's cranes to such *Zugvögel*, for as we follow them they play openly and finally stage Dante's idea of reading and writing. In *Inferno* 5, they too fly before the Pilgrim and signify their capacity to ensnare or to liberate. By surveying Dante's progressive references to cranes, we notice that they also mark an effort to extend the very idea of writing. While their configurations initially convey stories of figures who have been led astray, they ultimately set before the reader divinely illuminated signs. The cranes we have followed in this discussion show how Dante devised strategies to expand or open a narrative that Derrida would describe as logocentric. Ultimately, the crane figure does not limit the idea of writing but graphically extends it, by allowing Dante to constantly involve writing with questions of interpretative authority. Dante's poem would be a vehicle for meaning, a text where the letters crossing the page like the wedgelike patterns formed by cranes function as a lure that can ensnare or free the properly faithful reader.

My digression on *Zugvögel* may remind us as well of the connection between philology and philosophical hermeneutics. Curtius and Heidegger are not as distant from each other as we may think, for the simple reason that they both bear the stamp of nineteenth-century German philology. While Curtius surveys topoi within Western literature, Heidegger delineates philosophical topoi. Study of the relationship between them would make a valuable project. I want to emphasize their relation because it is far too frequently assumed that an abyss lies between their two enterprises. Theorists might look more carefully at medieval hermeneutics, just as medievalists could enhance their work by noticing how much they actually share with much critical inquiry. Dante's text is not simply a field in which to identify topoi, but a philosophical narrative that challenges readers constantly to negotiate meaning.

The trope acknowledges how words always pull the reader into negotiation and reminds us of how much of what Dante placed in the category of religion we, as descendants of the Enlightenment, place in the realm of interpretive theory. We desire to understand how meaning becomes generated through our interaction with texts, and Dante allows us to follow the progression of such meaning in abundance. The invitation to textual migration and transformation afforded by the crane topos ultimately challenges us to negotiate meaning between two different books—the Book of Scripture and the Book of Nature. For neither the Pilgrim nor the reader are meaning and understanding constituted solely in one or the other. Rather, meaning and understanding are attained through the integration of the two books in the reader's own experience.

Dante's cranes challenge us to undertake a kind of dialogical migration, or to enter an evolving hermeneutical procedure, involving the construing of figures that reach backward and forward into the text. Cesare Segre has described a process by which readers orient themselves by projecting or anticipating the movement of a plot or *fabula*.[26]

The discussion—which parallels Wolfgang Iser's notion of narrative blanks in interesting ways—is useful because it permits us to recognize that the plot itself is affirmed through the negotiations of smaller narrative structures.[27] As we follow Dante's cranes, they become part of our memorizing synthesis of the *Commedia*'s evolving narrative and contribute to its unfolding signification. The crane topos is not employed as an ornamental figure but as a constitutive metaphor. It is not a static figure drawn into the text to ornament an idea momentarily but a dynamic figure through which meaning becomes negotiated.

The crane topos attracted Dante because it figures social order and leadership intimately related to the act of writing and reading. Although the patterns perceived by the Pilgrim in *Inferno* tell stories of persons who have sinned, simultaneously, allusion to the wedgelike formations of cranes warns of the need for vigilance as one follows and learns from their negative examples. In *Purgatorio* 24 and 26, cranes reappear—but to admonish vigilance in writing and reading: although reading and interpretation appear as group activities in *Inferno* 5, here writing is portrayed as an act that has a bearing on political and poetic communities as well. While one poet may momentarily lead the flock, he too must be prepared to retire and make way for new voices, whether he be Guinezzelli, Arnaut, or Dante himself. The recapituation of earlier motifs of reading and writing occurs in *Paradiso* 18, as the Pilgrim strives to make out the text formed in the heavens by the Divine Illuminator. Here, too, the message embodied by angelic forms is intended not for the individual alone but for the whole community. But by far the most compelling message appears, not in the unfolding stages of the trope portrayed in *Inferno*, *Purgatorio*, and *Paradiso*, but in the configuration of the Pilgrim's entire voyage as a migration from *Inferno* to *Paradiso*, in which the reader participates through reading.

Georgia Institute of Technology

NOTES

1. Reinhold Köhler, "Und wenn der Himmel war Papier," *Kleinere Schriften*, ed. Johannes Bolte (Berlin: Verlag von Emil Felber, 1900), pp. 293–318.

2. For references to Heidegger and Derrida, see David Farrel Krell, "Daimon Life, Nearness and Abyss: An Introduction to Za-ology," *Research in Phenomenology*,

vol. 17, ed. John Sallis (Trenton, N.J.: Humanities Press, 1988), pp. 23–53. For Gadamer, see "Language and Concept Formation," in Hans-Georg Gadamer, *Truth and
Method* (New York: Crossroad Publishing, 1975), pp. 387–97; 390.

   3. See Augustine's amplification of Genesis 1:20 (Dixit etiam Deus: "Producant
aquae reptile animae viventis, et volatile super terram sub firmamento caeli"), in
Confessions 13: "The words of your messengers have soared like winged things above
the earth beneath the firmament of your Book, for this was the authority given to
them and beneath it they were to take wing wherever their journey lay. There is no
word, no accent of theirs that does not make itself heard, till their utterance fills
every land, till their message reaches the ends of the world. And this is because you,
O Lord, have blessed their work and multiplied it." Augustine *Confessions*, trans.
R. S. Pine-Coffin (Baltimore: Penguin Books, 1968), p. 328.

   4. Italian references are to *La Divina Commedia*, ed. C. H. Grandgent and rev.
Charles S. Singleton (Cambridge, Mass.: Harvard Univ. Press, 1972); translations are
from *The Divine Comedy*, Italian text with English translation and commentary by
John D. Sinclair, 3 vols. (New York: Oxford Univ. Press, 1961).

   5. Benvenuto da Imola's gloss may be cited as an example: "Et hoc faciebant a
simili, *sí come augelli surti di rivera*, idest, que surrexerunt de riperia, in qua moram
trahunt, *quasi congratulando a lor pasture*, id est, simul letantes de eorum pabulis
inventis, *fanno di sé or lunga schiera or tonda*; nam aliquando faciunt de se 'unam
lineam ordinatem in modum literarum alphabeti' ut dicit Lucanus; aliquando faciunt
de se coronam. Et nota quod comparatio est proprie de gruibus." For this gloss and
the others referred to in the text, see *La Divina Commedia*, ed. G. Giagi et al., 3 vols.
(Turin: Unione Tipografico-Editrice Torinese, 1939), vol. 3, *Paradiso*, pp. 412–13.

   6. Ernst R. Curtius, *European Literature and the Latin Middle Ages*, trans.
Willard R. Trask (New York: Harper & Row, 1963), p. 367.

   7. For medieval bestiaries, see Hennig Brinkmann, *Mittelalterliche Hermeneutik*
(Tübingen: Max Niemeyer Verlag, 1980), pp. 101–16; and Florence McCulloch, *Medi-
eval Latin and French Bestiaries* (Chapel Hill: Univ. of North Carolina [Studies in
Romance Languages and Literature 33], 1960). For general references to cranes, see
Hans Martin von Erffa, "Grus Vigilans": Bemerkungen zur Emblematik," *Philobiblon*
1 (Dec. 1957): 186–308; Hugh William Davies, *Devices of the Early Printers, 1457–
1560: Their History and Development* (London: Grafton & Co., 1935); and *Emblemata:
Handbuch zur Sinnbildkunst des XVI und XVII Jahrhunderts*, ed. Arthur Henkel and
Albrech Schöne (Stuttgart: J. B. Metzlersche, 1967), cols. 818–25. For cranes in Dante,
see Lawrence V. Ryan, "Stornei, Gru, Colombe: The Bird Images in Inferno V," *Dante
Studies* 94 (1976): 25–45.

   8. "Many indications of high intelligence are given by cranes. They will fly to a
great distance and high up in the air, to command an extensive view; if they see
clouds, and signs of bad weather they fly down again and remain still. They, furthermore, have a leader in their flight, and patrols that scream on the confines of the
flock so as to be heard by all. When they settle down, the main body goes to sleep
with their heads under their wing, standing first on one leg and then on the other,
while their leader, with his head uncovered, keeps a sharp lookout, and when he
sees anything of importance signals it with a cry." Aristotle *Historia animalium*,
trans. D'Arcy Wentworth Thompson, *The Works of Aristotle*, ed. J. A. Smith and
W. D. Ross (Oxford: Clarendon Press, 1910), vol. 4, bk. 9, p. 10.

   9. Pliny *Natural History*, trans. H. Rackham, 10 vols. (Cambridge, Mass.: Harvard Univ. Press [Loeb Classical Library], 1967), 10.30.

   10. Virgil *Aeneid*, trans. H. Rushton Fairclough, 2 vols. (Cambridge, Mass.: Harvard Univ. Press [Loeb Classical Library], 1974), 2.10.262–66; Statius *Thebaid*, trans.
J. H. Mozley, 2 vols. (Cambridge, Mass.: Harvard Univ. Press [Loeb Classical Library],

1961), 2.5.7–14; Lucan *De bello civili*, trans. J. D. Duff (Cambridge, Mass.: Harvard Univ. Press [Loeb Classical Library], 1951), 5.709–16.

11. See Hyginus, *Fabulae*, ed. H. I. Rose (Leyden: A. W. Sythoff, 1933), p. 170: "Parcae, Clotho, Lachesis, Atropos, invenerunt litteras Graecas septem, A B H T I Y; alii dicunt Mercurium ex gruum volatu, quae cum volant litteras exprimunt; Palamedes autem Nauplii filius invenit aequae litteras undecim."

12. Commentary on cranes appears in the following medieval authors: Basil the Great (*PG* 29.175); Ambrose (*PL* 14.241–42); Isidore of Seville (*PL* 82.460–61), Rabanus Maurus (*PL* 111.244); Hugh of St. Victor (*PL* 177.40–41); Pseudo-Hugh of St. Victor (*PL* 177.148); Eustathius (*PL* 53.950); and Albertus Magnus, *Animalium*, vol. 12, *Opera omnia*, ed. August Borgnet (Paris, 1891), 23.53. References to *PG* and *PL* are to *Patrologia series graeca*, 161 vols., and *Patrologia series latina*, 221 vols., ed. Jacques Paul Migne (Paris: P. Geuthner, 1844–1900). Subsequent references will be cited directly in the text.

13. "Ab iis igitur ordiamur, quae nostro usui se imitationem dederunt. In illis enim politia quaedam et militia naturalis, in nobis coacta atque servilis. Quam injusso et voluntario usu grues in nocte solicitam exercent custodiam. . . . At illa volens suscipit sortem, nec usu nostro invita et pigrior somno rununtiat: sed impigre suis excutitur stratis, vicem exsequitur, et quam accepit gratiam pari cura atque officio repraesentat. Ideo nulla desertio, quia devotio naturalis; ideo tuta custodia, quia voluntas libera. . . . Quid hoc pulchrius, et laborem omnibus et honorem esse communem, nec paucis arrogari potentiam, sed quadam in omnes voluntaria sorte transcribi? Antiquae hoc reipublicae munus, et instar liberae civitatis est. Sic ab initio acceptam a natura exemplo avium politiam homines exercere coeperunt; ut communis esset labor, communis dignitas, per vices singuli partiri curas discerent, obsequia imperiaeque dividerent, nemo esset honoris exsors, nullus immunis laboris. Hic erat pulcherimus rerum status, nec insolescebat quisquam perpetua postestate, nec diuturno servitio frangebatur. . . . Nos autem non solum de primo, sed etiam de medio saepe conendimus, et plurimos discubitus in convivio vindicamus: ac si semet delatum fuerit, volumus esse perpetuum."—("Let us, therefore, order ourselves on the model of those which gave themselves to us as models for imitation. In them we observe a certain natural political structure as well as military structure, arranged for ourselves and even for our service. . . . The crane willingly takes up his lot and does not give up his sleep with reluctance and sluggishness as we do. He rises from his bed energetically and accepts his turn. With what gratitude he accepts preparation for the service and even hastens to his duty. Therefore, there is no desertion because this is natural devotion; therefore, there is a secure watch because it is founded on free will. . . . What is more beautiful than labor and honor being common to all? Even the smallest authority is not demanded but by means of a certain voluntary assent it is assigned to all by lot. This was how ancient republics functioned and is the very model of a free society. Thus receiving the example of birds from nature, man from the earliest time began to practice politics so that work, as dignity, would be commonly shared. Each one determined that the tasks were to be shared in turn. No one was to be excluded from honor. No one was to be immune from labor. This was the most beautiful state of things, for no one either became insolent from too much authority or broken by daily slavery. . . . When we eat we not only occupy ourselves with the first places but often with those in the middle and seek to claim the first tables. If it were always left to ourselves we would want to be first"; *PL* 14.241–42). All subsequent translations are my own, unless otherwise indicated.

14. "Grues quippe illos significare possunt, qui in coenobiis communiter viventes, unius tamen ductum sequi non spernent, vigilias exercent, et pro invicem solliciti nocturnos cantus in psalmodiis edere non segnes fiunt. Unde dicitur: Grues una sequuntur et litterato ordine volant."—("Certainly cranes may signify those who, living together in a cloister, do not reject following a single leader. At night they practice vigilance and do not become sluggish in the singing of psalms. From whence it is said that cranes follow a single leader and fly in a lettered order"; (PL 111.244).

15. "Lapis, est Christus; pes, mentis affectus. Sicut enim aliquis pedibus incedit, sic mens suis affectibus quasi pedibus ad optata tendit. Si quis igitur ad custodiam sui vel fratrum vigilat, lapillum in pede, id est Christum in mente portet. . . . Possumus autem per vigiles intelligere quoslibet discretos fratres, qui communiter fratribus temporalia provident, et de singulis specialiter curam habent. Ad obsequia fratrum pro posse suo vigilant, ut ab eis incursus daemonum, et accessus saecularium repellant prudenter."—("The stone signifies Christ; their feet, the mind's disposition. Just as someone goes forward on their feet, the mind holds to its own affection as the feet to their desire. Therefore, if anyone watches out for his own safety or that of a brother, he carries in his feet a pebble, that is Christ in his mind. . . . We are able to see in such vigilance discerning brothers who communally provide for their brothers and who specifically, one after another, have charge. They watch for the allegiance of their brothers by their own ability so that they prudently repel from them the assaults of demons and the encroachment of the world"; PL 177.41).

16. Glossarium mediae et infimae latinitatis, ed. Du Cange [Charles de Fresne] (Niort: Firmin Didot, 1883–87).

17. Gian Roberto Sarolli, Prolegomena alla Divina Commedia (Florence: Leo S. Olschki Editore, 1971); see especially "I quattro sensi figurati: fondamenta strutturali della Commedia," pp. 144–87. For a setting that may describe a V-pattern used to warn readers, see Par. 2.1–6, which suggests the V-pattern a boat makes passing through the water.

18. "Marshalled again in squadrons and the stern discipline of rank, they are bidden to renew the march, each in his former place and under the same leader as before. Already the first dust is rising from the earth, and arms are flashing through the trees. Just so do flocks of screaming birds, caught by the Pharian summor, wing their way across the oaa from Paraetonian Nile, whither the fierce winter drove them; they fly, a shadow upon the sea and land, and their cry follows them, filling the pathless heaven. Soon will it be their delight to breast the north wind and the rain, soon to swim on the melted rivers, and to spend the summer days on naked Haemus." Statius Thebaid 2.5.7–14.

19. Brunetto Latini, Il tesor volgarizzato da Bono Giamboni, ed. P. Chabaillé (Bologna: Gaetano Romagnoli, 1877), pp. 185–86. Latini's account of the leader-crane's worn voice appears to draw on Isidore's comment, "At ubi raucescit, succedit alia" (PL 82. 460–61).

20. "['L] colmo del nostro arco è ne li trentacinque, tanto quanto questa etade ha di salita tanto dee avere di scesa; e quella salita è quella scesa e quasi lo tenere de l'arco, nel quale poco di flessione si discerne." Dante, Il Convivio, vol. 2, ed. G. Busnelli and G. Vandelli (Florence: Felice Le Monnier, 1964), 4.24; 306.

21. M. Val. Martialis Epigrammata, ed. W. M. Lindsay (Oxford: Oxford Univ. Press, 1965), 13.75; Martial, The Epigrams, ed. and trans. George Bell (London: n.p., 1890).

22. Bellini notes that the very term can specifically pertain to birds (Vocabolario universale della lingua italiana, ed. Bernardo Bellini et al. [Mantua: Editori Fratelli

Negretti, 1853]). Occurrences of *auguria* in Du Cange and in the *Mittellateinisches Wörterbuch* (Munich: C. H. Becksche Verlagsbuchhandlung, 1959) indicate that augury was firmly associated with birds in medieval Latin.

23. See Sarolli, "Dante scriba Dei: storia e simbolo," in his *Prolegomena* (above, n. 17), pp. 189–298. See also *Illuminated Manuscripts of the Divine Comedy*, ed. Peter Brieger et al., 2 vols. (Princeton: Princeton Univ. Press, 1969).

24. Paul Ricoeur, *Time and Narrative* (Chicago: Univ. of Chicago Press, 1984), pp. 52–89; 53.

25. For Heidegger's use of *Zug*, see John D. Caputo, *Radical Hermeneutics* (Bloomington: Indiana Univ. Press, 1987), pp. 59–92; 62.

26. Cesare Segre, *Structures and Time*, trans. John Meddemmen (Chicago: Univ. of Chicago Press, 1979), p. 11.

27. Wolfgang Iser, *The Act of Reading: A Theory of Aesthetic Response* (Baltimore: Johns Hopkins Press, 1978); also Iser, "Interaction between Text and Reader," in *The Reader in the Text: Essays on Audience and Interpretation*, ed. Susan R. Suleiman and Inge Crosman (Princeton: Princeton Univ. Press. 1980).

Thomas Aquinas and Siger of Brabant in Dante's *Paradiso*

LOUIS M. LA FAVIA

The fourth Heaven of Dante's *Paradiso*—the Heaven of the Sun, of the Sages—appears to be composed of opposed or conflicting elements that eventually reassemble themselves in unity or reconciliation. The author's intention was obviously to create a "concordia discors," which pervades like a continuo the entire theme of the Heaven of the Sages. This intention is apparent in several textual elements. To mention only the most evident, there is the scenic presentation of the characters—two dancing garlands representing two theological schools of opposite derivation, one of Platonic-Augustinian origin, the other, of Aristotelian-Averroistic origin; the "elocutio" of the characters— Saint Thomas, a Dominican, eulogizes Saint Francis and criticizes the Dominicans; Saint Bonaventure, a Franciscan, eulogizes Saint Dominic and criticizes the Franciscans; and the selection and juxtaposition of the "personae"—Thomas-Bonaventure, Bonaventure-Joachim a Fiori, Solomon-Nathan, and so on.

Against this background we find the strident opposition of Thomas Aquinas and Siger of Brabant who, once enemies on earth, are now more than friends in Heaven. In recent years this opposition has spurred research by scholars—particularly those of neo-scholastic extraction—resulting in a rediscovery of the historical Siger of Brabant. Nonetheless, some points concerning the precise knowledge that Dante

147

might have had of Siger's philosophical and theological thought have remained obscure, as well as the intellectual relationship Siger might have had with Thomas.

Thus, before delving to the heart of the question, I shall mention some interesting biographical details about the poet that might shed light on the psychological and cultural aspects of the thematic structure of the fourth Heaven of Dante's *Paradise*.

Dante might have seen Thomas Aquinas; he was nine years old when Thomas died in 1274. Two years before, Aquinas had traveled from Paris to Rome and stopped in Florence for the Dominican General Chapter on Pentecost Day, 1272. According to some biographers, Thomas was with the Dominicans when Fra Giovanni da Vercelli addressed the people of Florence, exhorting them to make peace with the other cities of Tuscany.[1] Very probably Dante, then seven years' old, saw the tall, handsome, imposing figure of Thomas. And just a few years later the young Dante attended the lectures of one of the strictest proponents and propagators of Aquinas's teaching, Fra Remigio de' Girolami da Firenze.[2]

Contrary to what some scholars think, the same possibility cannot be proposed in regard to Siger of Brabant, whose acquaintance with Dante is based on a story of Giovanni da Serravalle (which originated with and passed through G. Villani-Boccaccio-Benvenuto) regarding Dante's travels in his youth, for the purpose of study.[3] This story was subsequently elaborated upon by some scholars so as to represent the young Alighieri in the "Rue du Fouarre" (Petrarch's "fragosus straminum vicus," *Sen.* 9.18) at Paris listening to and attentively taking notes from the "lectiones" of "Magister Sigerius."[4] The truth is that Giovanni da Serravalle (as well as Domenico Bandini, less well known than da Serravalle but who reports the same story in a remaining fragment of his lost commentary on the *Comedy*)[5] misinterpreted the information in Benvenuto's Ferrarese commentary (still unpublished, in the Laurentian Codex Ashburnham 839, c. 6v),[6] which da Serravalle systematically transcribed and elaborated. Of equal improbability is S. Reinach's theory that the young Dante traveled from Florence to Orvieto[7] (a possibility even suggested by Brunetto Latini, according to another scholar)[8] to hear "Magister" Siger, who taught him the general introduction to philosophy and theology. The idea is certainly provocative, but it lacks the slightest hint of documentary support.

More influential in Dante's intellectual formation was the presence of the Dominican and Franciscan schools of theology in Florence. Almost all of Dante's life ran parallel to those decades of the first and stormiest period in the history of Thomism: the clash of the Franciscans and the Dominicans. Thomas's thought and the repercussions of that strife must have reached the youthful Dante as he started his philosophical education in Florence "ne le scuole de li religiosi e a le disputazioni de li filosofanti" (*Conv.* 2. 12.7) at Santa Croce or at Santa Maria Novella, the Florentine houses of the Franciscans and the Dominicans, respectively.

Concerning the theme of the fourth sphere of Dante's *Paradise*, let us recall that Dante had just passed three heavens, those of the Moon, Mercury, and Venus, and was now in the Heaven of the Sun: the Heaven of the wise men, the "Sapientes," the theologians. He had just thanked God for the special privilege of being on the planet—for the creatures, a visible image of the invisible Creator—when, with Beatrice, he was surrounded by a garland of twelve stars sparkling brilliantly, even against the effulgently bright background of the sun.

The stars are twelve spirits. Their leader is a Dominican, Thomas Aquinas. He introduces the companions of his circle (from the right, Albert of Cologne, Gratian, Peter Lombard, Solomon, Dionysius, Orosius, Boethius, Isidore of Seville, Bede, Richard of St. Victor, Siger of Brabant), delivers a splendid eulogy on Saint Francis, and deplores the deterioration of his own order.

When Thomas falls silent, a second garland, also consisting of twelve stars, gathers outside the first. The leader is the Franciscan Bonaventure da Bagnoregio, who introduces the spirits of his circle, delivers a splendid eulogy on Saint Dominic, and denounces his order's degeneracy. The structure has a contentious note. And Thomas's character emerges here as important in the history of his order, in the Church, and in theological thought as it was culturally fixed in Dante's mind.

Within fifty short years of the death of their founders (Dominic in 1221, Francis in 1226), the two great orders—which indeed had reshaped the thought of Western Christianity in the generation before Dante's birth, and of which the poet undoubtedly had a divinely providential concept of their appearance in the course of history[9]—had already distorted the particular purpose for which they had both been established.

In the *Divine Comedy*, Dante—obviously in keeping with the customary narrative technique of creating emblematic characters—needed a personality in each order who could be a scourge as well as a model, an impressive leading figure who could simultaneously criticize and spur a reorganization of his own order according to its original purpose. The poet saw, in the history of these two orders, Thomas and Bonaventure as their best representative figures. Each, as spokesman for his own circle, is an extoller as well as a censor. Each lauds the founder of the *other* order, reprimands his own, and recalls for each order its own founder.

The literary device, suggested by each order's courteous practice of inviting a member of the other to preach at the founder's feast, creates alternating, crossing lines of truly effective praise and blame. The resulting dramatic contrast vividly concretizes the conflicting reality the two orders had felt on earth—both in their internal life, overwhelmed by cupidity and temporal ambitions, and in their mutual relations, divided by hatred and contention. So the orders had thwarted the example of their founders, for whom "ad un fine fur l'opere sue" (*Par.* 10.42), as Thomas stresses, and "elli ad una militaro" (*Par.* 11.32), as Bonaventure in tandem remarks.

At the end of the thirteenth and beginning of the fourteenth centuries, the years of Dante's activity, the rivalries between these two orders were not only a matter of scandalous exhibition in the body of the Church but also had dangerous repercussions in the field of knowledge as transmitted in the primary temples of speculative thought in the West.

This situation was largely due to doctrinal controversies, aroused during the second half of the thirteenth century and caused by the new trend led by the Dominican Thomas Aquinas, in the philosophical and theological fields. Aquinas's deliberate choice of Aristotle as the preeminent guide of his thought evoked violent opposition from the Neoplatonic tradition.

To the conservative theologians Thomism seemed to undermine the entire Augustinian system, threatening the sanctioned dogmas of sound theology. "The house of God is full of fraudulent thinkers,"[10] stormed the traditionalists, who were predominantly led by the Franciscans Peter Olivi, Bonaventure da Bagnoregio, and John Peckam. The climax occurred in 1282 when the Franciscan General Chapter at Strassburg imposed—officially for its order—as the interpretation of

Thomism, William de La Mare's *Correctorium*,[11] a "correction" of Thomas Aquinas's system on the paradigm of Augustine and Bonaventure.

The entire work is nothing more than an openly neo-Augustinian attack on Thomism. A Dominican counterattack was inevitable. It called the *Correctorium* of William de La Mare *Corruptorium* (corruption), and a series of polemical writings under the title *Correctorium corruptorii* ("Correction of corruption") was issued. Esprit de corps bound the Dominicans to their "Frater Thomas," and a series of General Chapters imposed Aquinas's doctrine as normative for the order: "Cum doctrina venerabilis doctoris Fratris Thomae de Aquino sanior et communior reputetur et eam Ordo noster specialiter prosequi teneatur, inhibemus districte,"[12] with the obligation to punish severely (acriter) those who dared to disobey. An impressive example—which could have reached Dante—is the case of the Dominican professor Uberto Guidi, "florentinus," who, having publicly criticized Thomas's doctrine, was removed (ca. 1315) from his "chair" and punished by being made "to live on bread and water for ten days."[13] But what really suffered was sound and free research for truth. The ingenious intuitions of one mind became the autocracy of many.

It is against the background of such turbulent circumstances that we must view the characterization of Thomas Aquinas in the *Comedy*. Dante, with the figure of Aquinas and the cooperation of Bonaventure as his counterpart in the Heaven of the Sun, tries to reconcile opposites, to reestablish balance—at least in Heaven.

Another aspect of Thomas's presence in the *Comedy* is the remarkable intuition with which Dante perfectly captured the principal characteristic of Thomism in the history of theological thought, even when the system of Aquinas and his writings were still in the process of diffusion and study. In choosing Thomas as leader of a group of selected thinkers in contrast to Bonaventure, the speaker of another selected group, Dante showed that he recognized what later historians have called "intellectualism" and "voluntarism" in the Scholastic system of theology of that period—in other words, that in the development of the "disciplina theologica" between the end of the thirteenth century and the beginning of the fourteenth two trends took form. One, primarily intellectual under Aristotle's influence, had as its leader Aquinas, who was for the supremacy of the *intellect*, holding that *beatitudo*—the final natural good of the intellectual creature—is essentially an act of "knowledge," or an intuitive action. This trend was antithetical to the Franciscan school, which claimed supremacy for "voluntas," stressing as the final natural good of the human mind the activity of the "will." Evidently, Dante's main intention was to reconcile these opposites, bringing the two parts into a unity so that they would not be antagonistic but complementary.

This historical characteristic of Thomism is also fixed by Dante through some rhetorical refinements in the *Comedy*'s external literary structure. It is significant that Thomas's first appearance is in the tenth canto of the *Paradiso*. Each tenth canto of the poem is, in some way, the specific canto of the power of human reason as "intellectus." In canto 10 of the *Inferno*, Dante condemned the materialists, that is, those who have denied the intellect's power of acquiring metaphysical truth. In canto 10 of the *Purgatorio* is the turning point, for human reason, from physical to metaphysical reality. In canto 10 of the *Paradiso* are the theologians, those who pushed the power of the human intellect to the ultimate goal of metaphysical speculation: God.

Dante could have found Thomism's keynote in his favorite book by Thomas, the *Summa contra gentiles* (the only work of Thomas that Dante mentions by title and from which he reproduces passages), where Aquinas most clearly and drastically states: "In nullo alio quaerenda est ultima felicitas quam in operatione intellectus; cum nullum desiderium tam in sublime ferat sicut desiderium intelligentiae veritatis" (3.50). Dante's concept corresponds perfectly with the way in which historians interpreted Aquinas through many centuries: as the pure emotionless viewer of pure naked truth.

Although today, especially after the studies by B. Nardi and E. Gilson,[14] Dante's complete adherence to Aquinas's thought cannot be supported, it is nevertheless impossible to deny that in the *Divine Comedy* he assigned Thomas a unique standing among all the other characters: he appears in more cantos than any other character (five) and has the longest speech (almost three hundred verses). And it must be noted that at the time Dante was writing Thomas was not yet canonized (his canonization occurred in 1323) and harsh controversies still surrounded his doctrine.

One of the most debated aspects of the figure of Thomas Aquinas as presented by Dante is the unexpectedly high praise extended in the *Paradiso* by Thomas to one of the most contentious of his colleagues of the Faculty of the Arts in Paris and one of the most controversial thinkers of the thirteenth century, Siger of Brabant, against whom Thomas fought on earth and who is now side by side with him in Heaven among the "Sapientes," the wise men.

Siger was born in Brabant around 1225. By his thirties he was already one of the most distinguished professors of the University of Paris's arts faculty: "Magistrum magnum, in philosophia maiorem qui tunc esset Parisius,"[15] reported Giles of Rome, who met Siger about this time in Paris. Siger, like Thomas, was an Aristotelian and thus fiercely opposed by the Neoplatonic traditionalists. But during the decade from 1260 to 1270 Siger emerged as a leader of a movement within Aristotelianism, called by modern scholars Latin-Averroism, which its supporters claimed was the true interpretation of Aristotle's thought. Siger incurred stiff opposition from Aquinas, who was working to reconcile Aristotle with Christian thought. For Thomas the Aristotelian system was perfectly adaptable to Christian orthodoxy if only it were purged of Averroistic accretions. For Siger, on the contrary, Averroes was the only interpreter who truly understood Aristotle, although some of his fundamental principles were in opposition to Christian faith. In 1270 Aquinas launched against Siger the lucid treatise *De unitate intellectus contra Averroistas*, a systematic refutation of monopsychism. Siger barricaded himself behind the division of philosophy from theology—namely, the idea that reason can reach conclusions different from those of faith, but that any resultant unorthodoxy was Averroes's and Aristotle's, not his own. Thomas insinuated that Siger secretly (*in angulis*)[16] was concealing his own convictions behind the thought of Averroes.

In addition to the conflict within the Aristotelian school, we should note that both Thomas and Siger were criticized by more conservative theologians both for Aristotelianism and for some individual theses they developed (for example, on free will and determinism, the capability of the human mind, the eternity of the world, the interrelation between matter and spirit in creatures, the attributes and power of the first cause, and so on). In fact, a strong revival of anti-Aristotelianism had been spearheaded by the conservative Augustinists, mainly Franciscan thinkers. As a result of this, in December 1270 the bishop of Paris, Etienne Tempier, condemned thirteen propositions that were clearly Averroistic in tendency and could easily be traced to Siger of Brabant. The bishop had been pushed into this situation by the strong Augustinists of the university's theology faculty, against one of whom,

John Peckam, Thomas had written *De aeternitate mundi* in the early months of 1270.[17] Because of these anti-Aristotelian attitudes, Tempier's action could also be viewed as a criticism of the Aristotelian Thomas.

No names were specified in the condemnations. Both Thomas and Siger continued to work at the university. But jealousy and envy continued among the faculty, which later came to be divided into the "pars Sigerii" and that of his adversaries.[18] For Siger, Paris became an uncomfortable place, and he left the university. But the conservative theologians' influence persisted, and in March 1277 the bishop of Paris issued a more severe sentence: 219 propositions were condemned. Of them, sixteen are known to have been by Thomas Aquinas.

By 1277 Thomas had been dead for three years. Just a few months before the condemnation was issued, however, Siger, suspected of heresy, was summoned before the Inquisition. He appealed to the pope and traveled to Italy. Information regarding Siger around this time is almost nil. Between 1276—when he possibly left for Italy—and 1284—when we have the first record of his death as having already occurred—he could have met three popes, all involved in Dante's *Comedy*: John XXI (1276–77), "Pietro Spano, lo qual giù luce in dodici libelli" (*Par.* 12.134–35), the only pope Dante placed in Paradise, in the fourth Heaven among the Sages, with Siger, but in the opposite garland guided by Bonaventure; Nicolas III (1277–80) of the Orsini family, whom Dante fixed in Hell among the simonists (*Inf.* 19); and Martin IV (1281–84), fond of the "anguille di Bolzena e la vernaccia" (*Purg.* 24.24), in life Simon de Brion, who in 1266, as papal legate at Paris, had achieved a reconciliation with Siger, then the leader of dissenters in the Faculty of Arts (this is the first time that Siger's name is ever historically recorded). We do not know what happened between him and these popes. However, there is no document to prove that a pope ever condemned Siger. He remained for a few years in the papal curia, only to be murdered at Orvieto (as we know from sonnet 92 of the *Fiore*, a work disputedly attributed to Dante) on an uncertain date between 1281 and 1284, by his servant, a demented cleric.[19]

Siger was a prominent philosopher and, in the context of his time, a daring innovator. As Dante testifies, he was an impressive thinker for his generation. Strangely enough, he was ignored for centuries. Actually he is a rediscovery of the past century, and interest in him was kindled by a six-verse passage of the *Paradiso* (10.133–38). Now his works are published and studied. Curiously, he was as controversial in his own generation as he is in ours: for one scholar, Siger was an Aristotelian who became a heretic (Mandonnet);[20] for another, Siger was a heretic who became a Thomist (Van Steenberghen);[21] and for a third—stranger yet—Siger was a teacher of very secondary importance who had nothing to do with the doctrinal infighting and subsequent condemnations at Paris, whereby the critical-historical reconstruction of a hundred and fifty years of research is totally wiped out (Gauthier).[22]

For Dante, there was no doubt that Siger was a prestigious thinker, one of the wise men who enlightened the world. But Dante could not have been unaware of the polemical treatise of one of the leaders of his own theological school, Thomas's De unitate intellectus contra Averroistas, written against "Magister Sigerius." Nor could the poet have been ignorant of the Paris condemnations of 1270 and 1277, since some of those propositions totally undermined the very structure upon which his entire Comedy stood.[23]

Historians and literary critics are still puzzling over the significance of Dante's placement of Siger in Heaven among the Sages and having him praised there by his adversary on earth, Thomas Aquinas. Opinions are many, and they have all been presented in our time. The first commentators on the Comedy totally ignored this jarring Dantesque outcome. It seems they had very few elements on which to build their knowledge of the Brabantine teacher. They limit themselves to rewriting in prose what Dante wrote in verse. Citing only one of Siger's works, Lana, Ottimo, Buti, and Anonimo Fiorentino refer to him vaguely as a dialectic or a philosopher who taught in Paris.[24] Only Pietro Alighieri, in his first commentary of the year 1340, calls Siger "magnus philosophus et theologus";[25] but twenty years later he translated his father's verses verbatim.[26] Benvenuto da Imola, usually more generous with chronical information than any of the other commentators, writing about fifty years after Dante's death, confused Siger with the legendary "Doctor parisiensis"[27] mentioned not too many years earlier in Jacopo Passavanti's Lo specchio della vera penitenza by the name of "Maestro Ser Lò,"[28] whose story can also be found in Jacopo da Varazze's Legenda aurea,[29] which in turn can be traced back to the Speculum historiale by Vincent of Beauvais,[30] who had died some years before the true Siger began his disputations at the University of Paris. But more astonishing and inexplicable is the position of Dante's commentator, Giovanni da Serravalle, a Franciscan, a bishop, and one of the expert theologians of Pope Gregory XII at the Council of Constance (1415–17), who in a 1416 commentary on the *Comedy*—written during the intervals of the council for two English bishops previously associated with Oxford University—repeats the same story ("Siger–Ser Lò") as he had heard it from Benvenuto, whose lectures on Dante he had attended in Ferrara about thirty-five years before.[31]

With Siger's death a veil of oblivion was drawn over his memory—and probably by intention. At that time, indeed, and only within the span of a generation, when the strife between church and empire was rekindled by Henry VII (ca. 1310) and Louis of Bavaria (ca. 1324), the word *Averroist* had become, in one school of thought, almost synonymous with heretic, as can be seen in a work written specifically against Dante a few years after his death: *De reprobatione monarchiae contra Dantem,* by the Dominican Guido Vernani.[32] Commentators on the *Comedy,* even those presumably well versed in Scholasticism and theology, have ignored Siger for centuries.[33] His rediscovery can now be traced back to the year 1845, and was due to J. V. Le Clerc, who passed on his research to F. Ozanam who, in turn, published it in the second edition of his highly acclaimed work, *Dante et la philosophie catholique au triezième siècle.*[34] Later research on Siger became more intense, spurred primarily—with Renan's interest in Averroism[35]—by the nascent neo-scholasticism which produced the most solid scholars in the field of research and rediscovery of Siger.

Today, the figure of Siger of Brabant can be rather well delineated by drawing from both historical documents and his published works. Contemporary commentators on Dante generally refer to those neo-scholastics as their primary sources for the subject, particularly to Mandonnet, Van Steenberghen, Gilson, and Nardi, who were well versed in the Scholasticism of the thirteenth and fourteenth centuries, as well as in Siger and Dante studies.

These scholars explain Dante's placement of Siger in Paradise with the Sages, amid Thomas's praises, in different ways, sometimes in disagreement obviously based on ideas gathered from their own research on Siger, along with their particular conceptions of the factions and doctrinal conflicts of the time.

Pierre Mandonnet—among the pioneers in the rediscovery of Siger who made a substantial contribution to the reconstruction of the historical figure, the cultural environment, and the proper thought of the

Brabantine—was the first to point out the problem posed by Siger's presence in Dante's Paradise and to present a solution. Convinced of Dante's absolute adherence to Thomistic thought and belief that Averroism was a heretical doctrine, Mandonnet has maintained that Dante did not know the true thought of the Brabantine and therefore placed Siger in the Heaven of the Sages exclusively as a pure "Philosopher," a representative of Aristotelianism, and as in some way connected with Thomas.[36] Such a hypothesis cannot be sustained today, when we know that Dante was not at all the strict follower of Thomism that Mandonnet believed; [37] nor did Averroism constitute so compact and defined a unity of thought as to have been circumscribed within a proper system.[38] Besides, even Aristotelianism was not accepted without criticism, some of it coming even from Siger himself.[39]

F. Van Steenberghen, who found in Siger's works a gradual development of his philosophical thought—so much so that the Brabantine could later change from a radical Averroist to a true admirer and even disciple of Thomism—explains in this way the poet's decision to put Siger in the Heaven of the Sages with Thomas's eulogy.[40] It is necessary to point out that Van Steenberghen's affirmations on the progressive development of Siger's thought are not unanimously accepted by critics today, primarily because of the uncertain chronology of Siger's works. But even if such affirmations were consistent, the reason for such a deduction for Siger's presence in Dante's Paradise would rest on the same premises as Mandonnet's, which are untenable. Moreover, Van Steenberghen's explanation does not correspond precisely to the literary meaning of the Comedy's text. In fact, according to his conclusions, in the Heaven of the Sun we actually have a Thomist praising a Thomist, and this would not explain verse 138, Par. 10, which is Thomas's praise of Siger as the one who "silogizzò invidïosi veri," an expression that clearly makes Siger's persona the focal point of a controversy, which is not addressed in Van Steenberghen's solution. His explanation totally lacks recognition of the spirit of reconciliation on which Dante's creation of the Heaven of the Sun is structured. Consequently, it must be pointed out that this scholar's hypothesis does not take into account the symmetrical structural order with which Dante imbues images and figures in contraposition to illustrate those meanings the Sages pursued in their search for truth. In this case, the order is shown by the figures of Thomas-Siger as counterparts to Bonaventure-Joachim of Fiori, of the opposite circle. It is, of course, the usual logic of the hierarchy of concepts—derived from Aristotle—that obtains here for the poet in his diversified perspectives of the moral and physical structure of the *Comedy*'s world.

That was precisely what E. Gilson considered in solving the present problem. He has presented one of the most accurate and analytical studies we have on the subject by disputing, from various perspectives, the theses of both Mandonnet and Van Steenberghen.[41] According to Gilson, in the fourth Heaven, Dante intended his Sages to signify aspects of divine wisdom distributed among human beings, each aspect acting independently but living in harmony and thus bringing about—in this world—that justice and order which Dante theorized and dreamed of in his *Convivio* and *Monarchia*. In this case, Siger represents philosophy, autonomous in its own sphere, independent and separate from theology—in Gilson's own words, as "une science [Philosophy] de la raison naturelle pure, et la théologie, sagesse de la foi, n'a pas autorité sur la morale naturelle ni sur la politique dont cette morale pose les fondaments."[42] Some of Dante's modern commentators have received this solution well, particularly because of an implied autobiographical reflex—derivable from it—in which the poet can be seen as Siger. Dante, too, in fact, because of his Sigerian Averroistic leanings, had proposed dangerous truths—in his case, for the political-religious conflict between the "Imperium et Sacerdotium."

Gilson's solution was refuted, the year after it was published, by B. Nardi, on the premise that it is based on the fact, which Gilson took for granted as indisputable, that the *Comedy* is the poetic transposition of Dante's thought as found in the *Convivio* and the *Monarchia*. For Nardi—according to whom Dante in the *Comedy* subjected his whole thought to a profound revision, particularly in the relation between philosophy and theology[43]—and for many contemporary critics—in whose view Dante changed even his political theory (notwithstanding P. G. Ricci's studies indicating that the *Monarchia* was written after the *Paradiso*)[44]—the *Comedy* is still considered to be the last stage in the evolution of Dante's thought and a complete reversal of his initial thinking. In the *Comedy*, Dante's thesis of the equality of the powers of church and state, as upheld in the *Monarchia*, changed into one of the supremacy of the Church.[45]

But, leaving aside these controversial arguments and returning to more stable ground, there are positive contextual proofs—and, in my judgment, incontrovertible ones—that make it impossible to embrace

Gilson's theory. What is unconvincing about it is the idea that the poet would have wanted to place a representative of "pure philosophy" or "a mere philosopher" in his Heaven of the Sages, a "sphere" started with the "signum Trinitatis" (*Par.* 10.1–3), in the name of the divine Wisdom ("guardando nel suo Figlio" [*Par.* 10.1]), in an intellectual proceeding of a theological operation (the order of the universe—reflection of God—"gustato" and "rimirato" [*Par.* 10.6] by the human mind), and where it is explicitly stated that these characters are spirits of "la quarta famiglia de l'alto *Padre* che sempre la sazia, mostrando come *spira* e come *figlia*" (*Par.* 10.49–51).

In other words, if Dante placed Siger in the Heaven of the Sun, he did so because he did not truly consider him a mere philosopher but a theologian. Moreover, the precise concept of "Sapientia," which Dante must *signify* in his *Paradiso*, cannot by its *definition*—or by its very nature—not imply as object the divinity. Thus, Dante excludes the possibility of placing in the Heaven of the Sun, the reflection of divine light, any figure that does not in itself imply the science that is a reflection of the divinity. Dante had acquired this concept, not only from Scholastic or whatever ecclesiastical sources he may have used, but also from pagan writings (in whatever way they may be interpreted)—to be precise, from his "Seneca morale," who in writing to Lucilius, stated: "Dicam inter sapientiam et philosophiam quid intersit. Sapientia perfectum bonum est mentis humanae. Philosophia sapientiae amor est et adfectatio. Haec eo tendit, quo illa pervenit. Philosophia unde dicta est apparet. Ipso enim nomine fatetur quid amet. Sapientiam quidam ita finierunt ut dicerent divinorum et humanorum scientiam. Quidam ita sapientia est nosse divina et humana et horum causas."[46]

A more telling argument comes to us from Siger himself, who in one of his works clearly expressed what he meant by true "sapientia theologica"—the only kind the poet could signify in his *Paradiso*. In his *Quaestiones in metaphysicam*, which also deals with the difference between philosophy and theology, Siger endowed theology alone, syllogistically excluding theodicy, with the proper attribute of "Sapientia," the only one that fits Dante's Heaven of the Sun: "Illa scientia dicetur magis sapientia quae maiorem cognitionem et certiorem habet de primis principiis entium. Sed sicut ex praedictis apparet, theologia quae sacra scriptura est, ipsa maiorem et certiorem cognitionem habet de ipsis quam ista theologia, cum sint nota in ea per divinam revelationem, ad quam cognitionem non potest pertingere ratio humana per se, et ita nec ista theologia quae dicitur pars philosophiae, cum ipsa consideret solum illa quae per inventionem et rationem humanam, lumine et ratione naturali, sciri possunt. Hinc est quod illa est magis sapientia quam ista."[47] It is very clear: for Siger, the spirit of wisdom in the pursuit of the truth is that which is revealed by Holy Scripture, by Revelation, by theology. One last argument against Gilson's solution could be deduced from the condemnation of March 7, 1277—already mentioned—in which Aquinas and Siger were involved. In it, propositions which state, against the "sapientia theologica," that the only superior "sapientia" is the "sapientia huius mundi," were explicitly censured (Prop. 40: "Quod non est excellentior status quam vacare philosophiae"; and Prop. 154: "Quod sapientes mundi sunt philosophi tantum"—such condemnations could have been directly against Boethius of Dacia).[48]

A last solution to the problem that seems to have been accepted by Dante's current interpreters is the one expressed by Nardi in his studies on Siger and reiterated a quarter of a century later in Nardi's criticism of Gilson. Nardi believes that the poet placed Siger in his fourth Heaven to "rialzare la memoria d'un onesto pensatore, grandemente stimato dai suoi contemporanei, la quale giaceva sotto il peso dei colpi inferti dall'invidia, e mostrarci riconciliati nel cospetto della verità eterna due grandi pensatori a lui cari, senza settarismo di scuola."[49] This solution could well have been reached because of Nardi's own interpretation of the controversial explanation of the "individïosi veri" (*Par.* 10.138), which seems to have caused unjust suffering to the Brabantine thinker.

It is, however, this last explanation that has become the most widely accepted among Dante's commentators. It is still accepted and taught today, and some have wanted to combine it with Gilson's previously mentioned theory.[50] Such a solution, however, is not very convincing, especially if one ponders other reasons not considered by Nardi, specifically, two relevant facts—one chronological, the other logistic—present in the poet's mind when he was structuring his fourth sphere: the knowledge he might have had of Siger's intellectual personality at the time of writing and his criterion of selecting suitable characters for his fourth Heaven.

First, from some documents still extant, we know that at the time of Dante's writing Siger's intellectual personality was still well known and highly respected. But this does not mean that he did not have any adversaries. After all, the figure of Thomas Aquinas was also controversial at the same time. In the Pierre Dubois's *De recuperatione terrae sanctae*, written around 1306, a quarter-century after Siger's death, there is a clearly expressed eulogium to the excellent "Magister Sigerius": "Praecellentissimus doctor philosophiae magister Sigerius de Brabantia."[51] And in another passage the author refers to *Quaestiones naturales*, a compendium of selected sentences from the writings of Thomas, Siger, and other thinkers whom he recommends: "Item expediret quod quaestiones naturales haberent extractas de scriptis tam fratris Thomae, quam Sigerii et aliorum doctorum."[52] It is therefore inaccurate to say that Dante had to resurrect Siger's fame.

Second, one must keep in mind that when the poet was making his intellectual choice of the twenty-four sages, his selection could delve into a culture circumscribed by the limits neither of particular time nor space but one whose historical spectrum was universal in scope. Dante, in fact, was absorbed in the task of expressing the configuration of Christian knowledge within the history of the "humana civilitas." He viewed it as operating according to its continuity, propelled by the power of eternal values, and extending from antiquity up to the time of his contemporaries (Salomon-Siger). It is most improbable, therefore, that the poet would address himself primarily to local "groups" or "quarrels" for the purpose of judgment or a strictly contemporary critique. This, however, does not exclude the fact that Dante might have nurtured in his soul some of the sentiments expressed by Nardi, as well as by other scholars (particularly during the late-Romantic criticism at the end of the nineteenth and beginning of the twentieth centuries).[53] What should be clear is that these motives cannot have been the primary reasons for his idea of placing in his *Paradiso* Siger, as one who enlightened the world and was praised by Thomas. The solution to the problem can only be found by ascertaining what Dante could possibly have known about Siger and Averroes and how he accepted these thinkers in his own culture.

First, Dante's Averroes is not being tortured in Hell in the *Comedy* but is among the great spirits in a hemisphere of light in the Limbo of the *Sapientes pagani*. Also, it is well to note that Averroes was characterized by Thomas as "philosophiae peripateticae depravator,"[54] by the other theologians of the Faculty of Paris as "pravus hereticus," and by Duns Scotus as "maledictus." For Dante, Averroes is "wiser" than he (*Purg.* 25.63); Averroes is the mind who "il gran commento feo" (*Inf.* 4.144), and the poet twice cites him to strengthen his own ideas (*Conv.* 4. 13.8; *Mon.* 1. 3.9); Averroes belongs to the "filosofica famiglia" (*Inf.* 4.132) in the Noble Castle of Limbo. It must also be noted that Dante was neither unique nor exceptional in his favorable judgment of the thinker of Cordoba. Averroism of itself did not constitute a definitive system, one that could be included, perchance, in a specific condemnation. Also, Averroes's premises and Aristotelian interpretations were accepted and assumed in different ways by the various thinkers and followers of his thought. In the universities unorthodox thinkers as well as avowed Averroists were able to dispute such crucial questions as the relationship between reason and faith (in which Siger also participated), the existence of the soul, and so on, freely, and for centuries. One can point to the Averroism of Padua and Bologna, to Biagio of Parma, to Pomponazzi. The only exceptions to this freedom were some warnings issued to the local chapters. In fact, the only official church pronouncement was issued under Leo X in 1513.[55]

In regard to Siger, a thorough analysis of his *sententiae* shows that it is not always possible to cull from his works unorthodox—particularly controversial—elements.

On two of the main theses stated by Siger—one regarding the union of the intellect with the sensitive soul, the other regarding the creation of the nether world through the potential power of the heavens— Dante's position is very far from that of Aquinas and very close to that of Siger (who on the first thesis was very close to Albert of Cologne).[56] Moreover, in regard to the relationship between philosophy and theology, it should be noted that Siger speaks of "differences" not "divisions";[57] his "expression" runs parallel to that of Albert of Cologne,[58] a thinker no one has ever tried to condemn. (It is interesting to note that we find Albert here in the same garland with Siger and immediately to the right, as Siger is immediately to the left of Thomas [*Par.* 10.97 and 133].) There is no doubt that in Siger's texts—particularly those relating to the "bonum" of the human intellect—theology is openly assigned superiority over philosophy.[59] In contrast, in the *Convivio* Dante speaks of their relation in discordant terms. In the *Monarchia* he arrives at a separation of the two disciplines, though placing them at the same level. But in the *Commedia*, theology definitely reclaims its superiority, and philosophy becomes "ancilla theologiae." On the conflict between philosophical and theological truth, Siger never claimed the doctrine of the so-called two-fold truth, which seems to have been derived by Siger's adversaries from expressions in the texts, or Tempier's condemnation of the year 1270, or Thomas's *De unitate intellectus* (unless it is accurate to trace it back to Boethius of Dacia).

And now for the accusations of unorthodoxy: Siger was supposed to have hidden his own ideas behind his interpretation of the thought of Aristotle. However, in his commentaries he affirmed that he always faithfully presented Averroes's interpretation without discussing the value of Averroistic or Aristotelian truth in itself. On the other questions that touched more closely on the distinction between physics and metaphysics, Siger's mind was tormented by the doubt and conflict that his search for truth aroused, but in these passages of his writings, he had recourse to the maxim which he frequently repeated, almost like a refrain: "fidei adherendum est."

And, although some of Siger's adversaries believed him insincere, many facts may have led Dante to conclude the opposite. After the condemnation of 1270 (in which, it must be remembered, Siger's name was not mentioned), Siger had been able to continue teaching in Paris, which means that he either modified some of his positions or was able properly to justify himself. He showed great esteem for Thomas and Albert of Cologne ("praecipui viri in philosophia Albertus et Thomas," he wrote in one of his works).[60] Finally, there is the fact that when it came to the suspicious relations to the condemnation of 1277, Siger made his appeal to the pope himself, which certainly demonstrates how absolutely convinced he was that his own theses were perfectly orthodox. Siger did fear, however, that a judgment rendered in Paris could be negatively influenced by the envy of the university's faculty. Probably, such a possibility is alluded to in the *Divine Comedy* by Thomas when he introduces Siger:

> "Essa è la luce etterna di Sigieri,
> che, leggendo nel Vico de li Strami,
> silogizzò *invidïosi* veri."
> (*Par.* 10. 136–38)

But Dante could have found Siger's honesty in the scholar's own writings. Siger clearly stated in his *De anima intellectiva*, when discussing the crucial problem of the unity of the intellect: "Mihi dubium fuit a longo tempore quid vi naturalis rationis praedicto problemate sit tenendum, et quid senserit Philosophus de dicta quaestione, et ideo, in tali dubio, fidei adherendum est quae omnem rationem humanam superat" ("for a long time I was in doubt about what should be held on this problem on the basis of natural reason, and what the Philosopher [Aristotle] felt about it; in such a doubt, one must adhere to faith, which surpasses all human reason").[61] It is in relation to this statement, or more properly this open confession, that Thomas's words in the Comedy must be understood:

> "Questi onde a me ritorna il tuo riguardo,
> è 'l lume d'uno spirto che 'n pensieri
> gravi a morir li parve venir tardo"
> (Par. 10. 133–35)

—"in his [Siger's] grave thoughts, death seemed slow in coming," which means that Siger was eager to die, to see at last in Heaven the definitive end to his doubts.

Actually, the real, historical Siger, although stressing and fighting for the absolute power of human reason and its autonomy in the proper sphere of the mind's speculation, always recognized the possibility of error and the mind's limitations: the ultimate appeal had to be to faith, to theology. And this is precisely Dante's concept of human reason in the Comedy, as the poet perfectly personified it in the character of Virgil, from his first appearance at the edge of the "selva selvaggia aspra e forte" (Inf. 1.5) to his last silent walk and imminent disappearance in the "divina foresta spessa e viva" (Purg. 28.2). In this entire span of activity, Virgil possesses a high mastery and a thorough command of natural knowledge but also shows limitations and the potential to err, so that he must appeal, ultimately, to Beatrice—"theology."

More specifically, Siger recognizes that human reason—in its speculative and rational operation—is limited in its efforts to investigate the "quidditas" of an essence that is superior to the human. He does not deny, however, that this superior essence (God) may give to human reason a power (lumen gratiae) that might help it to know, in some "modus," this superhuman "quidditas." In fact, this is what happens to Dante at the end of his journey in the world beyond, when his mind perceives a direct vision of the two highest and deepest mysteries of any created mind, the Trinity and the humanity of God, in their own perfect symbiosis. Dante tells us only that the event *has* taken place; but *how* it has taken place is impossible for the human mind to grasp:

> "Qual è 'l geomètra che tutto s'affige
> per misurar lo cerchio, e non ritrova,
> pensando, quel principio ond'elli indige,
> tal era io a quella vista nova:
> veder volea come si convenne
> l'imago al cerchio e come vi s'indova;
> ma non eran da ciò le proprie penne;
> se non che [and here the *lumen gratiae* intervenes] la
>   mia mente fu percossa
> da un fulgore, in che sua voglia venne"
>
> (*Par.* 33.133–41)

So Siger is placed in Heaven, not exclusively as the symbol of pure philosophy, the activity of the human mind in its natural processes of logical reasoning, but as philosophy buttressed in its limitations by theology. In Dante's *Paradiso*, he stands as the mediator of the problematic nature of the correlation between physics and metaphysics, philosophy and theology, in man's attempts to find truth—and even to safeguard the faith, as Dante might have seen it.

In conclusion, to return to the two personae in opposition at the beginning of my discussion, I would like to say that Aquinas and Siger juxtaposed in *Paradiso* exemplify a sure sign of "concordia discors." Dante's choice of Thomas, Siger's great adversary on earth, as his great eulogist in Heaven is a highly original stroke of poetic intuition. The poet not only reveals to the reader an aspect of his speculative mind but also clearly places before the mind of every researcher and every scholar in every age the golden rule that Dante learned from Augustine and that must guide all those who seek truth: "In veritate unitas, in dubiis libertas, in errore caritas" (In matters of truth, let there be unity; in matters of doubt, let there be freedom; in matters of error, let there be charity").

Catholic University

NOTES

1. Cf. Angelo Waltz, O.P., *San Tommaso d'Aquino* (Rome: Edizioni Liturgiche, 1945), pp. 157–59; Robert Davidson, *Geschichte von Florenz* (Berlin: E. S. Mittler und sohn, 1896), 2:84.

2. Cf. Innocenzo Taurisano, O.P., "Discepoli e biografi di S. Tommaso," in *S. Tommaso d'Aquino O.P. Miscellanea Storica-Artistica* (Rome: Società Tipografica A. Manuzio, 1924), pp. 139–43; M. Grabmann, "Fra Remigio Girolami discepolo di S. Tommaso d'Aquino e maestro di Dante," *La scuola cattolica* 53 (1925): 267–81; 347–68.

3. Cf. Fratris Johannis De Serravalle, *Translatio et Comentum totius libri Dantis Aldigherii cum textu italico Fratris Bartholomei a Colle,* ed. Fr. Marcellino da Civezza, M.O., e Fr. Teofilo Domenichelli, M.O. (Prato: ex officina libraria Giachetti, Filii et Soc., 1891), pp. 15 and 21.

4. M. A. F. Ozanam, *Dante et la philosophie catholique au triezième siècle,* new ed. (Louvain: C. J. Fonteyn, Libraire-Editeur, 1847), pp. 259–65; *Commedia di Dante Allighieri . . .* esposta e commentata da Antonio Lubin (Padua: Stabilimento della Ditta Pessada), cf. note on *Par.* 10.133–38.

5. Lorenzo Mehus, *Ambrosii Traversarii generalis camaldulensium . . . Latinae Epistulae . . . Adcedit eiusdem Ambrosii Vita . . .* (Florence: ex Typographio Caeserao, 1759), p. clxix.

6. Benvenuto wrote: "Nam iste [Dante] dedit se in iuventute omnibus artibus liberalibus studio bononie padue etiam postea studuit parisiis in sacra theologia circa tres annos" (*Codex Laurentian Ashburnham 839,* c. 6v; hereafter *Cod. Laurent. Ashbur.*). G. da Serravalle, who followed only this Ferrarese commentary, interpreted the "postea" of this text as a temporal preposition still related to young Dante's education, while Benvenuto da Imola, as is evident from his last commentary, meant the "postea" to relate to the period of Dante's exile.

7. S. Reinach, "L'Enigme de Siger," *Revue historique* 151 (1926): 34–47.

8. Robert L. John, *Dante Templare* (Milan: Editore Ulrico Hoepli, 1987), p. 17 (Italian translation of *Dante* [Vienna: Spring-Verlag, 1946]).

9. Cf. *Par.* 11.28–35; 11.118–23; 12.106. As a consequence of v. 106, *Par.* 12, some commentators interpreted the "due ruote" of *Purg.* 29.107 as symbols of the two orders, Dominican and Franciscan. Cf. *Dante Alighieri, La Divina Commedia,* ed. Dino Provenzal (Verona: Edizioni Mondatori, 1949), 2:573–74, nn. 106–8, and 3:732–33, nn. 106–11; *Dante Alighieri, La Divina Commedia,* ed. Carlo Steiner and rev. Maria Dozzi Vasta (Turin: G. B. Paravia & C., 1966), 2:388, n. 107.

10. Cf. C. T. Martin, *Registrum epistolarum fr. Johannis Peckham archiepiscopi cantuariensis* (London: Longman and Co., 1885), 3:871.

11. Cf. Pierre Félix Mandonnet, *Siger de Brabant et l'averroïsme latin au XIIIme siècle* (Louvain: Institut supérieur de philosophie de l'Université, 1911), 1:402.

12. The formula was stated and reiterated at the Dominican General Chapters of Metz (1313), London (1314), and Bologna (1315); cf. Witold Wehr, "Tommaso D'Aquino," in *Enciclopedia Cattolica,* 12:281 (Vatican City: Ente per l'Enciclopedia Cattolica, 1959).

13. Cf. Innocenzo Taurisano, O.P., "Discepoli e biografi di S. Tommaso," in *S. Tommaso D'Aquino O.P.—Miscellanea Storica-Artistica* (Rome: Società Tipografica A. Manuzio, 1924), pp. 143–45. The severity of the punishment might be explained by the place and the time of Guidi's attack. The two Dominicans Remigio de' Girolami and Nicola Brunacci (called by Albert of Cologne "the second Thomas Aquinas") were strenuous propagators of Thomism, as well as the leading theologians of the Florentine "studium" (where Guidi gave his speech). At the same period, they were working with Fra Tolomeo da Lucca for the canonization of Thomas in order to authenticate his doctrine.

14. B. Nardi, *Dante e la cultura medioevale* (Bari: Laterza, 1942), pp. 186–209, and 244–54; idem, *Saggi di filosofia dantesca* (Milan: Perrella, 1930), pp. 35–48; E. Gilson, *Dante et la philosophie* (Paris: Librairie J. Vrin, 1939), pp. 151–222.

15. *In II Sententiae* dist. 17, Q. 2, a. I; Giles of Rome is one of the authors known by Dante (*Conv.* 4.xxiv. 9).

16. Thomas Aquinas, *De unitate intellectus contra Averroistas* 5.436.

17. Cf. I. Brady, "John Peckham and the Background to *De aeternitate mundi* of St. Thomas Aquinas," in *St. Thomas Aquinas 1274–1974* (Toronto: Pontifical Institute of Medieval Studies, 1974).

18. Cf. H. Denifle-E. Châtélain, *Chartularium Universitatis Parisiensis* (Paris: ex typis fratrum Delalain, 1889), 1:523 and 527.

19. Cf. "Martini continuatio brabantina," in *Monumenta germaniae historica*, p. 263: "Huius tempore [of emperor Rudolph, d. 1299] floruit Albertus de ordine Praedicatorum, doctrina et scientia mirabilis, qui magistrum Sygerium, natione Brabantinus, eo quod quasdam opiniones contra fidem tenuerat, Parisius subsistere non valens, Romanam curiam adiit ibique post parvum tempus a clerico suo quasi dementi perfossus periit." The chronicle must have been written around 1308 (see pp. 259–60).

20. See pp. 156–57 and p. 169 n. 36.

21. See pp. 157–58 and p. 169 n. 40.

22. R. A. Gauthier, "Notes sur Siger de Brabant. I. Siger en 1265," *Revue des sciences philosophiques et theologiques* 67 (1983): 201–32; and idem, "Notes sur Siger de Brabant. II. Siger en 1272–1275, Aubry de Reims et le scission des Normandes," *Revue des sciences philosophiques et theologiques* 68 (1984): 3–49. The author maintains that, during the conflict at the University of Paris in 1265–66, Siger was merely teaching his *Quaestiones in III de anima* and was only a secondary figure among the faculty, not its turbulent leader. Also, in the *Quaestiones in III de anima* there are no original ideas, but Siger borrows from Thomas's *Sententiae*; and even in his interpretation of Averroes, he borrows from other theologians. The original thought of the Brabantine does not go beyond the logical exercise of his *Impossibilia*. Moreover, the disturbances of the years 1272–75 were not caused by doctrinal conflicts but merely by infighting among the Normans of Low Normandy and the Normans of Rouen. No doubt, there are good points in Gauthier's research in analyzing some of Mandonnet's conclusions—of which, however, the critics were already suspicious. But the author completely neglected to examine and explain valuable documents regarding Siger's fame. His silence about these seriously weakens the entire body of his research and, in the particular case under consideration here, does not shed any light on the impact Siger might have had on Dante's culture.

23. A simple glance at these propositions makes the reader wonder why Dante put him in Paradise:

"1. The intellect of all men is one and numerically the same.
2. It is false or improper to say, 'Man understands.'
3. The will of man wills or chooses necessarily.
4. Everything that happens here in the sublunar world is governed by the necessity of celestial bodies.
5. The world is eternal.
6. There never was a first man.
7. The soul, which is the form of man inasmuch as he is man, corrupts on the corruption of the body.
8. The soul separated after death does not suffer from corporeal fire.

9. Free will is a passive power, not an active one; and it is moved necessarily by the appetible object.

10. God does not know singulars.

11. God does not know anything other than Himself.

12. Human actions are not governed by the providence of God.

13. God cannot grant immortality or incorruptibility to a corruptible or mortal thing."

Text abridged and reported in J. A. Weisheipl, O.P., *Friar Thomas d'Aquino, His Life, Thought, and Works* (Washington, D.C.: The Catholic University of America Press, 1983), p. 276.

24. Cf. *Commedia di Dante degli Allagherii col commento di Jacopo della Lana,* ed. Luciano Scarabelli (Bologna: Tipografia Regia, 1866), 3:177; *L'ottimo commento della Divina Commedia,* ed. Alessandro Torri (Pisa: presso Niccolò Capurro, 1829), 3:257; *Commento di Francesco da Buti sopra La Divina Commedia di Dante Allighieri,* ed. Costantino Giannini (Pisa: pei fratelli Nistri, 1860), 3:326–27; *Commento alla Divina Commedia d'anonimo fiorentino del sec. XIV,* ed. Pietro Fanfani (Bologna: presso Gaetano Romagnoli, 1874), 3:206.

25. Cf. *Petri Allegherii super Dantis ipsius genitoris Comoediam Commentarium,* ed. Vincentio Nannucci (Florence: apud Angelum Garinei, 1845), p. 623.

26. Cf. *Cod. Lauren. Ashbur. 841,* c. 267r (Pietro Alighieri's last commentary on the *Divine Comedy,* begun in ca. 1357/58).

27. Cf. *Cod. Lauren. Ashbur. 839,* c. 140v; see also *Benvenutus de Rambaldis de Imola Comentum super Dantis Aldigherij Comoediam,* ed. Jacopo Philippo Lacaita (Florence: Typis G. Barbèra, 1887), 5:47 (but in this commentary the story of Ser Lò is incomplete).

28. *Lo specchio della vera penitenza di Fr. Jacopo Passavanti fiorentino dell'Ordine de' Predicatori* (Milan: Società Tipografica dei Classici Italiani, 1808), 1:74–77 (on p. 74 is written, "Ser Lò, il quale insegnava Loica e Filosofia," a description commonly applied to Siger of Brabant by early commentators on the *Comedy*).

29. Jacopo da Varazze, *Legenda aurea,* on "All Souls' Day."

30. *Speculum historiale,* lib. 25, c. 89. Even before the account given there, a mention of the story of the "Doctor parisiensis" can be found in authors quoted by Duboulay in *Histoire de l'Université de Paris,* year 1172.

31. Cf. Fratris Johannis De Serravalle, *Translatio et Comentum totius libri Dantis Aldigherii* (n. 3 above), pp. 940–41.

32. Guido Vernani, *De reprobatione Monarchiae compositae a Dante Aligherio,* ed. Jarro [G. Piccini] (Florence: Bemporad e Figlio, 1906), pp. 8 and 10.

33. We have mentioned the case of Giovanni da Serravalle, a bishop and the official theologian for Pope Gregory XII at the Council of Constance, but three centuries later we have Pompeo Venturi (1732), followed by Baldassarre Lombardi (1791), Giosafatte Biagioli (1819), Antonio Cesari (1826), Brunone Bianchi (1854), Luigi Benassuti (1865), Giovanni Maria Cornoldi (1887), and even Giacomo Poletto, who published his commentary in the last decade of the nineteenth century (1894), a half-century after Ozanam's work (see *Dante et la philosophie catholique,* p. 15). The first commentator to capture some historical aspects of the real Siger seems to have been Domenico Palmieri (cf. *Commento alla Divina Commedia di Dante Alighieri,* ed. D. Palmieri (Prato: Tipografia Giachetti, Figlio e C., 1899), 3:167.

34. Ozanam, *Dante et la philosophie catholique* (n. 4 above), pp. 261ff.

35. "Averroès et l'Averroïsme" was J. E. Renan's dissertation for his doctorate in 1852. See Renan, *Averroès et l'Averroïsme—Essai historique*, 9th ed. (Paris: Calmann-Lévy, 1935).

36. Mandonnet, *Siger de Brabant et l'averroïsme* (n. 11 above), 1:307.

37. See above, n. 14.

38. Cf. G. Federici Vescovini, *Astrologia e Scienza—La crisi dell'aristotelismo sul cadere del Trecento e Biagio Pelacani da Parma* (Florence: Nuovedizioni Enrico Vallecchi, 1979), pp. 126ff.

39. "La filosofia e la scienza della natura dell'Occidente cristiano hanno origine con la recezione di Aristotele, che tuttavia è già all'inizio congiunta a una critica assolutamente autonoma, che, in parte, giunge a forme molto incisive. E questa critica, sia detto ancora una volta, non ha nulla a che vedere con le obiezioni mosse all'aristotelismo dal punto di vista della fede cristiana e della Chiesa, ma parla in nome della verità naturale. Grossatesta, Ruggero Bacone, Alberto Magno, Egidio Romano, perfino Sigieri di Brabante, trovano che in molti problemi e teorie specifiche Aristotele debba essere corretto, se non proprio respinto . . ."; cf. A. Maier, "Il principio della doppia verità," in *Scienza e filosofia nel medio evo* (Milan, 1984), p. 393.

40. F. Van Steenberghen, *Les Oeuvres et la doctrine de Siger de Brabant* (Brussels: Palais des Académies, 1938), pp. 78–79 and 182–83.

41. E. Gilson, *Dante et la philosophie* (Paris: Librairie Philosophique J. Vrin, 1939), pp. 256ff.

42. Cf. ibid., p. 270.

43. B. Nardi, "Dante e la filosofia," *Studi danteschi* 25 (1940; reprinted in B. Nardi, *Nel mondo di Dante* [Rome: Edizioni di storia e letteratura, 1944], pp. 209–45). It must be noted, however, that Nardi does not say here that in the *Commedia* Dante renounced his idea of the independence of the Empire from the Church; G. Giacalone must be corrected (*Dante Alighieri, La Divina Commedia*, ed. G. Giacalone [Rome: Angelo Signorelli editore, 1983], *Paradiso*, p. 103).

44. Cf. Pier Giorgio Ricci, "Monarchia," in *Enciclopedia dantesca* (Rome: Istituto della Enciclopedia Italiana, 1971), 3: 1000, cols. 2–1002, col. 1, and Bibliography.

45. "Le concezioni politiche della *Monarchia* e della *Commedia* nei riguardi della distinzione dei poteri e dei fini tra Impero e Papato, cioè delle due autorità terrene, sono in completa antitesi. La *Monarchia*, pur indicando l'amore dei romani per il bene pubblico, l'assistenza divina, la necessità che Cristo venisse giudicato da un tribunale romano e da un vicario imperiale, è una continua accusa al temporalismo della Chiesa e una celebrazione dell'autosufficenza dell'Impero, che può vivere senza la guida della Chiesa. La *Commedia*, invece afferma che l'Impero non fu voluto da Dio per se stesso, ma per un fine specifico, per *lo loco santo*, dove siede il successore di Pietro. Virgilio stesso non può condurre da solo il discepolo alla felicità terrena, e l'insufficienza della natura e della ragione viene integrata dalla grazia" (Giacalone, in *Dante Alighieri, Paradiso*, p. 103). Cf. also: Passerin d'Entrèves, *Dante as a Political Thinker* (Oxford: Clarendon Press, 1952); R. Montano, *Suggerimenti per una lettura di Dante* (Naples: Conte Editore, 1956), pp. 207ff.; *Comprendere Dante*, ed. R. Montano and U. Barra (Naples: G. B. Vico Editrice, 1976), pp. 291ff.

46. Seneca, *Epistulae ad Lucilium* 89. 4–5.

47. Cf. Siger of Brabant, *Quaestiones in metaphysicam*, ed. W. Dunphy (Louvain-la-Nueve: Editions de l'Institut supérieur de philosophie, 1981), p. 361.

48. Cf. B. Nardi, "L'averroismo di Sigieri e Dante," *Studi danteschi* 20 (1938): 101. But see also René Antoine Gauthier, "Notes sur Siger de Brabant, II Siger en

1272–1275, Aubry de Reims et la scission des Normands," *Revue des sciences philosophiques et theologiques* 68 (1984): 19, n. 30.

49. B. Nardi, "Sigieri di Brabante nella *Divina Commedia*," *Rivista di filosofia neoscolastica* (Apr.–Oct. 1911; Feb.–Apr. 1912), p. 70; and "Dante e la filosofia," p. 244.

50. Giacalone, ed., *Paradiso*, pp. 169–70, n. 133.

51. Pierre Dubois, *De recuperatione terrae sanctae*, published after a Vatican MS by Ed. Ch.-V. Langlois (Paris: A. Picard, 1891), pp. 121–22.

52. Ibid., loc. cit., n. 2.

53. Cf. Carlo Cipolla, "Sigieri nella Divina Commedia," *Giornale storico della letteratura italiana* 8 (Turin, 1886): 53–139; F. X. Kraus, *Dante, sein leben und sein werk, sein verhaltniss zur kunst und zur politik* (Berlin: G. Grote, 1897), p. 67; Gaston Paris, "Siger de Brabant," in *La Poésie du Moyen Age* (Paris: Librairie Hachette et C.ie, 1906), pp. 165–83; E. Gebhart, *L'Italie mystique* (Paris: Librairie Hachette et C.ie, 1906), p. 328.

54. Thomas Aquinas, *De unitate intellectus contra Averroistas* 2.156.

55. "De natura praesertim animae rationalis, quod videlicet mortalis sit, aut unica in cunctis hominibus, et nonnulli temere philosophantes, secundum saltem philosophiam verum id esse asseverent, . . . hoc sacro approbante Concilio damnamus et reprobamus omnes asserentes, animam intellectivam mortalem esse, aut unicam in cunctis hominibus. . . . Cumque verum vero minime contradicat, omnem assertionem veritati illuminatae fidei contrariam omnino falsam esse definimus." Cf. Henrich Denzinger and A. Schönmetzer, *Enchiridion Symbolorum* . . . (Barcinone: Herder, 1976), nos. 1440, 1441, pp. 353–54).

56. Cf. B. Nardi, "L'origine dell'anima secondo Dante," *Giornale critico della filosofia italiana* 12, no. 6 (1931) and 13, nos. 1–2 (1932).

57. We present a significant page in which Siger, through his "distinctiones," proves the superiority of theology over philosophy; at the same time, it is a palpable "sample" of Siger's "silogizzare," through which can be seen the appositeness of the poet's characterization of Siger (*Quaestiones in metaphysicam* 6, Q. 1, comm. 1): "Consequenter quaeritur qualiter differat scientia theologia quam prae manibus habemus, quae est pars philosophiae, et scientia theologia quae non est pars philosophiae sed est sacra scriptura, nam utraque dicitur theologia. Quomodo ergo differunt? Dicendum quod, sicut nunc mihi apparet, defferunt quantum ad sex: primo, quantum ad modos considerandi; secundo, quantum ad considerata in utraque; tertio, quia theologia quae est sacra scriptura, ipsa est magis universalis quam theologia quae est pars philosophiae; quarto, quia item est magis certa; quinto, quia ipsa etiam est practica, theologia quae est pars philosophiae, ipsa non est practica; sexto, quia theologia quae sacra scriptura est, est magis sapientia quam theologia ista.

Dico ergo quod differunt quantum ad modum considerandi, quia modus considerandi in ista theologia, quae est pars philosophiae, est procedere ex principiis quae sunt nota nobis via sensus, memoriae et experimenti, ex lumine et ratione naturali. Modus autem considerandi in theologia quae est sacra scriptura non est procedere ex principiis quae sint nota via sensus, memoriae et experimenti et lumine naturali, sed proceditur in ea ex principiis notis per divinam revelationem, sicut multis sanctis nota fuerunt per revelationem divinam. Deinde autem ex illis principiis, sic notis per revelationem divinam, proceditur per investigationem humanam, applicando ad alia, sicut ad conclusionem illius scientiae, illa principia.

Differunt etiam quantum ad considerata in eis, quia haec scientia theologia quae est pars philosophiae non extendit considerationem suam nisi usque ad ea quae per rationem humanam et per creaturas tantum possunt cognosci a nobis. Illa autem scientia theologia quae est sacra scriptura extendit considerationem suam ad ea quae sunt supra rationem humanam et quae per creaturas tantum non possunt cognosci: nam, sicut dictum est, ipsa considerat ea quae per revelationem divinam tantum possunt cognosci. Unde et quaecumque scibilia sunt per modum divinae revelationis, sive sint entia naturalia, sive divina, sive mathematica, sive quaecumque, in eo quod cadunt vel cadere possunt sub modo sciendi vel cognoscendi ea per revelationem divinam, considerat haec scientia theologia quae est sacra scriptura, quae non est pars philosophiae.

Differunt etiam tertio, quia theologia quae est sacra scriptura est magis universalis, quod patet ex praedictis. Nam si ipsa considerat omnia illa quaecumque possunt cadere sub ratione divinae revelationis, tunc haec non tantum possunt esse principia scientiarum particularium, sed etiam conclusiones particularium scientiarum. Sed scientia haec theologia quae est pars philosophiae non intromittit se de conclusionibus aliarum scientiarum particularium, sicut Commentator dicit. Ideo illa scientia theologia magis est universalis quam ista.

Differunt quarto, quia theologia quae sacra scriptura est magis est certa quam ista theologia quae est pars philosophiae. Et hoc etiam apparet ex praedictis quia, sicut dictum est, theologia quae est pars philosophiae procedit ex principiis notis via sensus, memoriae et experimenti, et ita in cognitione suorum principiorum potest cadere error, ut sic cognoscuntur sicut in hac scientia cognoscuntur. Sed theologia sacra scriptura procedit ex principiis notis per divinam revelationem. In tali autem cognitione non potest cadere error. Et ideo, quia principia ex quibus procedit scientia theologia quae est sacra scriptura sunt magis nota et certa quam principia ex quibus procedit scientia theologia quae est pars philosophiae, et cuius principia sunt magis nota, eius conclusiones sunt magis notae et certiores, et per consequens tota scientia magis certa, hinc est quod theologia sacra scriptura est certior.

Differunt etiam quinto per hoc quod illa est practica, ista vero non. Et quod theologia quae est sacra scriptura sit practica et non tantum speculativa, apparet per duas rationes. Quarum prima est quia, sicut dictum est, illa considerat omnia illa quae cognosci possunt per revelationem divinam; haec autem possunt esse non solum speculabilia, verum etiam practica, id est factibilia vel agibilia. Ergo practibilia vel agibilia ipsa considerat in quantum ipsa possunt cadere sub revelatione divina, vel sub cognitione quae est per eam. Ergo ipsa aliquo modo est practica scientia. Hoc etiam patet alia ratione, nam si ipsa considerat ea quae imprimuntur in nobis per revelationem divinam, tunc ex ipsa impressione apparet quod est activa: ita quod, sicut theologia quae est pars philosophiae est scientia una speculativa, sic et theologia quae est sacra scriptura est scientia una practica seu activa, et non tantum speculativa, sicut ex praedictis patet. Haec autem theologia nullo modo est practica. Ergo etc.

Differunt etiam sexto per hoc quod theologia quae est sacra scriptura magis est sapientia quam ista. Quod apparet sic. Nam dicit Aristoteles in principio *primi libri* huius scientiae, quod illa scientia dicitur sapientia quae considerat de primis causis et primis principiis, ut de Deo et aliis substantiis separatis. Tunc arguo: illa scientia dicetur magis sapientia quae maiorem cognitionem et certiorem habet de primis principiis entium. Sed sicut ex praedictis apparet, theologia quae sacra scriptura est, ipsa maiorem et certiorem cognitionem habet de ipsis quam ista theologia, cum sint nota in ea per divinam revelationem, ad quam cognitionem non potest pertingere ratio humana per se, et ita nec ista theologia quae dicitur pars philosophiae, cum ipsa consideret solum illa quae per inventionem et rationem humanam, lumine et ratione naturali, sciri possunt. Hinc est quod illa est magis sapientia quam ista. Sic ergo quantum mihi videtur nunc, ipsae differunt in his sex iam dictis. Ex quibus iam dictis apparet quod pessime volunt procedere illi qui in illa scientia volunt procedere in omnibus modo demonstrativo. Principia enim demonstrationis debent esse nota via sensus, memoriae et experimenti. Principia autem illius scientiae nota sunt, ut visum est, per revelationem divinam." *Siger of Brabant, Quaestiones in metaphysicam*, ed. W. Dunphy (Louvain-la-Nueve: Editions de l'Institut supérieur de philosophie, 1981), pp. 359–61.

58. "Dico quod nihil ad me de Dei miraculis cum ego de naturalibus disseram" (Albert of Cologne *De gener. et corr.* 1.1.22); "Theologica autem non conveniunt cum physicis in principiis, quia fundantur super revelationem et inspirationem, et non super rationem; et ideo de illis in philosophia non possumus disputare" (*Metaphisicorum libri XII*, 1.10, tract. 3. c. 7); see also: Albert of Cologne *De anima* 3. 2. 1; *De somno et vigilia* 1. 1.1 and 3.1.12.

59. See above, n. 57.

60. Siger of Brabant, *Quaestiones de anima intellectiva*, in Mandonnet (n. 11 above), 2:152. Also relevant is the gracious letter of condolence (mentioned by L. Pietrobono in his commentary on the *Divine Comedy* [*La Divina Commedia di Dante Alighieri*, commentata da L. Pietrobono, D.S.P.; Turin: Società Editrice Internazionale, 1946, 3:125, note 136]) that Siger, as soon as he heard of Thomas's death, sent to the Dominican General Chapter assembled in Lyon.

61. Siger of Brabant, *Quaestiones de anima intellectiva*, in Mandonnet, 2:169.

Poetic Discourse and Courtly Love: An Intertextual Analysis of *Inferno* 5

MICHELANGELO PICONE

To begin my analysis of *Inferno* 5, I would like to clarify two assumptions that underlie my reading of this famous episode. The first concerns the interpretative framework within which I develop my analysis. The *Commedia* in general, and the canto of Francesca in particular, represents the palinode of the Arthurian romances. In other words, Dante offers us a rewriting of the "Arturi regis ambages pulcerrime" ("the most attractive wanderings of King Arthur's knights") in his poetic text. He uses narrative patterns taken from the Arthurian tradition when structuring this episode; but while he recalls the Old French *romans*, at the same time he endows them with a totally new meaning. Dante thus brings the profane *fabula* of the worldly Arthurian knights back to the sphere of the divine *historia* of the otherworldly knight (the *actor* of the *Commedia*) who recounts the ultimate human adventure, the search for eternal truth. Since I have dwelt at length upon this topic in a recent article of mine, I will not develop this theoretical perspective further.[1]

My second presupposition is of a historical and also less controversial nature. The course of Dante's poetical and cultural development is—broadly speaking—not linear but interrupted. Let me explain. There exists within Dante's literary career a discontinuity between the *Vita nuova* and the *Commedia* on the one hand, and the *Convivio* and the *De vulgari eloquentia* on the other. The *Vita nuova* and the *Commedia*—that is, the first and the last of Dante's works, represent an exaltation of Beatrice as an image of divine truth: they describe the journey of faith. The *Convivio*, along with the Latin treatise on language and poetry, represents instead an exaltation of the Donna Gentile, or of an image of rational and philosophical truth: they therefore describe the journey of reason.[2] It is precisely while pursuing this journey of reason that the Pilgrim comes to lose his way in the "selva oscura," the dark wood of the first canto of *Inferno*; and it is only through the direct intervention of the celestial Beatrice that he once again finds the right path.

This discontinuity explains why in the *De vulgari eloquentia*, as well as in the *Convivio*, Dante gives a positive judgment of the magnificent adventures of the knights of the Round Table—hallmark of the Arthurian romances and ultimate symbol of Old French civilization—whereas in the *Commedia* that judgment is reversed.[3] In the *Commedia*, in fact, a thorough consideration of the French literary tradition is conspicuously absent, while the Provençal and the Italian literatures are not only fully represented but also treated as exemplary. The few allusions to the Arthurian tradition that do exist are completely negative, a clear sign of Dante's rejection of the culture to which that tradition belongs. I would venture to explain away this opposition between the two Dantes by saying that the Pilgrim of the *Commedia* enters into competition with the Arthurian knights. He is, in fact, the true Perceval, the true Galahad, to whom is granted the sublime privilege of directly contemplating the Being of which the sought-after Grail is merely a symbol: God.

From this narrative perspective, I consider the *Commedia* to be a profoundly anti-French work—even more, a work that realizes a new *translatio studii*. As a matter of fact, the poet of the *Commedia* can be thought of as the anti–Chrétien de Troyes; just as, from the allegorical perspective, he can be thought of as the anti–Guillaume de Lorris, or the anti–Jean de Meun, and the *Commedia* itself considered as the anti–*Roman de la Rose*. (I have stated this point simply and quickly, knowing very well that further discussion would take us too far from our central focus.)[4]

I shall end these rather lengthy but necessary preliminary observations by restating my initial axiom: not only is the poet of the *Com-*

media the new knight of Romance culture, but the *Commedia* is the *new* book of modern civilization as opposed to the *old* book of the Arthurian tradition. Dante therefore applies to his profane scripture the same hermeneutical criteria followed in the Sacred Scriptures: that is, the typological approach, a special brand of the *allegoria in factis*.[5] The *novitas* of Dante's poetry lies in the new meaning attributed to "love"; the language of *eros* expressed in the *Commedia* differs from that expressed in the French narrative tradition. It is exactly this double articulation of the language of erotic desire (the true language of desire revealed by the *Commedia* and the false language of desire displayed by the French romances) which characterizes the whole episode of Francesca, to which we now turn.

There is no doubt that *Inferno* 5 represents the privileged locus of the Arthurian presence in the entire *Commedia*.[6] It is here, in fact, that the echoes of the courtly romances actually constitute a metaliterary system. We can note the precise intention on the part of Dante the poet to offer a final and global judgment on the Arthurian tradition. Namely, the judgment offered by the *Commedia* is stated *sub specie aeternitatis*, while that contained in the *De vulgari eloquentia* is stated only *sub specie poesis*.

The most evident sign of Dante's intention to cancel definitively the memory of the Arthurian courtly world is the fact that the French romance is directly evoked in this canto. When the Pilgrim interrogates Francesca about the "prima radice" (125), the "first root" of her sinful love (that is, of the love that led her to eternal damnation), Francesca replies by recalling the cultural model according to the conventions of which her amorous adventure with Paolo was born, developed, and reached its tragic end. This textual model is, more precisely, the French prose *Roman de Lancelot* (the tradition now known as the Vulgate Cycle):

> Noi leggiavamo un giorno per diletto
> di Lancialotto come amor lo strinse;
> soli eravamo e sanza alcun sospetto.
> Per più fiate li occhi ci sospinse
> quella lettura, e scolorocci il viso;
> (127–31)

One day, for pastime, we read of Lancelot, how love constrained him;
we were alone, suspecting nothing. Several times that reading urged our
eyes to meet and took the color from our faces.[7]

It is this reading of the exemplary love story of the "romanesque"
characters Lancelot and Guinevere that guides the steps of the "no-
vella-like" characters, the modern lovers Paolo and Francesca. However, in this passage Dante views literature not as a medium to reach
integration but rather as an instrument of alienation. Let us note that
the lovers are alone during their reading ("soli," meaning without the
guide of an experienced interpreter): their *lectura* is therefore characterized by a cognitive *défaillance* ("senza alcun sospetto," says
Francesca). Singleton's translation somewhat banalizes this very important syntagmo, when he renders it as "suspecting nothing," as if
Francesca were concerned with her love affair being discovered by
someone! In reality, Francesca here indicates the lack of knowledge
that characterized her own, and Paolo's, experience with love. The
unguided journey through the labyrinth of the French *roman* is the
direct cause of the fateful existential interpretation that leads them
astray:

> ma solo un punto fu quel che ci vinse.
> Quando leggemmo il disïato riso
>   esser basciato da contanto amante,
>   questo, che mai da me non fia diviso,
> la bocca mi basciò tutto tremante.
>
> (132–35)

but one moment alone it was that overcame us. When we read how the
longed-for smile was kissed by so great a lover, this one, who never shall
be parted from me, kissed my mouth all trembling.

It is the literary kiss of Lancelot and Guinevere that induces the actual
kiss of Paolo and Francesca. It is a textual "punto" that causes the
moral and religious crisis, bringing the lovers dangerously close to the
"doloroso passo" (114).[8] Literature, then, is responsible for the particular sinful action for which Paolo and Francesca are paying an eternal price:

Galeotto fu 'l libro e chi lo scrisse:
quel giorno più non vi leggemmo avante.
(136–37)

A Gallehaut was the book and he who wrote it [the French *auctor*]; that
day we read no farther in it.

Let us synthesize the results of our analysis so far. Paolo and Francesca's love experience closely follows the pattern of Lancelot and
Guinevere's paradigmatic love. In fact, their erotic action develops
according to the book of Lancelot and follows the subtly enchanting
cultural code recently imported from northern France. The lovers from
Rimini try to elevate their concrete and historical reality to the level
of the fascinating and exemplary reality of the Arthurian court. That
is, in their *imitatio* of the perfect secular love of Lancelot and Guinevere, they strive to achieve the same perfection of the knights and ladies
("le donne antiche e' cavalier," 71) that they so greatly admire.[9] However, in applying the literary model of the French *roman* to their own
lives they forget the divine dimension of love; they lose sight of the
pole of *caritas* toward which all human love should be oriented. They
therefore fail to attain the ultimate Object of every amorous quest: God.
This is the reason why Dante issues his negative judgment in the *Commedia*—a judgment that concerns, not only the historical love of Paolo
and Francesca, but also the exemplary love of Lancelot and Guinevere.

The *Commedia* thus becomes the new book of properly oriented
love, the love that can reveal the nature of Francesca's sin and at the
same time explain the reason behind her eternal punishment. In this
view, the entire canto appears to be constructed in a double perspective, which allows for two levels of meaning and analysis. The first is
the level of the *littera* and of the *sensus historialis*. The particular story
of Paolo and Francesca needs to be contrasted with its cultural
model—that is, with the Arthurian *roman*—in terms of its constructive
elements. The second is the level of the *sententia* and of the *sensus
allegoricus*. At this level, the eternal judgment explicitly regards the
concrete occurrence of Paolo and Francesca's love story but implicitly
relates to the timeless love story of Lancelot and Guinevere. This two-

fold judgment is handed down by the author of the *Commedia*. He is able to pronounce it because he is the only poet of the Romance tradition to attain, by virtue of his other-worldly journey, divine revelation—the only poet to discover the sacred sources of the Word. For Dante, to be a poet means exactly that: to rediscover, after the Fall, the original Word, the original language.

We have seen, then, that in the episode of Francesca the *matière* follows the paradigm of the profane *Roman de Lancelot*. It is through this continuous confrontation, or *collatio* (if I may use this technical term taken from textual criticism), with the French book that the plot of our episode is realized. The stylistic and thematic organization of the canto therefore reflects the modeling presence of the Arthurian *Roman*. On the other hand, the *senefiance*, or deep meaning, is conveyed by the sacred book of the *Commedia*, through which the final truth is revealed. The underlying *sensus* of Francesca's love can be deciphered in terms of the supreme interpretative code to which only Dante the poet possesses the key. It is this code that transmits the ultimate meaning of the episode: that is, the condemnation of the Arthurian romance written in the *langue d'oïl*, and the consecration of Dante's divine poem written in the *lingua di sì*.

Of the many points in *Inferno* 5 which I could present to demonstrate my thesis, I will discuss only one here: the punishment to which Francesca and all the other lustful souls are condemned. Let us recall that they are eternally swept by a "bufera . . . che mai non resta" (31)—an infernal hurricane, or sea-storm, that never rests.[10] Now the problem is the following: what is the correspondence between sin and punishment? How does the extremely rigorous law of *contrapasso* (according to which the penalties are assigned in Hell) apply here? In what way does the image of a "hurricane" translate, on a visual and a poetical level, the sin of lust? The answer given by most commentators (that is, by those who have asked themselves this question) is the obvious one: the passion of love naturally suggests the idea of a storm that sweeps one away. In my opinion, no such psychological reasoning can fully clarify the problem. We need to delve into Dante's text, to search for an intertextual reason, in order to discover a more satisfying explanation.

Let us read, for example, lines 31–33:

> La bufera infernal, che mai non resta,
>   mena li spirti con la sua rapina;
>   voltando e percotendo li molesta.

The hellish hurricane, never resting, sweeps along the spirits with its rapine; whirling and smiting, it torments them.

Here we find the terms *bufera* ("hurricane") and *mena* ("sweeps along"): the verb *menare* represents the punitive action executed by the *bufera*. Now, *menare* can be considered thematic in the entire episode, a true key-word. In fact, we find it repeated in three other places in this same canto.

It recurs first in lines 40–43:

> E come li stornei ne portan l'ali
>   nel freddo tempo, a schiera larga e piena,
>   così quel fiato li spiriti mali
> di qua, di là, di giù, di sù li mena;

And as their wings bear the starlings along in the cold season, in wide, dense flocks, so does that blast the sinful spirits; hither, thither, downward, upward, it drives them.

It is interesting to note here (in addition to the association *fiato/mena*, which recalls that of *bufera/mena* previously mentioned) the contrifugal activity of the wind: its movement is not unidirectional, but chaotic.

Menare crops up again in lines 76–78:

> Ed elli a me: "Vedrai quando saranno
>   più presso a noi; e tu allor li priega
>   per quello amor che i mena, ed ei verranno."

And he to me, "You shall see when they are nearer to us; and do you entreat them then by that love which leads them, and they will come."

Here, significantly, the subject of *menare* is not *bufera* but *amor*. This implies that the love of Paolo and Francesca possesses the same destructive power as the infernal storm: it has become the eternal representation of the particular type of love practiced by Francesca on earth.

Another occurrence of *menare* is found in lines 112–14:

> Quando rispuosi, cominciai: "Oh lasso,
>   quanti dolci pensier, quanto disio
>   menò costoro al doloroso passo!"

When I answered, I began, "Alas! How many sweet thoughts, what great desire, brought them to the woeful pass!"

Here Dante laments the fact that the amorous adventure of Paolo and Francesca, born under the sign of a well-directed desire, could have come to such a "doloroso passo," to such a tragic end: the death of their souls.

These three passages clearly demonstrate how the action of love on earth and the action of the storm in the hereafter have the same negative and tragic value. Just as the mortal love of Francesca constituted the antithesis of divine love, so the storm is the antithesis of the perfect centripetal movement that God's love imparts to the stars (let us remember that God is defined at the end of *Paradiso* as "l'amor che move il sole e l'altre stelle").

It is precisely this use of the verb *menare* that provides us with the textual proof of Dante's intention to correct the Arthurian tradition and its language of desire. *Mener* is, in fact, a technical verb in courtly romances, one that we often find used in conjunction with the term embodying the entire knightly quest: *aventure*.[11] Let us recall here only a few of the many instances in which this verb appears. One of the most typical ways to describe the sense of the chivalrous quest is the following:

> il ne quierent onques droit chemin ains vont tout adés ainsi comme aventure les *maine* . . .
>
> the wandering knights never follow the right path, instead they let themselves be driven by the spirit of adventure . . .

We see here the characteristic opposition between *droit chemin* and *aventure*, between an orderly and a disorderly movement. The erring knight naturally tends to follow the latter.

Another brief example will further clarify this point: "[Lancelot] chevaucha comme aventure le *mena* . . ." ("the knight rode as adventure drove him . . ."). We cannot find a more representative expression than this (it is almost a romanesque cliché) to qualify the meaning of *aventure* in the Arthurian context. In fact, the essence of the "cavalleria errante" seems to be the continuous abandonment to adventure, no matter how capricious and motiveless it may be. To go astray in search of extraordinary epiphanies, letting oneself be transported by chance or by irrational forces like the *fol'amor* or love-passion—this is the distinctive feature of the chivalrous civilization with which Francesca totally identifies herself.

For the critical perspective I am developing here, the most interesting occurrence of the verb *mener* is probably the one contained in the prose *Roman de Tristan*, the other paradigmatic Arthurian text whose echo resounds in Francesca's episode.[12] In this passage Guinevere sends a letter to Isolde in order to console her for Tristan's presumed betrayal. The letter includes the following definition of love: "d'amors, m'est il avis, ne puet l'en mie toz jorz joie avoir, enz devons savoir certenement que puis qu'amors est chose humene, et des choses humenes est ausi com de la roe de Fortune qui l'ome *moine* a sa volenté, ore desus, ores dejus, or en joie, or en corroz; et por ce dient li plusor que amors est humene chose, qu'ele est muable ausi come li venz . . ." (Curtis ed., 2:173). Rather than translate this passage, I shall provide a brief summary of its content. Man cannot always experience joy through love; since love is a human reality, and all human realities are controlled by Fortune, who drives man at her will—now downward, now upward [cf. 43], now in joy, now in sorrow—many say that Love is a changeable reality, exactly like the wind.

Here one can immediately notice two decisive and revealing elements for the understanding of *Inferno* 5. First, the presence of the verb *mener*, whose subject here is *Fortune*; and second, the analogy drawn between *amors* and *venz*, love and the wind, on the basis of the common trait *muabilité* ("mutability").

I shall now proceed to a more detailed analysis of the excerpt we have just quoted. It is clearly constructed as a syllogistic statement:

(a) First premise. Love is a totally mundane reality ("chose humene")—a reality, that is, which is completely inscribed within the limits of human possibilities.

(b) Second premise. Insofar as it is a human reality, love is subject to the influence of "Fortune," who (according to medieval iconography) incessantly spins her wheel and constantly changes man's condition: he who finds himself at the top will soon enough find himself at the bottom; he who now experiences joy, will soon experience pain. "Fortune," in fact, "mene l'ome a sa volenté."

(c) Conclusion. Isolde, who is now unhappy because she has been forsaken by Tristan, will once again find joy in a requited love.

It is clear that the love-passion theorized here by Guinevere is identical to the form of love that Francesca followed in her own amorous experience with Paolo. Francesca also couches the description of her love in a syllogistic line of reasoning,[13] but with a radical difference. The conclusion here is not optimistic and positive as in Guinevere's statement; it is pessimistic and tragic. The conclusion of Francesca's love is not eternal life but eternal death.

Francesca offers us her own version of the Arthurian *fol'amor* in the three famous *terzine* memorized by all readers of the *Commedia*— *terzine* that are constructed according to the rhetorical principle of anaphoric repetition of the word *amore*.

Let us read the first *terzina*:

> Amor, ch'al cor gentil ratto s'apprende,
>   prese costui de la bella persona
>   che mi fu tolta; e 'l modo ancor m'offende.
>   (100–102)

Love, which is quickly kindled in a gentle heart, seized this one for the fair form that was taken from me—and the way of it afflicts me still.

For Francesca, love kindles noble hearts, not on the basis of spiritual beauty (which mirrors the beauty of God), but on the basis of physical beauty (in fact, Francesca speaks of "bella persona," of Paolo's fairness). It is therefore an exclusively passionate form of love that manifests itself suddenly ("ratto"), irresistibly ("s'apprende/prese"), and irrationally ("il modo ancor m'offende"). It is a love that goes against *mezura* ("immoderata cogitatio," as Andreas Capellanus would have put it), and thus is called *fol'amor*: a carnal sin that defies reason. It is no accident that Dante defines the lustful as "i peccator carnali / che la ragion sommettono al talento" (38–39), "the carnal sinners who subject reason to desire."

Let us move on to the second *terzina*:

> Amor, ch'a nullo amato amar perdona,
>   mi prese del costui piacer sì forte,
>   che, come vedi, ancor non m'abbandona.
> (103–5)

Love, which absolves no loved one from loving, seized me so strongly with delight in him, that, as you see, it does not leave me even now.

This particular love is characterized by the law of reciprocity, which inextricably links the hearts of those who are conquered by it; and its participants do not act of their own free will but are driven by a force within them. This force is a magical one, such as that associated with the love-potion of Tristan and Isolde. The kind of love in question possesses so strong a power that it can reach beyond the natural limits of death ("che, come vedi, ancor non m'abbandona"). Indeed, in the case of Paolo and Francesca, love breaks the order that governs their particular section of Hell. They are allowed to go together ("que' due che 'nsieme vanno," 74), unlike all other sinners belonging to the same group ("de la schiera ov'è Dido," 85), who are condemned to go one-by-one. It is worthwhile to recall at this point that one of the fundamental themes of the Tristan legend is precisely the burial of the two lovers *together*, in adjacent tombs. In some versions of the myth, two trees actually grow from the tombs, so that their branches may intertwine eternally. This theme is known as "les arbres entrelacés" and symbolizes the victory of love over death.

We now come to the final lines of Francesca's discourse:

> "Amor condusse noi ad una morte.
>   Caina attende chi a vita ci spense."
> (106–7)

"Love brought us to one death. Caina awaits him who quenched our life."

In her conclusion, Francesca emphasizes the tragic end of her love—tragic not only at the existential level (the two lovers are killed, in a situation similar to that of the *Roman de Tristan*, by the betrayed husband), but at the spiritual level as well (they are eternally exiled from God in the circle of the lustful). At the moment of death, therefore, Francesca's love found, not its ultimate consecration (as in the case of Tristan and Isolde), but its definitive condemnation. Furthermore, being together ("insieme") in Hell does not signify, as it did in the Tristan legend, the continuation of love beyond the boundary of death, but stands for eternal punishment. The proximity of the two lovers has the function of reminding them of their ill-directed love; it is a perpetual reminder of the fact that they did not succeed in identifying the true object of human love: that is, God.

In conclusion, Francesca, in recounting her love story, reveals herself as a disciple of a theory of love that can be identified with the Arthurian treatment of *fol'amor*. Her existential model is Guinevere, or, as we have seen, Isolde. Francesca's particular type of *folie* leads her, first, to follow a love which is only earthly and profane (subject, as such, to the laws of Fortune, particularly that of death); and second, to believe that she has found the perfect object of love in Paolo (that is, in a mere human being, no matter how beautiful and gallant he may be).

In contrast to Francesca's ill-directed language of desire stands the language of desire of Dante the poet, a language that is correctly oriented. The Pilgrim, in fact, is first a follower of a love that is not earthly but divine (Beatrice defines him in *Inferno* 2.61 as: "l'amico mio e non de la ventura"—a follower of Beatrice, true love, not of Fortune, profane love); and second, he is the author of the *Vita nuova* (in the *libello*, the *actor*'s amorous experience is projected beyond the *speculum* of Beatrice to the direct contemplation of the divine image, "oltre la spera che più larga gira").[14]

In this respect, the *Commedia* becomes the locus of the restoration of the original Word. In it the language of disorderly desire receives an exemplary correction. The erotic quest of the Arthurian knights and ladies, along with the quest of their imitators Paolo and Francesca, undergoes a *recantatio*—that is, a total rewriting—in the quest of the new Christian knight, the Pilgrim who, following in the footsteps of Beatrice, searches for the true image of God. Therefore, at the end of his sacred poem, Dante can claim the crown of the poet par excellence of the Romance tradition. He is, in fact, the poet who has restored the alienated Word to its divine source, the poet who has succeeded in finding the prelapsarian correspondence between *nomina* and *res*.

McGill University

NOTES

1. See Michelangelo Picone, "Dante e la tradizione arturiana," *Romanische Forschungen* 94 (1982): 1–18.

2. The critic who has most convincingly defended this position is John Freccero, in his *Dante: The Poetics of Conversion* (Cambridge, Mass.: Harvard Univ. Press, 1986), especially pp. 186–94.

3. For a general survey of Dante's allusions to Arthurian literature, see Daniela Branca Delcorno, "Romanzi arturiani," *Enciclopedia dantesca*, 4:1028–30; more particularly, for the judgment offered in the *De vulgari eloquentia*, see Pier Vincenzo Mengaldo, *Linguistica e retorica di Dante* (Pisa: Nistri Lischi, 1978), pp. 294–303.

4. For a more detailed analysis, see the article cited in n. 1, above.

5. See the studies of various authors gathered in *Dante e le forme dell'allegoresi* (Ravenna: Longo, 1987).

6. The cultural and hermeneutical problems presented by this canto are carefully investigated by Francesco Mazzoni in his *Lectura; Casa di Dante in Roma: Inferno* (Rome: Bonacci, 1977), pp. 97–143.

7. All passages from the *Commedia* follow the text established by Giorgio Petrocchi, *La Commedia secondo l'antica vulgata* (Milan: Mondadori, 1966); the English translation is that of Charles S. Singleton, *The Divine Comedy* (Princeton: Princeton Univ. Press, 1970).

8. See the seminal essay by René Girard, "The Mimetic Desire of Paolo and Francesca," in *"To Double Business Bound": Essays on Literature, Mimesis and Anthropology* (Baltimore: Johns Hopkins Univ. Press, 1978), pp. 1–8; see also Susan Noakes, *Timely Reading: Between Exegesis and Interpretation* (Ithaca, N.Y.: Cornell Univ. Press, 1988), pp. 38–67.

9. The pertinent analysis may be found in the masterful article by d'Arco Silvio Avalle, ". . . de fole amor," in *Modelli semiologici nella Commedia di Dante* (Milan: Bompiani, 1975), pp. 97–121.

10. For a treatment of the nautical metaphor in the *Commedia* and in Petrarch's *Canzoniere*, see Michelangelo Picone, *Lectura Petrarce: Il sonetto CLXXXIX* (Florence: Olschki, 1989).

11. Fundamental for this point is the research done by Erich Köhler, *Ideal und Wirklichkeit in der höfischen Epik* (Tübingen: Max Niemeyer Verlag, 1970).

12. Pio Rajna already stressed the importance of the Tristan theme in this episode: see "Dante e i romanzi della Tavola Rotonda," *Nuova Antologia* 55 (1920): 223–47. For a more recent critical development, see Paolo Valesio, "Regretter: genea-

logia della ripetizione nell'episodio di Paolo e Francesca," *Yearbook of Italian Studies* 4 (1980): 87–104.

13. See the excellent metrical analysis offered by Mario Fubini, *Metrica e poesia* (Milan: Fetrinelli, 1962), pp. 178–80.

14. See Michelangelo Picone, *Vita Nuova e tradizione romanza* (Padua: Liviana, 1979), especially pp. 27–72.